D0577307

Betty Crocker's
New American
★★ Cooking ★★

Betty Crocker's
New American Cooking
** **

Random House, Inc. New York

Copyright © 1983 by General Mills, Inc., Minneapolis, Minnesota

All rights reserved under International and Pan-American Copyright Conventions. Published in the United States by Random House, Inc., New York, and simultaneously in Canada by Random House of Canada Limited, Toronto.

Library of Congress Cataloging in Publication Data   Crocker, Betty. Betty Crocker's New American Cooking.

Includes index. 1. Cookery, American. I. Title. II. Title: New American Cooking.
TX715.C92163   1983   641.5973   83-42780

Manufactured in the United States of America   24689753   First Edition

ISBN 0-394-52307-5

There's a new American way of living today . . . and there's a new American style of cooking to match. Americans care about physical fitness and good nutrition now as never before. We are conscious of calories and seek a well-balanced diet of lighter meals and more healthful snacks. We eat less red meat and more poultry and fish, more fresh vegetables and fruits, more whole grain cereals and flour. We are turning to cooking methods requiring less fat, such as poaching, steaming, baking and stir-frying. We are using less salt and more lemon, garlic, onions, spices and herbs.

Our population is more diversified than ever before, and so we borrow from our rich ethnic heritage the pasta of Italy, the lively seasonings of Mexico and the crisp-tender texture of food from the Orient. And we are regularly experimenting with once unfamiliar, exotic ingredients now found in most markets.

Above all, both men and women are finding new interest in the kitchen, not only to enjoy fine restaurant-quality food at home but also to cook creatively for the pure pleasure of it. New American cooking is more than a way of eating; it is fast becoming a national pastime. And cooking schools, cookbooks and new kinds of kitchen equipment all contribute to this enthusiasm for delicious and healthful food.

For these reasons, *Betty Crocker's New American Cooking* is more than a collection of 350 new and inspired recipes. It is also a common-sense guide to good nutrition. Each recipe is tagged with its calorie count per serving, and good sources of important nutrients are identified for many recipes. At the close of each chapter, you'll find a comprehensive chart of the computer-calculated nutrients in every recipe. And to interpret and focus all of this information, we've assembled an introductory guide to what is best in nutrition trends today. So turn the page, read, cook, eat — and enjoy all the pleasures of *Betty Crocker's New American Cooking*.

Contents

★★★

Introduction
★★★

NEW AMERICAN COOKING — WHAT IT MEANS

The newest trend in American cooking means emphasis on vegetables and fruits, reduced servings of high-fat foods, moderate use of sugar and salt, use of whole grains and cereals as inexpensive sources of protein, vitamins, minerals and dietary fiber. It means today's and yesterday's ingredients assembled in fresh ways to reflect the recent awakening to good nutrition and physical fitness. It also means an increased awareness of nutrition which has resulted in many concerns about how nutrition relates to good health.

PROTEIN

Proteins occur naturally in foods of animal and plant origin. Meat, milk and eggs — foods of animal origin — are said to provide "good quality" or complete protein because they contain all of the eight essential amino acids which the body cannot manufacture. Cereal grains, legumes and nuts — foods of plant origin — are low in one or more of the essential amino acids and thus are said to be "lower quality" or incomplete protein.

About 20 percent of our total body weight is protein. All the necessary enzymes in our body are proteins and some proteins, like insulin, are hormones. Proteins work together to clot blood after a cut and to act as antibodies which help fight off infections. We can obtain energy from protein, but this is very inefficient and expensive.

Is a high-protein, low-carbohydrate diet low in calories? No. Equal amounts (weight) of protein and carbohydrates contain the same number of calories. In addition, many of the foods high in protein are also high in fat, which contains twice as many calories as protein or carbohydrates. Such diets have their dangers because they cause dizziness, nausea, weakness and fainting.

Is animal protein necessary to be well nourished? No. Ovolacto vegetarians who eliminate meat only from their diets obtain good quality protein from dairy products and eggs. Strict vegetarians who consume no foods from animal origin can obtain protein of adequate quantity and quality by combining complementary protein-containing foods of plant origin, such as rice and dried beans.

CARBOHYDRATES

Unfortunately, carbohydrate foods are often misunderstood. Many people associate the word fattening with carbohydrates, but it should be understood that carbohydrates contain more calories than protein — four calories per gram. Because many protein foods, such as meat, contain fat with a higher count of nine calories per gram, a high-protein diet may actually be higher in calories than a high-carbohydrate diet.

Americans are encouraged by nutritionists to increase the amount of carbohydrates in the diet — especially whole grain foods, fruits and vegetables. Again, the rule is to eat a varied balanced diet. There are two categories of carbohydrates — simple and complex. Simple carbohydrates include sugar found naturally in some foods and sweeteners, such as honey, molasses and granulated, brown and powdered sugar. Complex carbohydrates occur naturally in plants and include the starches in vegetables and grains as well as the fiber of many fruits, vegetables, legumes and whole grains.

Sugar

The body does not discriminate among sources of sugar. Regardless of whether a sugar is added to a food or whether it occurs naturally in food, it is used in the same way by the body.

Is it necessary to add sugar to processed foods? Yes. Sugar adds flavor, acts as a preservative, as in jellies and jams, is needed as "food" for yeast in breads, contributes to the browning of baked products, helps to hold moisture in some products so the shelf life can be extended and adds "mouthfeel" and texture to some foods, such as candies and baked products.

Is sugar addictive? No. There is no substantiated evidence that sugar is addictive or that the amount of sugar eaten early in life creates an increased desire for sweets later.

Does eating sugar *cause* obesity? No. The basic cause of overweight is an excess consumption of calories whether they are from fats, protein or carbohydrates and an inadequate amount of exercise. Studies have shown that obese people actually eat less sugar than those of normal weight.

Does eating sugar *cause* diabetes? No. Eating too much sugar does not cause diabetes. Medical scientists believe heredity and obesity are the most important contributing factors.

Does the consumption of starches and sugar *cause* hypoglycemia or "low blood sugar"? No. "Low blood sugar" is a popular subject and of concern to many people who blame their diets for their irritability and difficulty in coping with problems. However, true hypoglycemia is a rare condition. The control of hypoglycemia, like diabetes, often involves a reduction in the intake of starches and sugar. But also like diabetes, sugar is not its main cause.

Does sugar consumption *cause* behavioral problems in children? No. At the present time there is no accepted evidence that hyperkinesis or other behavioral problems are caused or increased by consuming sugar-containing foods.

Dietary Fiber

Fiber is the part of plant foods that cannot be completely digested by the body. This means that when fiber is eaten, it merely passes through the digestive tract. It is also known as roughage or bulk.

Does it help to have fiber in the diet? Yes. One of the most well-documented benefits of fiber is its ability to relieve constipation.

Can dietary fiber *help minimize* some health problems? Sometimes. It is believed by some

scientists to prevent and/or treat a wide variety of problems, including obesity, diabetes, appendicitis and cancer of the colon. However, fiber has not yet been proven to cure any of these diseases. But for normal healthy individuals, a moderate increase in fiber in the diet may be helpful.

FAT AND CHOLESTEROL

Fat

Fat is a nutrient found in many foods. The main functions of fat in the diet are to supply energy, provide essential fatty acids and aid in the transportation of the fat-soluble vitamins A, D, E and K. The body needs fat to insulate and cushion the organs. However, there is a great concern today about the relationship of fat and cholesterol in the diet and its relationship to heart disease.

Is eating fat *related* to heart disease? Somewhat. Americans often get 40 percent of their calories from fat. The American Heart Association suggests limiting it to 30 percent because it may reduce the risk of heart disease for some people.

Cholesterol

Cholesterol is a complex fatlike substance that is found only in animal tissue. About half of the cholesterol in the body is produced by the body, while the rest comes from the diet. The most concentrated sources are organ meats but egg yolks also contain a significant amount.

Does our body need cholesterol? Yes. It is an important part of nearly all tissues — especially the brain and nerves. Sunlight converts one form of cholesterol in the skin to vitamin D. Cholesterol also is needed to produce certain hormones and to aid in fat digestion.

Is it bad to eat foods containing cholesterol? No. It is the amount of cholesterol in the blood that is a risk factor for heart disease. Scientists have shown that for most people, the amount of cholesterol eaten does not change the amount in the blood. However, people with a family history of heart disease and high blood cholesterol should consult their physician concerning diet.

VITAMINS AND MINERALS

Vitamins

Vitamins are compounds that are necessary for normal growth, reproduction and maintenance of health. Most vitamins are not formed in the body, but must be supplied from a source outside the body. Two exceptions are vitamin D, formed in the skin when in sunlight, and vitamin K, formed in the intestines.

Vitamins are divided into two groups: those soluble in fat (A, D, E and K), which means they can be stored in the fatty tissue of the body, and those soluble in water (the B vitamins, including thiamin, niacin, riboflavin, B_6 and B_{12} and vitamin C). This means the excess vitamins can be eliminated from the body and are not stored. Also, the water-soluble vitamins can be more easily lost during cooking.

Are Americans consuming enough of the B vitamins? Yes. This is true for the B vitamins, niacin, riboflavin and thiamin, because they are part of the enrichment of breads and cereals. However, many Americans do not eat the recommended amount of vitamin B_6. Good sources of B_6 are meats, nuts and whole grains.

Does our body store vitamin C? No. Because it is water soluble, it is not stored and should be consumed daily. For average adults, 60 milligrams is the recommended daily intake.

Do large amounts of vitamin C *prevent* colds? No. To date, there is little evidence that large doses affect how often people get colds, the types of cold symptoms they have or how long the cold lasts. Because excessive intake may have some unfavorable side effects, large amounts of vitamin C are not recommended without medical advice.

Is it necessary for healthy individuals to take vitamin pills? No. An adequate, well-balanced diet of at least 1200 calories each day will provide all the needed vitamins for the prevention of disease and promotion of health, as well as other nutrients also essential to health.

Are natural vitamin pills better than synthetic vitamin pills? No. Vitamins are the same whether they are from a natural source or synthetic. The body cannot tell the difference between them. However, often vitamin pills labeled natural will cost more.

Minerals

Minerals also are important to the body because they are part of a rigid skeleton, are needed to help nerves and muscles function and are oxygen carriers. The most prevalent minerals are calcium, phosphorus, sodium, potassium, chlorine and magnesium. The trace minerals — those needed in smaller amounts — are iron, zinc, manganese, copper and iodine. Even smaller amounts of fluoride, selenium, chromium and others are required.

Especially good sources of minerals are whole grain and fortified cereal products, green leafy vegetables, milk and milk products as well as meat, fish and legumes.

Sodium/Salt

Common table salt is a combination of sodium and chloride — both needed to help regulate the balance of water in the body. Salt is about 40 percent sodium which means a teaspoon of salt contains about 2000 milligrams of sodium — about the weight of two paper clips.

Does our body need sodium? Yes. Sodium is necessary for normal nerve and muscle activity, which play a vital role in the heart beating as well as in body movement and coordination.

Will reducing salt intake *prevent* high blood pressure? No. For the majority of individuals who are healthy and have no history of high blood pressure, there is no reason to believe that drastically reducing salt intake will prevent high blood pressure. However, consult your physician about salt intake if you have high blood pressure.

Do most people consume more sodium than the body needs? Yes. The daily intake by adults is equivalent to the amount of sodium in 2 to 2¼ teaspoons of salt — the body needs about ⅛ teaspoon of salt (200-300 milligrams sodium) each day. About one-third of this amount is added as salt to foods as they are cooked and eaten. About one-fourth of the sodium occurs naturally in foods, and the remaining amount comes from processed foods.

WATER—THE FORGOTTEN NUTRIENT

Water makes up about 70 percent of the human body and is second only to oxygen as being essential for life. We can last only four days without water.

Because water is involved in so many body functions, maintenance of water balance is crucial. Balance is attained when we ingest at least as much water as we lose. Drinking six or more cups of liquids — including juices and broths — per day helps provide some of the water that is needed to maintain water balance. Sodium and potassium are the principal minerals responsible for the body's water balance along with adequate protein.

GUIDELINES TO UNDERSTANDING NUTRITION INFORMATION

- *The first ingredient* in the ingredient list was used to calculate the nutrition information. For example, when "plain yogurt or dairy sour cream" was listed, the nutrition was figured using plain yogurt.
- *The lower weight or smaller measurement* was used to calculate the nutrition content when a range was given for an ingredient.
- *"If desired"* ingredients were not included in the nutrition calculations.
- *Nutrition information* was given for all recipes, but has not been calculated for the variations which sometimes follow. A salmon variation following a tuna recipe will have different calorie and nutrient values.
- *A good source of nutrient(s),* stated beneath the recipe title, is identified if a serving contains 25 percent of more of the U.S. Recommended Daily Allowance for that nutrient.

UNDERSTANDING THE BASIC FOOD GROUPS

If you use the Basic Food Groups below as a guide in planning meals, you will be meeting your nutritional needs.

Food Group	Recommended Daily Amounts	Nutrient Contributions
Milk, Yogurt and Cheese	Children under 9 years, 2 to 3 servings Children 9 to 12 years, 3 servings Teens, 4 servings Adults, 2 servings 1 serving = 1 cup milk or yogurt, 1¼ ounces cheese	Calcium, Phosphorus, Protein, Riboflavin, Vitamin A, Vitamin D
Meat, Fish, Poultry, Nuts and Dried Beans	2 servings 1 serving = 2 to 3 ounces lean, cooked meat, fish or poultry or ½ to ¾ cup cooked dried beans or 1 egg	Iron, Niacin, Protein, Riboflavin, Thiamin, Vitamin B$_{12}$ (animal products only)
Breads and Cereals (Whole grain, enriched and fortified)	4 servings 1 serving = 1 slice bread or 1 cup dry cereal or ½ cup cooked cereal, rice or pasta	Carbohydrate, Iron, Niacin, Riboflavin, Thiamin
Vegetables and Fruits	4 servings Include one good source of vitamin C daily. Frequently include deep yellow or dark green vegetables. 1 serving = 1 cup fresh or ½ cup cooked	Carbohydrate, Vitamin A, Vitamin C
Fats, Sweets and Alcohol	The number of servings depends on the individual's calorie needs	Supply fatty acids and Vitamin E

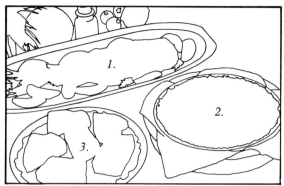

1. Baked Fish with Grapefruit Sauce, 2. Seafood Rice Pie, 3. Swordfish with Cucumber

Marinated Swordfish

Good source of protein, niacin and vitamin A

1 - pound swordfish steak, about 1 inch thick
2   tablespoons olive or vegetable oil
2   teaspoons lemon juice
2   large cloves garlic, crushed
$\frac{1}{2}$ teaspoon dried oregano leaves
$\frac{1}{8}$ teaspoon salt
     Dash of pepper
4   lemon wedges

Cut fish steak into 4 serving pieces. Place in ungreased square baking dish, 8 × 8 × 2 inches. Mix oil, lemon juice, garlic and oregano; pour over fish. Cover and refrigerate, turning fish occasionally, 4 hours.

Remove fish from marinade; reserve marinade. Place fish on rack in broiler pan; brush with marinade. Set oven control to broil and/ or 550°. Broil fish with tops 2 to 3 inches from heat until light brown, about 5 minutes. Turn carefully; brush with remaining marinade. Broil until fish flakes easily with fork, 5 to 8 minutes longer. Sprinkle with salt and pepper; garnish with lemon wedges.

4 servings; 260 calories each.

☆ ☆ ☆ ☆ ☆

Swordfish with Cucumber

Good source of protein, niacin and vitamin A

$1\frac{1}{2}$ - pound swordfish steak, about 1 inch thick
$\frac{1}{4}$ cup lemon juice
2   tablespoons olive or vegetable oil
2   cloves garlic, crushed
$\frac{1}{4}$ teaspoon chili powder
$\frac{1}{8}$ teaspoon ground cloves
1   teaspoon salt
1   large cucumber
1   tablespoon olive or vegetable oil
1   tablespoon lemon juice
$\frac{1}{8}$ teaspoon salt
$\frac{1}{4}$ teaspoon fennel seed

Cut fish steak into 6 serving pieces. Place in ungreased square baking dish, 8 × 8 × 2 inches. Mix $\frac{1}{4}$ cup lemon juice, 2 tablespoons oil, the garlic, chili powder, cloves and 1 teaspoon salt; pour over fish. Cover and refrigerate at least 2 hours.

Cut cucumber lengthwise into fourths; remove seeds. Cut each fourth lengthwise into thin slices. Remove fish from marinade; reserve marinade. Place fish on rack in broiler pan. Set oven control to broil and/or 550°. Broil fish with tops 2 to 3 inches from heat until light brown, about 5 minutes. Turn carefully; brush with marinade. Broil until fish flakes easily with fork, 5 to 8 minutes longer.

Heat 1 tablespoon oil in 10-inch skillet over medium heat until hot. Add cucumber. Cook and stir just until cucumber is crisp-tender, about 2 minutes. Toss with 1 tablespoon lemon juice, $\frac{1}{8}$ teaspoon salt and the fennel seed. Serve cucumber with fish.

6 servings; 265 calories each.

☆ ☆ ☆ ☆ ☆

Fish with Dressing

Good source of protein, niacin and vitamin A

1   medium onion, chopped (about ½ cup)
1   medium stalk celery, chopped (about ½ cup)
¼   cup margarine or butter
1   can (4 ounces) mushroom stems and pieces
2   cups coarsely crushed unseasoned croutons
1   medium carrot, shredded
¼   cup snipped parsley
½   teaspoon salt
¼   teaspoon pepper
¼   teaspoon ground sage
1   egg, slightly beaten
4   fish steaks, 1 inch thick (about 2 pounds)
½   teaspoon salt
2   tablespoons lemon juice
    Paprika

Cook and stir onion and celery in margarine in 2-quart saucepan over medium heat until celery is tender; remove from heat. Stir in mushrooms (with liquid), croutons, carrot, parsley, ½ teaspoon salt, the pepper, sage and egg.

Place fish steaks in greased jelly roll pan, 15½ × 10½ × 1 inch; sprinkle with ½ teaspoon salt, the lemon juice and paprika. Spoon crouton mixture around fish. Cook uncovered in 350° oven until fish flakes easily with fork, 35 to 40 minutes. Cut fish steaks into halves.

8 servings (½ fish steak and ½ cup dressing); 300 calories each.

☆ ☆ ☆ ☆ ☆

Sweet-Sour Fish Bake

Good source of protein and niacin

1   can (8 ounces) pineapple chunks in juice
¼   cup sugar
¼   cup vinegar
1   teaspoon soy sauce
¼   teaspoon salt
1   small clove garlic, finely chopped
2   tablespoons cornstarch
2   tablespoons cold water
1   small green pepper, cut into ½-inch strips
2   fish steaks (about ¾ pound)
½   teaspoon salt
1   tomato, cut into 8 wedges

Drain pineapple; reserve juice. Add enough water to juice to measure 1 cup. Heat pineapple juice, sugar, vinegar, soy sauce, ¼ teaspoon salt and the garlic to boiling in 2-quart saucepan. Mix cornstarch and water; stir into sauce. Boil and stir 1 minute. Stir in pineapple chunks and green pepper. Place fish steaks in ungreased baking dish, 8 × 8 × 2 inches; sprinkle with ½ teaspoon salt. Pour pineapple mixture over fish. Cook uncovered in 350° oven until fish flakes easily with fork, 25 to 30 minutes. Add tomato wedges during the last 5 minutes of cooking.

4 servings; 210 calories each.

☆ ☆ ☆ ☆ ☆

BUYING FRESH AND FROZEN FISH

Fish is a high-protein food and only two or three ounces is needed to provide the required protein for one serving. Use the following guidelines to determine how much fish per serving to purchase: whole (or eviscerated) about ¾ pound; pan-dressed (ready to cook) about ½ pound; steaks (cross-section slices) about ⅓ pound and fillets (sides cut lengthwise away from the backbone) about ¼ pound.

All fresh fish should smell fresh, but not too strong. The flesh should be firm and spring back when pressed. When selecting whole fresh fish, look for bright, clear eyes that bulge, shiny bright-looking scales that are close to the skin and reddish pink gills.

When purchasing frozen fish, select fish that is frozen solid. It should be tightly wrapped with little or no air space between fish and wrapping. The fish should not be discolored or have excess ice crystals and should have little or no odor.

Mustard-Topped Fish

Good source of protein and niacin

4	*small halibut, 1 inch thick*
$\frac{1}{2}$	*teaspoon salt*
$\frac{1}{8}$	*teaspoon pepper*
2	*tablespoons margarine or butter, melted*
2	*egg whites*
$\frac{1}{4}$	*cup grated Parmesan cheese*
2	*tablespoons Dijon-style mustard*
2	*tablespoons chopped green onions (with tops)*

Sprinkle fish steaks with salt and pepper. Place fish on rack in broiler pan; brush with 1 tablespoon of the margarine. Set oven control to broil and/or 550°. Broil fish with tops 2 to 3 inches from heat until light brown, about 5 minutes. Turn; brush with remaining margarine. Broil until fish flakes easily with fork, 5 to 8 minutes. Beat egg whites until stiff but not dry. Fold in cheese, mustard and onions. Spread mixture over fish. Broil until tops are golden brown, about 1½ minutes.

8 servings; 140 calories each.

☆ ☆ ☆ ☆ ☆

Fish with Radishes

Good source of protein and vitamin A

1	*pound fish fillets*
$\frac{1}{2}$	*teaspoon salt*
$\frac{1}{8}$	*teaspoon pepper*
1	*teaspoon shredded orange peel*
$\frac{1}{4}$	*cup orange juice*
$\frac{1}{4}$	*teaspoon ground cinnamon*
1	*small onion, thinly sliced*
$\frac{1}{4}$	*cup sliced radishes*

If fish fillets are large, cut into 5 serving pieces. Sprinkle both sides of fish with salt and pepper. Place fish in ungreased square baking dish, $8 \times 8 \times 2$ inches. Mix orange peel, orange juice and cinnamon; pour evenly over fish. Place onion and radish slices over fish. Cover and cook in 350° oven until fish flakes easily with fork, 20 to 30 minutes. Garnish with orange wedges if desired.

5 servings; 110 calories each.

☆ ☆ ☆ ☆ ☆

Mustard-Topped Fish, and Chili Skillet Fish

Chili Skillet Fish

Good source of protein

1   pound fish fillets
1   medium onion, thinly sliced
2   tablespoons olive or vegetable oil
½   teaspoon salt
¼   teaspoon coarsely ground pepper
1   can (4 ounces) chopped green chilies, drained
10 pimiento-stuffed green olives
¼   cup dry white wine
1   tablespoon lemon juice
    Lemon wedges

If fish fillets are large, cut into 5 serving pieces. Place onion in oil in 10-inch skillet. Place fish on onion; sprinkle with salt and pepper. Spoon chilies on fish; top with olives. Mix wine and lemon juice; pour over fish. Heat to boiling; reduce heat. Cover and simmer until fish flakes easily with fork, about 10 minutes. Serve with lemon wedges.

5 servings; 165 calories each.

☆ ☆ ☆ ☆ ☆

Oven-Fried Fish

Good source of protein

1   pound fish fillets
2   tablespoons cornmeal
2   tablespoons dry bread crumbs
¼   teaspoon salt
¼   teaspoon paprika
⅛   teaspoon dried dill weed
    Dash of pepper
¼   cup milk
3   tablespoons margarine or butter, melted

Move oven rack to position slightly above middle of oven. Heat oven to 500°. Cut fish fillets into 2 × 1½-inch pieces. Mix cornmeal, bread crumbs, salt, paprika, dill weed and pepper. Dip fish into milk, then coat with cornmeal mixture. Place fish in well-greased rectangular pan, 13 × 9 × 2 inches. Pour margarine over fish. Cook uncovered until fish flakes easily with fork, about 10 minutes.

5 servings (about 5 pieces); 165 calories each.

☆ ☆ ☆ ☆ ☆

Fish with Cabbage

Good source of protein and vitamin A

1   *pound pike or sea bass fillets*
1   *tablespoon vegetable oil*
1   *teaspoon cornstarch*
1   *teaspoon soy sauce*
1/2 *teaspoon salt*
    Dash of pepper
1   *tablespoon cornstarch*
1   *tablespoon cold water*
3   *tablespoons vegetable oil*
2   *cloves garlic, finely chopped*
1   *small head green cabbage (about 1 pound),*
    cut into 1½-inch pieces
1/2 *cup chicken broth (page 56)*
1/2 *cup chili sauce*
1/2 *to 1 teaspoon red pepper sauce*
3   *green onions (with tops), cut into 1-inch pieces*

Cut fish fillets into strips, 2 × 1 inch. Toss fish, 1 tablespoon oil, 1 teaspoon cornstarch, the soy sauce, salt and pepper. Cover and refrigerate 30 minutes. Mix 1 tablespoon cornstarch and the cold water. Heat 3 tablespoons oil in 12-inch skillet or wok over high heat until hot. Add fish and garlic; cook and stir until fish turns white, about 3 minutes. Add cabbage; cook and stir 3 minutes. Stir in chicken broth, chili sauce and pepper sauce; heat to boiling. Stir in cornstarch mixture; cook and stir 1 minute. Stir in onions.

6 servings (about 1 cup); 220 calories each.

☆ ☆ ☆ ☆ ☆

Garlic Cod

Good source of protein

1   *pound cod fillets*
1/4 *teaspoon salt*
    Dash of pepper
2   *tablespoons margarine or butter, melted*
1   *tablespoon lemon juice*
1/2 *teaspoon onion powder*
1/4 *teaspoon paprika*
5   *large cloves garlic, finely chopped*
2   *tablespoons margarine or butter*
1   *tablespoon olive or vegetable oil*
5   *lemon wedges*

If fish fillets are large, cut into 5 serving pieces. Sprinkle both sides with salt and pepper. Mix melted margarine, the lemon juice, onion powder and paprika. Dip fish into margarine mixture. Place in ungreased square pan, 9 × 9 × 2 inches. Pour remaining margarine mixture over fish. Cook uncovered in 350° oven until fish flakes easily with fork, 25 to 30 minutes. Cook and stir garlic in 2 tablespoons margarine and the oil over medium heat until garlic is brown; spoon over fish. Garnish with snipped parsley if desired. Serve with lemon wedges.

5 servings; 230 calories each.

□ *Microwave Directions:* If fish fillets are large, cut into 5 serving pieces. Sprinkle both sides with salt and pepper. Mix melted margarine, the lemon juice, onion powder and paprika. Dip fish into margarine mixture. Arrange fish with thickest parts to outside edges in ungreased microwavable dish, 8 × 8 × 2 inches. Pour remaining margarine mixture over fish. Cover tightly and microwave on high (100%) 2 minutes; rotate dish ½ turn. Microwave until fish flakes easily with fork, 2 to 4 minutes longer. Let stand 3 minutes. Place garlic, 2 tablespoons margarine and the oil in 2-cup microwavable measure. Cover loosely and microwave until garlic is brown, 4 to 5 minutes; pour over fish. Serve with lemon wedges.

☆ ☆ ☆ ☆ ☆

Cod with Marinated Tomatoes

Cod with Marinated Tomatoes

Good source of protein

2   medium tomatoes, chopped (about 1½ cups)
¼   cup sliced green onions (with tops)
2   tablespoons vinegar
2   tablespoons water
1   tablespoon capers
½   teaspoon salt
¼   teaspoon red pepper sauce
1   pound cod fillets
1   teaspoon salt

Mix tomatoes, onions, vinegar, water, capers, ½ teaspoon salt and the pepper sauce in glass jar or bowl. Cover and let stand at room temperature at least 4 hours.

If fish fillets are large, cut into 5 serving pieces. Heat 1½ inches water and 1 teaspoon salt to boiling in 10-inch skillet; reduce heat. Place fish in single layer in skillet. Heat to boiling; reduce heat. Simmer uncovered until fish flakes easily with fork, 4 to 6 minutes. Remove fish with slotted spoon. Drain tomato mixture; spoon over fish.

5 servings; 125 calories each.

☐ *Microwave Directions:* Prepare tomato mixture as directed. Arrange fish with thickest parts to outside edges in ungreased microwavable dish, 8 × 8 × 2 inches. Cover tightly and microwave on high (100%) 3 minutes; rotate dish ½ turn. Microwave until fish flakes easily with fork, 2 to 4 minutes longer. Remove fish with slotted spoon. Drain tomato mixture; spoon over fish.

☆ ☆ ☆ ☆ ☆

Creamed Cod and New Potatoes

Good source of protein

1½ pounds new potatoes (about 12)
1 pound cod fillets
1 medium onion, sliced
3 slices lemon
1 teaspoon salt
2 peppercorns
    Cream Sauce (below)
2 tablespoons snipped parsley

Pare narrow strip around center of each potato. Heat 1 inch salted water (1 teaspoon salt to 1 cup water) to boiling. Add potatoes. Cover and heat to boiling; reduce heat. Simmer until tender, 20 to 25 minutes; drain.

If fish fillets are large, cut into 5 serving pieces. Heat 1½ inches water, the onion, lemon, salt and peppercorns to boiling in 10-inch skillet; reduce heat. Place fish in single layer in skillet. Heat to boiling; reduce heat. Simmer uncovered until fish flakes easily with fork, 4 to 6 minutes. Remove fish with slotted spoon; place on serving platter and keep warm. Strain broth; reserve 1¼ cups for Cream Sauce. Prepare Cream Sauce. Arrange potatoes on platter with fish; pour sauce over top. Sprinkle with parsley.

Cream Sauce

1 small onion, finely chopped (about ¼ cup)
¼ cup margarine or butter
3 tablespoons all-purpose flour
1 tablespoon Dijon-style mustard
½ teaspoon salt
¼ teaspoon pepper
1¼ cups reserved fish broth
1 cup half-and-half

Cook and stir onion in margarine in 1½-quart saucepan over low heat until onion is tender, about 5 minutes. Blend in flour, mustard, salt and pepper. Cook over low heat, stirring constantly, until smooth and bubbly; remove from heat. Stir in reserved fish broth and the half-and-half. Heat to boiling, stirring constantly. Boil and stir 1 minute.

5 servings; 370 calories each.

☐ *Microwave Directions:* Prepare potatoes as directed. If fish fillets are large, cut into 5 serving pieces. Place onion, lemon, salt, peppercorns and 1 cup hot water in microwavable dish, 8 × 8 × 2 inches. Arrange fish with thickest parts to outside edges of dish. Cover tightly and microwave on high (100%) 4 minutes; rotate dish ½ turn. Microwave until fish flakes easily with fork, 3 to 5 minutes longer. Remove fish with slotted spoon; place on serving platter and keep warm. Strain broth; reserve 1 cup. To prepare Cream Sauce, place onion and margarine in 1½-quart microwavable casserole. Microwave uncovered on high (100%), stirring every minute, until onion is tender, 2 to 3 minutes. Blend in flour, mustard, salt and pepper; stir in reserved fish broth and the half-and-half. Microwave, stirring every minute, until sauce is thickened, 4 to 6 minutes. Continue as directed.

☆ ☆ ☆ ☆ ☆

Orange Almond Trout

Good source of protein, niacin and vitamin C

1 pound trout fillets
¼ cup sliced almonds
1 medium onion, sliced
¼ cup margarine or butter
½ cup all-purpose flour
1 teaspoon salt
½ teaspoon paprika
⅛ teaspoon pepper
2 oranges, pared and sectioned

If fish fillets are large, cut into 5 serving pieces. Cook and stir almonds and onion in margarine in 10-inch skillet until onion is tender; remove with slotted spoon and keep warm. Mix flour, salt, paprika and pepper. Coat fish with flour mixture. Cook fish in same skillet over medium heat, turning carefully, until brown, about 10 minutes. Top with almonds and onion; garnish with orange sections.

5 servings; 375 calories each.

☆ ☆ ☆ ☆ ☆

Sesame Perch

Good source of protein

1   pound ocean perch fillets
1/4 teaspoon salt
2   tablespoons margarine or butter
2   tablespoons vegetable oil
1   tablespoon sesame seed
1   lemon, cut into halves
1   teaspoon dried basil leaves
2   tablespoons snipped parsley

If fish fillets are large, cut into 5 serving pieces; sprinkle both sides with salt. Heat margarine and oil in 10-inch skillet over medium heat until hot. Cook fish, turning fish carefully, until brown on both sides, about 10 minutes. Remove fish; keep warm.

Cook and stir sesame seed in same skillet over medium heat, until golden brown, about 5 minutes; remove from heat. Squeeze lemon over sesame mixture; stir in basil. Pour over fish. Sprinke with parsley.

5 servings; 190 calories each.

☆ ☆ ☆ ☆ ☆

Flounder in Wine

Good source of protein

1   pound flounder fillets
1/2 teaspoon salt
1/2 teaspoon paprika
1/8 teaspoon pepper
1/3 cup sliced leeks
4   ounces mushrooms, sliced (about 1 1/2 cups) or
     1 can (4 ounces) mushroom stems
     and pieces, drained
2   tablespoons margarine or butter
1/2 cup dry white wine
1/4 cup sliced almonds
3   tablespoons grated Parmesan cheese

If fish fillets are large, cut into 5 serving pieces. Arrange in ungreased square baking dish, 8 × 8 × 2 inches; sprinkle with salt, paprika and pepper. Cook and stir leeks and mushrooms in margarine until leeks are tender; stir in wine. Pour mushroom mixture over fish; sprinkle with almonds and cheese. Cook uncovered in 375° oven until fish flakes easily with fork, about 25 minutes.

5 servings; 295 calories each.

☆ ☆ ☆ ☆ ☆

Sesame Perch

Red Snapper with Vegetable Sauce

Good source of protein and vitamin A

1	pound red snapper fillets
2	medium carrots, thinly sliced (about 1 cup)
1	large onion, chopped (about 1 cup)
1	medium stalk celery, thinly sliced (about ½ cup)
1	large clove garlic, finely chopped
1	tablespoon instant chicken bouillon
½	teaspoon dried rosemary leaves
2	tablespoons margarine or butter
1	cup water
½	cup dry white wine
½	teaspoon salt
⅛	teaspoon pepper
2	tablespoons cornstarch
2	tablespoons cold water

If fish fillets are large, cut into 5 serving pieces. Cook and stir carrots, onion, celery, garlic, chicken bouillon and rosemary in margarine in 10-inch skillet over medium heat just until carrots are crisp-tender, about 10 minutes. Place fish on vegetables. Pour 1 cup water and the wine over fish; sprinkle with salt and pepper. Heat to boiling; reduce heat. Cover and simmer until fish flakes easily with fork, 8 to 10 minutes. Remove fish with slotted spoon; keep warm. Mix cornstarch and 2 tablespoons water; stir into vegetable mixture. Heat to boiling; boil and stir 1 minute. Spoon vegetable mixture over fish.

5 servings; 175 calories each.

☆ ☆ ☆ ☆ ☆

Red Snapper with Vegetable Sauce

Hot Pepper Snapper

Good source of protein and vitamin C

1   can (16 ounces) whole tomatoes
1   medium onion, chopped
2   large cloves garlic
1   or 2 canned jalapeño peppers
1/4   cup sunflower nuts
1/4   teaspoon ground cumin
1   pound red snapper fillets
1/4   teaspoon salt
1   cup coarsely crushed corn chips

Place half of the tomatoes (with liquid), onion, garlic, peppers, sunflower nuts and cumin in blender container. Cover and blend on high speed until smooth, about 10 seconds. Repeat with remaining half of ingredients.

If fish fillets are large, cut into 5 serving pieces. Place fish in ungreased rectangular baking dish, 12 × 7½ × 2 inches; sprinkle with salt. Pour tomato mixture evenly over fish; sprinkle with corn chips. Cook uncovered in 350° oven until fish flakes easily with fork, 25 to 30 minutes.

5 servings; 205 calories each.

□ *Food Processor Directions:* Place tomatoes (with liquid), onion, garlic, peppers, sunflower nuts and cumin in workbowl fitted with steel blade. Cover and process until smooth, 10 seconds.

□ *Microwave Directions:* Prepare tomato mixture as directed. If fish fillets are large, cut into 5 serving pieces. Arrange fish with thickest parts to outside edges in ungreased microwavable dish, 8 × 8 × 2 inches; sprinkle with salt. Pour tomato mixture over fish. Cover tightly and microwave on high (100%) 5 minutes. Sprinkle with corn chips; rotate dish ½ turn. Microwave uncovered until fish flakes easily with fork, 2 to 3 minutes longer. Let stand 3 minutes.

☆ ☆ ☆ ☆ ☆

Creole Fish Stew

Good source of protein, niacin and vitamin A

2   medium onions, sliced
2   teaspoons chili powder
2   tablespoons margarine or butter
1   can (28 ounces) whole tomatoes
1/2   cup peanut butter
1/2   teaspoon salt
1   package (10 ounces) frozen sliced okra
1   pound cod fillets, cut into ½-inch slices
1   small green pepper, chopped (about ½ cup)

Cook and stir onion and chili powder in margarine in 4-quart Dutch oven over medium heat until onion is tender, about 5 minutes. Stir in tomatoes (with liquid), peanut butter and salt. Break up tomatoes with fork. Heat to boiling; reduce heat. Cover and simmer 20 minutes. Rinse okra under running cold water; drain. Stir okra, fish and green pepper into tomato mixture. Heat to boiling; reduce heat. Cover and simmer until fish flakes easily with fork and okra is done, about 10 minutes. Sprinkle with peanuts if desired.

8 servings (about 1 cup); 240 calories each.

☆ ☆ ☆ ☆ ☆

STORING FRESH AND FROZEN FISH

Store fresh fish covered in the coldest section of your refrigerator and plan to use it within a day or two. Freeze fish tightly wrapped in moistureproof, vaporproof wrap, or place in freezer container and cover with cold water.

If you have leftover cooked fish, place it in a tightly covered container and refrigerate no longer than three days, or wrap, label and freeze no longer than three months. Use in place of canned tuna or salmon or in recipes that use flaked, cooked fish.

Thaw frozen fish in the refrigerator, allowing about twenty-four hours for a 1-pound package. If it is necessary to thaw it faster, place the moistureproof package of frozen fish in cold water. Use immediately after thawing. Do not thaw fish at room temperature.

Chili Fish Stew

Good source of protein

1	medium onion, thinly sliced
2	large cloves garlic, crushed
2	tablespoons olive or vegetable oil
1	tablespoon chili powder
3	cups chicken broth (page 56)
1	can (4 ounces) chopped green chilies
4	medium tomatoes, coarsely chopped (about 3 cups)
1	medium green pepper, chopped (about 1 cup)
1	pound frozen fish fillets, partially thawed and cut into 1-inch pieces
1	can (4¼ ounces) tiny shrimp, rinsed and drained
1	teaspoon salt
1½	cups plain yogurt
	Snipped cilantro or parsley

Cook and stir onion and garlic in oil in 4-quart Dutch oven until onion is tender, about 5 minutes. Add chili powder; cook and stir 2 minutes. Add chicken broth and green chilies (with liquid). Heat to boiling; reduce heat. Cover and simmer 20 minutes. Stir in tomatoes, green pepper, fish, shrimp and salt. Heat to boiling; reduce heat. Cover and simmer until fish flakes easily with fork, about 3 minutes. Gradually stir in yogurt; heat just until hot (do not boil). Sprinkle with cilantro.

9 servings (about 1 cup); 175 calories each.

☆ ☆ ☆ ☆ ☆

Red Snapper Stew

Good source of vitamin A

1	medium onion, sliced
2	tablespoons margarine or butter
4	cups chicken broth (page 56)
2	medium carrots, cut crosswise into ¼-inch slices
½	cup uncooked regular rice
1	tablespoon lemon juice
1	teaspoon salt
¼	teaspoon dried dill weed
¼	teaspoon dried thyme leaves
¼	teaspoon pepper
1	package (10 ounces) frozen baby Brussels sprouts
1½	pounds red snapper fillets, cut into 1-inch pieces
1	cup sliced mushrooms

Cook and stir onion in margarine in 4-quart Dutch oven over medium heat until onion is tender, about 5 minutes. Stir in chicken broth, carrots, rice, lemon juice, salt, dill weed, thyme and pepper. Heat to boiling; reduce heat. Cover and simmer until rice is tender, about 20 minutes. Rinse Brussels sprouts under running cold water to separate; drain. Stir into rice mixture. Heat to boiling; reduce heat. Cover and simmer 5 minutes. Stir in fish and mushrooms; simmer until fish flakes easily with fork, 5 to 8 minutes longer.

8 servings (about 1 cup); 110 calories each.

☆ ☆ ☆ ☆ ☆

FISH — THE FAT AND THE LEAN

There are two classifications of fish: fat and lean. Fish classified as fat contain oil throughout their flesh and are best for baking because they remain moist after cooking. Lean fish have less oil and are better when cooked with the addition of a small amount of fat. It is best to substitute fish from within the same classification. One lean fish (halibut, pike, sea bass, cod, ocean perch, flounder, red snapper, smelt or swordfish) can be substituted for another lean fish in a recipe and the same is true for fat fish (lake trout, white fish and salmon).

Whether fat or lean, fish provide good protein with fewer calories than most red meat: a serving of lean fish has only about half the calories of an equal serving of most red meats. A serving of fat fish has about 20 percent less fat than an equal serving of most red meats. In recent years, as people have become more weight-and-health conscious, consumption of fish has increased.

Fish and Vegetable Soup

Good source of protein, niacin and vitamin A

1	small cucumber
2	cans (10¾ ounces each) chicken broth
2⅓	cups water
1	tablespoon soy sauce
⅛	teaspoon ground ginger
	Dash of pepper
2	ounces uncooked vermicelli
½	pound fish fillets, cut into ½-inch slices
1	can (4½ ounces) tiny shrimp, rinsed and drained
1	cup sliced mushrooms or 1 can (4 ounces) mushroom stems and pieces, drained
5	cups torn spinach (about 4 ounces)
¼	cup sliced green onions (with tops)

Cut cucumber lengthwise into halves; remove seeds. Cut each half crosswise into thin slices. Heat chicken broth, water, soy sauce, ginger and pepper to boiling in 3-quart saucepan; stir in vermicelli. Heat to boiling; cook uncovered just until tender, about 4 minutes. Stir in cucumber, fish, shrimp and mushrooms. Heat to boiling; reduce heat. Simmer uncovered until fish flakes easily with fork, about 1 minute. Stir in spinach until wilted. Sprinkle each serving with green onions.

6 servings (about 1 cup); 160 calories each.

☆ ☆ ☆ ☆ ☆

Fish and Vegetable Soup

Stuffed Baked Fish

Good source of protein and vitamin A

2 - to 2½-pound whole fish (whitefish, pike, red
    snapper, salmon, lake trout or bass)
1½ cups cooked brown or regular rice
½ cup cut-up dates or raisins
¼ cup sliced green onions (with tops)
1 teaspoon finely shredded lemon peel
¼ teaspoon salt
⅛ teaspoon ground cinnamon
⅛ teaspoon turmeric
¼ cup margarine or butter, melted
2 tablespoons lemon juice
1 lemon, cut into wedges

Remove head from fish. Mix rice, dates, on-ions, lemon peel, salt, cinnamon and turmeric. Spoon rice mixture into cavity of fish. Close opening with wooden picks or skewers; lace with string. Place remaining rice mixture in greased casserole; cover and refrigerate. Place in oven with fish the last 20 minutes of cook-ing. Place fish in greased shallow roasting pan. Mix margarine and lemon juice; brush fish with margarine mixture. Cook uncovered in 350° oven, brushing occasionally with marga-rine mixture, until fish flakes easily with fork, about 1 hour. Remove wooden picks and string. Serve fish with lemon wedges. Garnish with lemon roses and parsley if desired.

8 servings; 260 calories each.

NOTE: To make lemon rose, cut thin slice from stem end of lemon. Starting just above cut end, cut around lemon in a continuous motion to form a spiral of peel. Carefully curl peel spiral to resemble a rose.

☆ ☆ ☆ ☆ ☆

Steamed Fish with Ginger

Good source of protein and vitamin A

2 - pound whole pike or sea bass
2 tablespoons lemon juice
1 tablespoon vegetable oil
1 teaspoon salt
2 teaspoons finely chopped gingerroot
2 green onions
    Ginger Sauce (below)

Remove head from fish. Slash fish crosswise 3 times on each side. Mix lemon juice, oil, salt and gingerroot; rub cavity and outside of fish. Cover and refrigerate 1 hour.

Place fish on rack over water in steamer or roaster (water should not touch bottom of rack; if necessary, elevate rack by placing on custard cups). Cover tightly and heat to boil-ing; reduce heat. Steam over boiling water until fish flakes easily with fork, about 20 min-utes. (Add boiling water if necessary.)

Cut green onions into 2-inch pieces; cut pieces into thin strips. Prepare Ginger Sauce. Care-fully remove skin from fish; place fish on serv-ing platter. Pour half of the Ginger Sauce over fish; sprinkle with green onions. Serve with remaining Ginger Sauce.

Ginger Sauce

1 tablespoon finely chopped gingerroot
1 teaspoon finely chopped garlic
2 tablespoons vegetable oil
½ cup dry white wine
¼ cup soy sauce
¼ cup chili sauce
½ teaspoon sugar
4 to 6 drops red pepper sauce
1 tablespoon cornstarch
2 tablespoons cold water

Cook and stir gingerroot and garlic in oil in 1-quart saucepan until light brown. Stir in wine, soy sauce, chili sauce, sugar and red pepper sauce. Heat to boiling; reduce heat. Cover and simmer 10 minutes. Mix corn-starch and cold water; stir into ginger mixture. Heat to boiling; boil and stir 1 minute.

7 servings; 220 calories each.

☆ ☆ ☆ ☆ ☆

Steamed Fish with Ginger, and Stuffed Baked Fish

Baked Fish with Grapefruit Sauce

Good source of protein and vitamin A

2 - to 2½-pound whole fish (whitefish, pike,
      salmon, lake trout or bass)
1   teaspoon salt
⅛   teaspoon dried dill weed
1   small onion, sliced
1   lemon, sliced
¼   cup margarine or butter, melted
2   tablespoons lemon juice
      Grapefruit Sauce (below)

Remove head from fish. Rub cavity of fish with salt and sprinkle with dill weed. Place onion and lemon in cavity. Place fish in greased jelly roll pan, 15½ × 10½ × 1 inch. Mix margarine and lemon juice; brush fish with margarine mixture. Cook uncovered in 350° oven, brushing occasionally with margarine mixture, until fish flakes easily with fork, about 1 hour. Prepare Grapefruit Sauce; serve over fish. Garnish with fresh dill weed or parsley if desired.

Grapefruit Sauce

½   cup unsweetened pink grapefruit juice
⅛   teaspoon salt
      Dash of dried dill weed
1   teaspoon cornstarch
1   tablespoon cold water
1   pink grapefruit, pared and sectioned

Heat grapefruit juice, salt and dill weed to boiling in 1½-quart saucepan. Mix cornstarch and cold water; stir into grapefruit juice. Heat to boiling; boil and stir 1 minute. Carefully stir in grapefruit sections.

8 servings; 200 calories each.

Oven-Fried Smelt

Good source of protein

¼   cup margarine or butter
2   tablespoons vegetable oil
⅓   cup all-purpose flour
½   teaspoon onion powder
¼   teaspoon garlic powder
½   teaspoon dry mustard
½   teaspoon paprika
1   pound smelt

Heat margarine and oil in jelly roll pan, 15½ × 10½ × 1 inch, in 425° oven until margarine is melted. Mix remaining ingredients except fish. Coat fish with flour mixture; place in pan. Cook uncovered 5 minutes; turn fish. Cook uncovered until fish flakes easily with fork, about 5 minutes longer.

4 servings (about 8 fish); 260 calories each.

Tuna-Hominy Casserole

Good source of niacin and protein

1   can (20 ounces) hominy, drained
1   can (8 ounces) tomato sauce
2   cans (6½ ounces each) tuna in water, drained
1   medium green pepper, chopped (about 1 cup)
1   small onion, chopped (about ¼ cup)
½   teaspoon ground cumin
½   cup shredded Cheddar cheese (about 2 ounces)

Mix hominy, tomato sauce, tuna, green pepper, onion and cumin in ungreased 1½-quart casserole; sprinkle with cheese. Cook uncovered in 350° oven until hot and cheese is melted, about 30 minutes.

☐ Microwave Directions: Mix all ingredients except cheese in 1½-quart microwavable casserole. Cover and microwave on high (100%) 3 minutes; stir. Microwave until hot, 4 to 6 minutes longer; sprinkle with cheese. Cover and let stand until cheese melts, about 3 minutes.

6 servings (about ¾ cup); 170 calories each.

Tuna Patties with Radish Sauce

Good source of niacin and protein

1   *can (6¹/₂ ounces) tuna in water, drained*
2   *cups cooked rice*
¹/₄ *cup chopped water chestnuts*
¹/₄ *cup sliced green onions (with tops)*
2   *eggs, slightly beaten*
1   *tablespoon cornstarch*
¹/₄ *teaspoon salt*
¹/₄ *cup vegetable oil*
     Radish Sauce (below)
2   *tablespoons sliced green onions (with tops)*

Mix tuna, rice, water chestnuts, ¹/₄ cup green onions, the eggs, cornstarch and salt. Heat oil in 10-inch skillet over medium heat. Drop mixture by ¹/₄ cupfuls, four at a time, into hot oil, spreading to form patties. Fry until golden brown and firm, turning once, about 6 minutes; keep warm. Prepare Radish Sauce. Serve over patties; sprinkle with 2 tablespoons green onions.

Radish Sauce

2   *cloves garlic, finely chopped*
2   *tablespoons vegetable oil*
1   *cup sliced radishes*
³/₄ *cup water*
1   *tablespoon soy sauce*
2   *teaspoons cornstarch*
1   *tablespoon cold water*

Cook and stir garlic in oil until light brown. Add radishes; cook and stir 2 minutes. Stir in ³/₄ cup water and the soy sauce; heat to boiling. Mix cornstarch and 1 tablespoon water; stir into radish mixture. Cook and stir 1 minute.

4 servings (3 patties); 435 calories each.

☆ ☆ ☆ ☆ ☆

Tuna with Vegetables

Good source of protein and niacin

1   *small eggplant (about 1 pound),*
     cut into ¹/₂-inch pieces
2   *stalks celery, sliced (about 1 cup)*
1   *large onion, sliced*
1   *medium green pepper, chopped (about 1 cup)*
3   *tablespoons olive or vegetable oil*
3   *tablespoons red wine vinegar*
2   *teaspoons sugar*
1   *teaspoon dried basil leaves*
³/₄ *teaspoon salt*
¹/₂ *teaspoon dried oregano leaves*
3   *medium tomatoes, chopped (about 2¹/₂ cups)*
2   *cans (6¹/₂ ounces each) tuna in water, drained*
¹/₄ *cup snipped parsley*
¹/₄ *cup grated Parmesan cheese*

Cook eggplant, celery, onion and green pepper in oil in 10-inch skillet over medium heat, stirring occasionally, until onion is tender, about 5 minutes. Stir in vinegar, sugar, basil, salt and oregano. Heat to boiling; reduce heat. Cover and simmer until eggplant is tender, about 7 minutes. Stir in tomatoes and tuna. Heat uncovered, stirring occasionally, just until tuna is hot, about 5 minutes. Stir in parsley; sprinkle with cheese.

6 servings (about 1 cup); 190 calories each.

☆ ☆ ☆ ☆ ☆

Tuna with Vegetables

Tuna Crepe Cups

Tuna Crepe Cups

Good source of protein

> Crepes (below)
> 1/4 cup finely chopped onion
> 1/4 cup finely chopped green pepper
> 1 can (6½ ounces) tuna in water, drained
> 4 eggs
> 1 cup milk
> ½ teaspoon salt
> ½ teaspoon dry mustard
> ⅛ teaspoon cayenne pepper
> 1/4 cup grated Parmesan cheese

Prepare Crepes. Carefully fit 1 crepe in each of 12 greased muffin cups, 2½ × 1¼ inches. Divide onion, green pepper and tuna among crepe-lined cups. Beat eggs, milk, salt, mustard and cayenne pepper until smooth. Pour about 3 tablespoons egg mixture into each cup. Sprinkle with cheese. Cook in 350° oven until knife inserted in center comes out clean, 20 to 25 minutes. (If edges of crepes begin to brown before eggs are set, cover with aluminum foil.) Let stand 5 minutes before serving.

Crepes

> 1 cup all-purpose flour
> 1/4 teaspoon baking powder
> 1/4 teaspoon salt
> 1¼ cups milk
> 1 egg
> 1 tablespoon margarine or butter, melted

Mix flour, baking powder and salt. Stir in remaining ingredients. Beat with hand beater until smooth. Lightly butter 6-inch skillet; heat over medium heat until bubbly. For each crepe, pour scant 1/4 cup of the batter into skillet; immediately rotate skillet until thin film of batter covers bottom. Cook until light brown. Run wide spatula around edge to loosen; turn and cook other side until light brown. Stack crepes, placing waxed paper between each. Keep crepes covered to prevent them from drying out.

6 servings; 290 calories each.

SALMON CREPE CUPS: Substitute 1 can (7¾ ounces) salmon, drained, cleaned and flaked, for the tuna.

Fitting Crepes into Cups

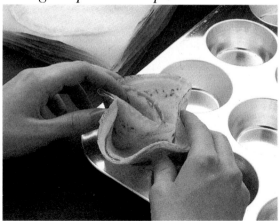

Carefully pleat each crepe to fit in each greased muffin cup.

☆ ☆ ☆ ☆ ☆

Tuna-Zucchini Soup

Good source of niacin and protein

6   slices bacon
1   medium onion, chopped (about ½ cup)
1   stalk celery, chopped (about ½ cup)
1   can (6½ ounces) tuna in water, drained
2½   cups chicken broth (page 56)
1   cup milk
1   cup shredded Cheddar cheese (about 4 ounces)
¼   teaspoon red pepper sauce
1   medium zucchini, shredded (about 1 cup)
1   teaspoon lemon juice

Fry bacon in 3-quart saucepan until crisp. Remove with slotted spoon and drain; crumble and reserve. Remove all but 2 tablespoons bacon fat. Cook and stir onion and celery in bacon fat until onion is tender, about 5 minutes. Stir in tuna, chicken broth, milk, cheese and pepper sauce. Heat, stirring occasionally, until tuna is hot and cheese is melted, about 7 minutes. Place 2 cups soup at a time in blender container. Cover and blend on medium speed until smooth, about 15 seconds. Repeat with remaining soup. Stir zucchini and lemon juice into soup; garnish with reserved bacon.

6 servings (about 1 cup); 205 calories each.

SALMON-ZUCCHINI SOUP: Substitute 1 can (7¾ ounces) salmon, drained, cleaned and flaked, for the tuna.

————— ☆ ☆ ☆ ☆ ☆ —————

Tuna-Potato Salad

Good source of protein and niacin

2   pounds potatoes (about 6 medium)
1   teaspoon instant chicken bouillon
⅓   cup hot water
⅓   cup dry white wine
2   cans (6½ ounces each) tuna in water, drained
½   cup sliced green onions
     Tarragon Dressing (below)
     Lettuce leaves
3   slices bacon, crisply fried and crumbled

Heat 1 inch salted water (½ teaspoon salt to 1 cup water) to boiling. Add potatoes. Cover and heat to boiling; reduce heat. Simmer until tender, 30 to 35 minutes; drain and cool. Cut potatoes crosswise into ¼-inch slices. Dissolve chicken bouillon in hot water; add wine. Pour over potatoes, tuna and onions. Cover and refrigerate, stirring occasionally, at least 4 hours. Prepare Tarragon Dressing; gently toss with tuna mixture. Spoon onto lettuce; sprinkle with bacon. Garnish with green onion pieces if desired.

Tarragon Dressing

3   tablespoons olive or vegetable oil
2   tablespoons vinegar
1   clove garlic, finely chopped
1   teaspoon Dijon-style mustard
¾   teaspoon dried tarragon leaves
⅛   teaspoon pepper
1   teaspoon salt

Shake all ingredients in tightly covered jar.

6 servings (about 1⅓ cups); 255 calories each.

SALMON-POTATO SALAD: Substitute 1 can (15½ ounces) salmon, drained and flaked, for the tuna.

————— ☆ ☆ ☆ ☆ ☆ —————

Tuna-Bean Salad

Good source of protein, niacin, vitamins C and D

3 medium green peppers
   Basil Dressing (below)
2 cans (16 ounces each) cannellini or
      Great Northern beans, drained
2 cans (6½ ounces each) tuna in water, drained
⅓ cup sliced ripe olives
1 bunch leaf lettuce
1 medium tomato, cut into 16 wedges

Set oven control to broil and/or 550°. Place peppers on rack in broiler pan. Broil peppers with tops 4 to 5 inches from heat until skin blisters and turns brown, about 5 minutes on each side. Wrap in towel; let stand 5 minutes. Remove skin, stems, seeds and membranes from peppers; cut peppers into ¼-inch slices.

Prepare Basil Dressing; toss with peppers, beans, tuna and olives. Cover and refrigerate, stirring occasionally, at least 4 hours. Spoon on lettuce leaves; garnish with tomato wedges.

Basil Dressing

⅓ cup olive oil
¼ cup lemon juice
2 tablespoons snipped parsley
1 tablespoon Dijon-style mustard
1 teaspoon dried basil leaves
½ teaspoon salt
½ teaspoon grated lemon peel

Shake all ingredients in tightly covered jar.

6 servings (about 1 cup); 300 calories each.

☆ ☆ ☆ ☆ ☆

Tuna-Stuffed Tomatoes

Good source of protein and niacin

½ cup bulgur (cracked wheat)
½ cup cold water
2 cans (6½ ounces each) tuna in water, drained
¼ cup finely chopped onion
2 tablespoons lemon juice
¼ teaspoon salt
¼ teaspoon dried basil leaves
¼ teaspoon dried oregano leaves
4 drops red pepper sauce
6 large tomatoes
   Lettuce leaves
2 tablespoons grated Parmesan cheese
24 pitted ripe olives

Cover bulgur with cold water. Let stand until bulgur is tender and water is absorbed, about 1 hour. Mix bulgur, tuna, onion, lemon juice, salt, basil, oregano and pepper sauce. Cover and refrigerate at least 3 hours.

Remove stem ends from tomatoes. Cut each tomato into 4 slices. Place the 2 end slices from each tomato, cut sides up, on lettuce leaves. Spoon about ¼ cup tuna mixture on each slice; sprinkle with Parmesan cheese. Top with remaining tomato slices; garnish with ripe olives. Repeat with remaining tomatoes.

6 servings; 225 calories each.

☆ ☆ ☆ ☆ ☆

Tuna-Stuffed Tomatoes

Marinated Tuna with Pasta

Good source of protein

2   cans (6½ ounces each) tuna in water, drained
2   medium tomatoes, chopped (about 1½ cups)
1   small onion, thinly sliced and separated
       into rings
½   cup pitted small ripe olives
2   cloves garlic, crushed
2   tablespoons olive or vegetable oil
2   tablespoons snipped parsley
½   teaspoon salt
½   teaspoon dried basil leaves
¼   teaspoon dried oregano leaves
⅛   teaspoon coarsely ground pepper
2   cups uncooked pasta bows (farfalle)

Mix all ingredients except pasta bows. Cover and refrigerate at least 2 hours but no longer than 24 hours.

Cook bows as directed on package; drain. Immediately toss with tuna mixture. Serve on lettuce and garnish with anchovies if desired.

5 servings (about 1 cup); 315 calories each.

☆ ☆ ☆ ☆ ☆

Crustless Salmon Quiche

Good source of protein, niacin, calcium and vitamin D

1   can (15½ ounces) salmon, drained and flaked
1   cup shredded Swiss cheese (about 4 ounces)
1   medium onion, chopped (about ½ cup)
2   tablespoons all-purpose flour
4   eggs
1   cup milk
¾   teaspoon salt
⅛   teaspoon red pepper sauce

Toss salmon, cheese and onion with flour. Spread in greased pie plate, 9 × 1¼ inches. Beat eggs slightly; beat in remaining ingredients. Pour egg mixture over salmon mixture. Cook uncovered in 350° oven until knife inserted in center comes out clean, 35 to 40 minutes. Let stand 10 minutes before cutting.

6 servings; 280 calories each.

CRUSTLESS TUNA QUICHE: Substitute 2 cans (6½ ounces each) tuna in water, drained, for the salmon.

☆ ☆ ☆ ☆ ☆

Salmon with Artichokes

Good source of protein, niacin and vitamin D

4   slices bacon, cut into ½-inch pieces
1   medium onion, sliced
1   medium stalk celery, diagonally sliced
1   package (10 ounces) frozen artichoke hearts
1   package (10 ounces) frozen green peas
¼   cup water
½   teaspoon salt
¼   teaspoon dried tarragon leaves
¼   teaspoon pepper
1   can (15½ ounces) salmon, drained and flaked
1   jar (2 ounces) diced pimiento, drained
1   tablespoon lemon juice
3   cups hot cooked spaghetti

Fry bacon in 10-inch skillet until crisp. Remove with slotted spoon and drain on paper towel; reserve. Cook and stir onion and celery in bacon fat until onion is tender, about 5 minutes. Stir in artichokes, peas, water, salt, tarragon and pepper. Heat to boiling; reduce heat. Cover and simmer until vegetables are tender, about 10 minutes. Stir in salmon, pimiento and lemon juice; heat just until salmon is hot. Toss with spaghetti; sprinkle with reserved bacon.

8 servings (about 1 cup); 215 calories each.

TUNA WITH ARTICHOKES: Substitute 2 cans (6½ ounces each) tuna in water, drained, for the salmon.

☐ *Microwave Directions:* Place bacon in 2-quart microwavable casserole. Cover with paper towel and microwave on high (100%), stirring every 2 minutes until crisp, 3 to 4 minutes. Remove with slotted spoon and drain on paper towel; reserve. Stir onion and celery into bacon fat. Microwave uncovered, stirring every minute, until onion is tender, 2 to 3 minutes. Stir in artichokes, peas, 2 tablespoons water, the salt, tarragon and pepper. Cover tightly and microwave 5 minutes; stir. Cover and microwave until vegetables are almost tender, 3 to 5 minutes. Stir in salmon, pimiento and lemon juice. Cover and microwave until salmon is hot, 2 to 3 minutes longer. Toss with spaghetti; sprinkle with reserved bacon.

══════════ ☆ ☆ ☆ ☆ ☆ ══════════

Salmon-Wild Rice Soup

A good source of protein and niacin.

3   slices bacon, cut into ½-inch pieces
1   medium onion, sliced
1   medium stalk celery, thinly sliced
4   ounces mushrooms, sliced (about 1½ cups) or
        1 can (4 ounces) mushroom stems
        and pieces, drained
2   tablespoons all-purpose flour
½   teaspoon dry mustard
¼   teaspoon dried rosemary leaves
2   cans (10¾ ounces each) chicken broth
1   cup cooked wild rice
1   can (15½ ounces) salmon, drained and flaked
1   cup half-and-half
        Snipped parsley

Fry bacon in 3-quart saucepan until crisp. Remove bacon with slotted spoon and drain on paper towel; reserve. Cook and stir onion, celery and mushrooms in bacon fat until celery is tender. Stir in flour, mustard and rosemary. Cook over low heat, stirring constantly, until bubbly; remove from heat. Stir in chicken broth and rice. Heat to boiling; reduce heat. Cover and simmer 10 minutes. Stir in reserved bacon, the salmon and half-and-half. Heat, stirring occasionally, until hot. Sprinkle with parsley.

6 servings (about 1 cup); 280 calories each.

TUNA-RICE SOUP: Substitute 2 cans (6½ ounces each) tuna in water, drained, for the salmon and 1 cup cooked regular rice for the wild rice.

══════════ ☆ ☆ ☆ ☆ ☆ ══════════

Cold Poached Salmon

Good source of protein and niacin

2   *cups water*
1   *cup dry white wine*
1   *small onion, sliced*
1   *stalk celery (with leaves), chopped*
4   *parsley sprigs*
1   *teaspoon salt*
5   *peppercorns*
1   *bay leaf*
¼   *teaspoon dried thyme leaves*
¼   *teaspoon dried tarragon leaves*
4   *salmon steaks, 1 inch thick (about 2 pounds)*
    Green Sauce (below)

Heat water, wine, onion, celery, parsley, salt, peppercorns, bay leaf, thyme and tarragon to

Cold Poached Salmon

boiling in 12-inch skillet; reduce heat. Cover and simmer 5 minutes. Place fish in skillet; add water, if necessary, to cover. Heat to boiling; reduce heat. Simmer until fish flakes easily with fork, 12 to 15 minutes. Carefully remove fish with slotted spatula; place on wire rack to drain. Carefully remove skin; cut fish lengthwise into halves. Cover and refrigerate until cold, at least 4 hours. Prepare Green Sauce; serve with fish.

Green Sauce

1   *cup parsley sprigs*
1½   *cups creamed cottage cheese (large curd)*
1   *tablespoon lemon juice*
1   *tablespoon milk*
½   *teaspoon dried basil leaves*
½   *teaspoon salt*
⅛   *teaspoon pepper*
4   *to 6 drops red pepper sauce*

Place all ingredients in blender container. Cover and blend on high speed, stopping blender occasionally to scrape down sides, until smooth, about 3 minutes.

8 servings; 245 calories each.

☐ *Food Processor Directions for Green Sauce:* Place all ingredients in workbowl fitted with steel blade. Cover and process until smooth, about 15 seconds.

☐ *Microwave Directions for Fish:* Rinse fish steaks under gently running cold water. Place fish in ungreased microwavable dish, 12 × 7½ × 2 inches. Place onion, celery, parsley, salt, peppercorns, bay leaf, thyme and tarragon on fish. Pour 1 cup water and ½ cup wine over fish. Cover tightly and microwave on high (100%) 3 minutes; rotate dish ½ turn. Microwave until small ends of fish flake easily with fork, 5 to 7 minutes. Let stand 3 minutes. Continue as directed.

☆ ☆ ☆ ☆ ☆

Salmon-Squash Salads

Good source of protein, niacin and vitamin C

    Sesame Dressing (below)
 1 small zucchini, thinly sliced (about 1½ cups)
 1 small yellow summer squash, thinly sliced
        (about 1½ cups)
 2 medium stalks celery, sliced (about 1 cup)
 1 small onion, sliced and separated into rings
 1 cup sliced mushrooms
    Lettuce cups or leaves
 1 can (15½ ounces) salmon, chilled, drained
        and flaked
12 cherry tomatoes

Prepare Sesame Dressing. Toss zucchini, summer squash, celery, onion and mushrooms. Spoon into lettuce cups on each of 6 plates. Place salmon chunks on center of vegetable mixture; top with 2 cherry tomatoes. Spoon Sesame Dressing over salads.

Sesame Dressing

 1   tablespoon sesame seed
 ⅓   cup white wine vinegar
 1   tablespoon sugar
 2   tablespoons vegetable oil
 1   teaspoon dry mustard
 ½   teaspoon salt
 1   large clove garlic, crushed

Cook and stir sesame seed over medium heat until golden brown; cool. Shake seed and remaining ingredients in tightly covered container. Refrigerate until chilled, about 2 hours. Remove garlic and shake before serving.

6 servings (about 1 cup); 220 calories each.

TUNA-SQUASH SALADS: Substitute 2 cans (6½ ounces each) tuna in water, chilled and drained, for the salmon.

━━━━━━━━ ☆ ☆ ☆ ☆ ☆ ━━━━━━━━

Salmon Sandwiches

Salmon Sandwiches

Good source of protein, niacin, thiamin and vitamin C

 1   can (15½ ounces) salmon, drained and flaked
 1   small green pepper, chopped (about ½ cup)
 ½   cup salted peanuts
 ¼   cup sliced green onions
 ⅓   cup chili sauce
 1   teaspoon dry mustard
 2   to 4 drops red pepper sauce
 6   6-inch Whole Wheat Pocket Breads (page 207)
        or 6 purchased pocket breads
 3   cups shredded lettuce
 2   cups alfalfa sprouts
 ¾   cup chili sauce

Mix salmon, green pepper, peanuts, onions, ⅓ cup chili sauce, the mustard and pepper sauce. Cut or tear breads crosswise into halves. Fill each half with about ¼ cup lettuce and ¼ cup salmon mixture; top with sprouts. Serve with chili sauce.

6 servings; 505 calories each.

TUNA POCKET SANDWICHES: Substitute 2 cans (6½ ounces each) tuna in water, drained, for the salmon.

━━━━━━━━ ☆ ☆ ☆ ☆ ☆ ━━━━━━━━

Shrimp Soufflé

Shrimp Soufflé

Good source of protein

½   pound raw shrimp
¼   cup finely chopped onion
¼   cup margarine or butter
¼   cup all-purpose flour
½   teaspoon salt
     Dash of cayenne pepper
1   cup milk
4   eggs, separated
¼   teaspoon cream of tartar
     Savory Sauce (below)

Peel shrimp. Make shallow cut lengthwise down back of each shrimp; wash out sand vein. Cut shrimp into ½-inch pieces. Cook and stir onion in margarine in 2-quart saucepan over medium heat until onion is tender, about 5 minutes. Add shrimp; cook and stir just until shrimp are pink, about 3 minutes. Remove shrimp with slotted spoon; reserve. Blend flour, salt and cayenne pepper into margarine. Cook over low heat, stirring constantly, until smooth and bubbly; remove from heat. Stir in milk. Heat to boiling, stirring constantly. Boil and stir 1 minute. Remove from heat; stir in shrimp.

Heat oven to 325°. Butter 6-cup soufflé dish or 1½-quart casserole. Beat egg whites and cream of tartar in large bowl on high speed until stiff but not dry. Beat egg yolks in small bowl until very thick and lemon colored, about 5 minutes; stir into shrimp mixture. Stir about ¼ of the egg whites into shrimp mixture. Fold shrimp mixture into remaining egg whites. Carefully pour into soufflé dish. Cook uncovered until knife inserted halfway between center and edge comes out clean, 50 to 60 minutes. Prepare Savory Sauce. Divide soufflé into sections with 2 forks. Serve soufflé immediately with sauce.

Savory Sauce

1   tablespoon margarine or butter
1   tablespoon all-purpose flour
½   teaspoon dried savory leaves
⅛   teaspoon pepper
¾   cup milk
¼   cup dry white wine

Heat margarine in 1-quart saucepan over low heat until melted. Blend in flour, savory and pepper. Cook over low heat, stirring constantly, until mixture is smooth and bubbly; remove from heat. Stir in milk. Heat to boiling, stirring constantly. Boil and stir 1 minute. Stir in wine; heat just to boiling.

5 servings; 275 calories each.

NOTE: 1 can (4¼ ounces) tiny shrimp, rinsed and drained, can be substituted for the cut-up cooked shrimp.

☆ ☆ ☆ ☆ ☆

Shrimp with Almonds

Good source of protein

½	pound raw shrimp
1	teaspoon cornstarch
4	large stalks bok choy
2	tablespoons cornstarch
3	tablespoons soy sauce
1	package (6 ounces) frozen pea pods
2	tablespoons vegetable oil
½	cup blanched almonds
⅛	teaspoon salt
2	tablespoons vegetable oil
1	teaspoon finely chopped gingerroot
1	teaspoon finely chopped garlic
4	ounces mushrooms, sliced (about 1½ cups)
1	can (8½ ounces) sliced bamboo shoots, drained
½	cup chicken broth (page 56)

Peel shrimp. Make shallow cut lengthwise down back of each shrimp; wash out sand vein. Cut shrimp lengthwise into halves; cut each half crosswise into halves. Toss shrimp and 1 teaspoon cornstarch. Cover and refrigerate about 30 minutes.

Separate bok choy leaves from stems. Cut leaves into 2-inch pieces; cut stems diagonally into ¼-inch slices. (Do not combine leaves and stems.) Mix 2 tablespoons cornstarch and the soy sauce. Rinse pea pods under running cold water to separate; drain.

Heat 2 tablespoons oil in 12-inch skillet or wok over high heat until hot. Add almonds; cook and stir until golden brown, about 1 minute. Remove almonds from skillet with slotted spoon; drain on paper towels. Sprinkle with salt. Add 2 tablespoons oil to skillet. Add shrimp, gingerroot and garlic; cook and stir until shrimp are pink. Remove shrimp with slotted spoon; reserve.

Add bok choy stems to skillet; cook and stir 2 minutes. Add bok choy leaves, mushrooms and bamboo shoots; cook and stir 1 minute. Stir in chicken broth; heat to boiling. Stir in cornstarch mixture; cook and stir until thickened, about 10 seconds. Stir in shrimp and pea pods; heat just until shrimp are hot. Sprinkle with almonds.

4 servings (about 1 cup); 335 calories each.

☆ ☆ ☆ ☆ ☆

Seafood Rice Pie

Good source of protein

1½	cups hot cooked rice
1	egg white
1	tablespoon snipped chives
1	can (6½ ounces) crabmeat, drained and cartilage removed
1	can (4½ ounces) tiny shrimp, rinsed and drained
⅓	cup finely chopped onion
1	jar (2 ounces) diced pimiento, drained
½	cup shredded mozzarella cheese (about 2 ounces)
3	eggs
1	egg yolk
1¼	cups milk
½	teaspoon salt
⅛	teaspoon cayenne pepper
1	avocado, cut into 8 slices
8	cherry tomato halves

Heat oven to 350°. Mix rice, egg white and chives with fork. Pour into greased pie plate, 9 × 1¼ inches. Spread rice mixture evenly with rubber spatula on bottom and up side of pie plate (do not leave any holes). Cook uncovered 5 minutes.

Sprinkle crabmeat, shrimp, onion, pimiento and cheese in rice crust. Beat eggs, egg yolk, milk, salt and cayenne pepper with hand beater until smooth. Pour over seafood mixture. Bake until knife inserted 1 inch from edge comes out clean, 25 to 30 minutes. Immediately run knife around edge to loosen crust. Let stand 10 minutes before cutting. Cut into wedges; top each with avocado slice and cherry tomato half.

8 servings; 240 calories each.

☆ ☆ ☆ ☆ ☆

Mussel Stew

Oyster Casserole

Good source of protein, riboflavin, thiamin, calcium and iron

1	medium onion, chopped (about $1/2$ cup)
2	medium stalks celery, chopped (about 1 cup)
2	tablespoons margarine or butter
2	tablespoons all-purpose flour
$1/2$	teaspoon salt
$1/4$	teaspoon ground sage
$1/8$	teaspoon ground thyme
$1/8$	teaspoon pepper
1	cup milk
3	cups hot cooked rice
1	pint oysters, well drained
$1/2$	cup grated Parmesan cheese
$1 1/2$	cups fresh bread crumbs
$3/4$	teaspoon dry mustard
$1/4$	cup margarine or butter, melted

Cook and stir onion and celery in 2 table-spoons margarine in 2-quart saucepan until onion is tender, about 5 minutes. Stir in flour, salt, sage, thyme and pepper. Cook over low heat, stirring constantly, until bubbly; remove from heat. Stir in milk. Heat to boiling, stirring constantly. Boil and stir 1 minute. Stir in rice. Spoon rice mixture into ungreased baking dish, $8 \times 8 \times 2$ inches, or 2-quart casserole. Arrange oysters on top. Mix cheese, bread crumbs, mustard and $1/4$ cup margarine; sprinkle over oysters. Cook uncovered in 375° oven until oysters are done and crumbs are light brown, about 30 minutes.

5 servings (about $3/4$ cup); 515 calories each.

☆ ☆ ☆ ☆ ☆

Mussel Stew

Good source of vitamin A

6	slices bacon
1	large onion, chopped (about 1 cup)
2	cloves garlic, finely chopped
1	can (28 ounces) whole tomatoes
$1/4$	cup snipped parsley
1	teaspoon Worcestershire sauce
$1/4$	teaspoon dried thyme leaves
$1/8$	teaspoon red pepper sauce
2	dozen mussels

Fry bacon in 4-quart Dutch oven until crisp. Remove bacon with slotted spoon; crumble and reserve. Remove all but 2 tablespoons bacon fat. Cook and stir onion and garlic in bacon fat until onion is tender. Stir in tomatoes (with liquid), parsley, Worcestershire sauce, thyme and pepper sauce. Break up tomatoes with fork. Place mussels on top. Heat to boiling; reduce heat. Cover and simmer un-til mussels open, about 5 minutes. Place 6 mussels in each of 4 shallow bowls; spoon tomato mixture over mussels. Sprinkle with reserved bacon.

4 servings; 220 calories each.

☆ ☆ ☆ ☆ ☆

Crabmeat Roll-Ups

Crabmeat Roll-Ups

Good source of protein

1	can (6½ ounces) crabmeat, drained and cartilage removed
½	cup shredded Swiss or Monterey Jack cheese (about 2 ounces)
1	small zucchini, shredded (about ½ cup)
¼	cup finely chopped celery
¼	cup finely chopped onion
3	tablespoons chili sauce
½	teaspoon salt
10	slices white sandwich bread
3	tablespoons margarine or butter, melted
	Avocado Sauce (below)

Mix crabmeat, cheese, zucchini, celery, onion, chili sauce and salt. Remove crusts from each slice of bread. Roll each slice to about ¼ inch thickness. Spoon crabmeat mixture across center of each slice of bread. Bring sides of bread up over crabmeat mixture; secure with wooden picks. Place roll-ups, seam sides down, in ungreased baking dish, 13 × 9 × 2 inches; brush with margarine. Cook uncovered in 350° oven until golden brown and hot, about 25 minutes. Prepare Avocado Sauce; serve over roll-ups.

Avocado Sauce

½	cup plain yogurt or dairy sour cream
½	teaspoon salt
1	medium tomato, chopped and drained
1	medium avocado, chopped

Heat yogurt and salt just until warm. Gently stir in tomato; heat 1 minute. Remove from heat; carefully stir in avocado.

5 servings (2 roll-ups); 390 calories.

TUNA ROLL-UPS: Substitute 1 can (6½ ounces) tuna in water, drained, for the crabmeat.

APPETIZER ROLL-UPS: Omit Avocado Sauce. Cut each roll-up into 3 pieces. 30 appetizers.

☆ ☆ ☆ ☆ ☆

Squid and Scallop Salad

Good source of protein and vitamin C

1/2   pound bay scallops
1   pound cleaned squid, cut into pieces
1/3   cup vegetable oil
1/4   cup lemon juice
1   tablespoon snipped parsley
1   clove garlic, finely chopped
1/4   teaspoon dried oregano leaves
1/8   teaspoon salt
1   small red onion, sliced and separated into rings
1/4   cup small pitted ripe olives
       Lettuce leaves
1   lemon, cut into wedges

Heat 2 quarts salted water (1 teaspoon salt) to boiling; reduce heat. Add scallops. Simmer until opaque, about 1 minute. (Do not drain water.) Remove with slotted spoon and drain; reserve. Place squid in same water. Cover and cook until tender, about 30 minutes; drain.

Shake oil, lemon juice, parsley, garlic, oregano and salt in tightly covered container. Toss with scallops, squid, onion and olives. Cover and refrigerate, stirring occasionally, at least 4 hours. Serve on lettuce leaves with lemon.

6 servings (about 1/2 cup); 240 calories each.

☆ ☆ ☆ ☆ ☆

Scallops in Wine Sauce

Good source of protein

4   ounces mushrooms, sliced (about 1 1/2 cups)
1   small leek (with green top), sliced (about 1/3 cup)
2   tablespoons margarine or butter
2   tablespoons olive or vegetable oil
1/2   cup dry white wine
1/8   teaspoon dried tarragon leaves
1   pound scallops
2   teaspoons cornstarch
2   tablespoons cold water
3   cups shredded lettuce
1   lemon, cut into wedges

Cook and stir mushrooms and leek in margarine and oil in 10-inch skillet 5 minutes. Stir in wine and tarragon. Heat to boiling; add scallops. Reduce heat; cook uncovered, stirring occasionally, until scallops turn white, 3 to 4 minutes. Mix cornstarch and water; stir into scallop mixture. Heat to boiling; boil and stir 1 minute. Spoon scallop mixture over lettuce; garnish with lemon wedges.

5 servings; 230 calories each.

☆ ☆ ☆ ☆ ☆

HOW TO PURCHASE SHELLFISH

Shellfish can be purchased live, partially or completely prepared as well as commercially frozen. Live mussels and clams should have tightly closed shells; however, an open shell will close when tapped if it is alive. If the mussel is not alive, do not use it for cooking. Two live mussels will make a sound like rocks when they are cracked together.

Just-caught shellfish are often commercially frozen for shipment in prime condition to locations thousands of miles from the sea. Solidly frozen seafood can be stored in the freezer for two to four months. Properly frozen packages of seafood are hard, never soft, to the touch and are free of ice crystals and frost. Avoid seafood with a strong, rancid odor or with white or discolored patches, which indicate freezer burn.

Oysters, scallops and clams are partially prepared when purchased shucked in their own liquid. Raw shrimp are available either with shells or completely shelled. Crab and shrimp can be purchased fully cooked in the deli or seafood section of many supermarkets. The flesh of partially prepared and prepared shellfish should be firm and spring back when pressed, indicating freshness.

Scallops in Wine Sauce, and Squid and Scallop Salad

Nutrition Information Per Serving or Unit

Recipe and Page Number	Protein	Carbo-hydrates	Fat	Sodium	Potas-sium	Protein	Calcium	Iron
		Grams		Milligrams		Percent U.S. Recommended Daily Allowance		
Baked Fish with Grapefruit Sauce, 28	16	7	12	440	425	34	0	4
Chili Fish Stew, 24	22	8	6	665	650	46	10	10
Chili Skillet Fish, 17	18	5	8	600	325	40	4	10
Cod with Marinated Tomatoes, 19	26	3	1	755	505	56	4	6
Cold Poached Salmon, 36	36	2	10	445	600	80	4	10
Crabmeat Roll-Ups, 41	15	31	23	1235	645	30	20	10
Creamed Cod and New Potatoes, 20	31	26	16	490	855	64	10	10
Creole Fish Stew, 23	22	13	11	465	670	48	8	10
Crustless Salmon Quiche, 34	26	6	17	765	400	56	44	10
Fish and Vegetable Soup, 25	23	12	2	890	525	36	8	16
Fish with Cabbage, 18	13	12	13	630	520	28	4	6
Fish with Dressing, 15	33	22	9	648	740	60	8	14
Fish with Radishes, 16	13	3	5	270	335	28	0	4
Flounder in Wine, 21	31	4	17	550	725	68	8	12
Garlic Cod, 18	26	2	13	320	415	56	4	6
Hot Pepper Snapper, 23	22	14	7	350	625	42	6	12
Marinated Swordfish, 14	32	2	14	70	30	70	4	10
Marinated Tuna with Pasta, 34	16	38	11	325	260	30	4	16
Mussel Stew, 40	10	14	14	390	570	24	4	12
Mustard-Topped Fish, 16	23	1	5	350	470	52	6	4
Orange Almond Trout, 20	23	19	23	545	240	50	4	6
Oven-Fried Fish, 17	18	5	9	400	290	40	6	8
Oven-Fried Smelt, 28	18	15	14	115	70	40	4	6
Oyster Casserole, 40	20	62	21	1340	395	40	32	44
Red Snapper Stew, 24	13	6	4	740	475	24	4	8
Red Snapper with Vegetable Sauce, 22	19	11	6	765	520	42	6	8
Salmon Sandwiches, 37	28	63	16	1320	730	52	24	22

Nutrition Information Per Serving or Unit

Recipe and Page Number	Protein	Carbo-hydrates	Fat	Sodium	Potas-sium	Protein	Calcium	Iron
	Grams			Milligrams		Percent U.S. Recommended Daily Allowance		
Salmon-Squash Salads, 37	17	11	12	585	665	38	24	10
Salmon-Wild Rice Soup, 35	24	14	14	1105	645	44	24	10
Salmon with Artichokes, 35	17	21	7	515	400	30	16	14
Scallops in Wine Sauce, 42	22	6	11	305	700	50	14	22
Seafood Rice Pie, 39	15	16	13	580	445	28	14	12
Sesame Perch, 21	18	2	12	305	305	40	4	8
Shrimp Soufflé, 38	12	12	20	480	270	26	16	10
Shrimp with Almonds, 39	13	19	23	980	670	30	10	18
Squid and Scallop Salad, 42	22	7	14	335	600	48	8	10
Steamed Fish with Ginger, 27	19	6	13	1085	495	42	0	6
Stuffed Baked Fish, 27	19	17	13	300	480	34	0	6
Sweet-Sour Fish Bake, 15	22	28	1	570	670	50	4	8
Swordfish with Cucumber, 14	32	3	14	415	85	70	4	10
Tuna-Bean Salad, 32	22	20	15	780	660	40	8	22
Tuna Crepe Cups, 30	21	20	14	485	250	40	20	12
Tuna-Hominy Casserole, 28	20	14	4	905	355	44	10	12
Tuna Patties with Radish Sauce, 29	19	36	24	1200	470	34	6	16
Tuna-Potato Salad, 31	20	21	10	1240	605	40	4	12
Tuna-Stuffed Tomatoes, 32	20	19	8	865	555	40	10	16
Tuna with Vegetables, 29	19	10	8	865	495	42	10	12
Tuna-Zucchini Soup, 31	19	5	12	800	365	42	20	8

Poultry
★ ★ ★

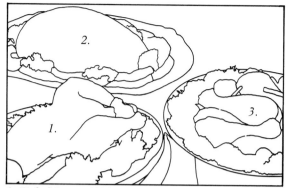

1. Herbed Lemon Chicken, 2. Turkey with Pineapple,
3. Chicken with Duchess Potatoes.

Herbed Lemon Chicken

Good source of protein and niacin

    Herbed Stuffing (below)
2½ - *to 3-pound broiler-fryer chicken*
  ¼ *cup margarine or butter, melted*
  2 *tablespoons lemon juice*
  ½ *teaspoon dried oregano leaves*
  1 *small clove garlic, finely chopped*

Prepare Herbed Stuffing. Fill wishbone area of chicken with stuffing first. Fasten neck skin to back with skewer. Fold wings across back with tips touching. Fill body cavity lightly. Tie or skewer drumsticks to tail. Place chicken, breast side up, on rack in shallow roasting pan. Mix remaining ingredients; generously brush over chicken. Roast uncovered in 375° oven, brushing with margarine mixture 2 or 3 times, until thickest parts are done and drumstick meat feels very soft, about 1¾ hours.

Herbed Stuffing

  ½ *cup chopped celery (with leaves)*
  1 *small onion, chopped (about ¼ cup)*
  ⅓ *cup margarine or butter, melted*
  2 *tablespoons lemon juice*
  ¾ *teaspoon salt*
  ½ *teaspoon dried sage leaves*
  ¼ *teaspoon dried thyme leaves*
  ⅛ *teaspoon pepper*
  3 *cups soft bread cubes*

Mix all ingredients except bread cubes. Toss with bread cubes.

7 servings; 270 calories per serving.

☆ ☆ ☆ ☆ ☆

Gingered Chicken with Vegetables

Good source of protein and niacin

2½ - *to 3-pound whole broiler-fryer chicken*
  ¼ *cup margarine or butter, melted*
  ¼ *teaspoon paprika*
  ¼ *teaspoon ground ginger*
  2 *packages (6 ounces each) frozen pea pods*
  1 *medium onion, chopped (about ½ cup)*
  ½ *teaspoon ground turmeric*
  ¼ *teaspoon ground ginger*
  2 *tablespoons margarine or butter*
  8 *ounces medium mushrooms*
  1 *teaspoon salt*
  2 *teaspoons lemon juice*
  8 *cherry tomatoes, cut into halves*

Fold wings of chicken across back with tips touching. Tie drumsticks to tail. Place chicken, breast side up, on rack in shallow roasting pan. Mix ¼ cup margarine, the paprika and ¼ teaspoon ginger; generously brush over chicken. Roast uncovered in 375° oven, brushing with margarine mixture 2 or 3 times, until thickest parts are done and drumstick meat feels very soft, about 1¼ hours.

About 15 minutes before chicken is done, rinse pea pods under running cold water to separate; drain. Cook and stir onion, turmeric and ¼ teaspoon ginger in 2 tablespoons margarine in 10-inch skillet over medium heat until onion is almost tender, about 3 minutes. Stir in pea pods, mushrooms, salt and lemon juice. Cook uncovered, stirring occasionally, until pea pods are hot, about 5 minutes. Stir in cherry tomatoes; heat just until hot. Serve vegetables with chicken.

7 servings; 255 calories per serving.

☆ ☆ ☆ ☆ ☆

Chicken Potato Roast

Good source of protein and niacin

2½ - to 3-pound whole broiler-fryer chicken
1 medium apple, cut into fourths
1 medium onion, cut into fourths
2 large cloves garlic, cut into fourths
8 medium potatoes
½ cup margarine or butter, melted
1 teaspoon dried thyme leaves
1 teaspoon paprika
½ teaspoon salt

Fold wings of chicken across back with tips touching. Place apple, onion and garlic in body cavity. Tie drumsticks to tail. Place chicken, breast side up, on rack in shallow roasting pan. Cut potatoes crosswise into ¼-inch slices about ¾ of the way through. Place on rack around chicken. Mix remaining ingredients; brush over chicken and potatoes. Roast uncovered in 375° oven, brushing chicken and potatoes with margarine mixture every 30 minutes, until thickest parts of chicken are done and potatoes are tender, 1¾ to 2 hours.

7 servings; 335 calories per serving.

☆ ☆ ☆ ☆ ☆

Chicken with Gravy

Good source of protein and niacin

2½ - to 3-pound whole broiler-fryer chicken
1 tablespoon margarine or butter, softened
½ teaspoon salt
¼ teaspoon ground allspice
1 tablespoon margarine or butter
¼ cup water
Gravy (below)

Fold wings of chicken across back with tips touching. Tie drumsticks to tail. Mix softened margarine, salt and allspice; brush over chicken. Heat 1 tablespoon margarine in 4-quart Dutch oven over medium heat until melted. Cook chicken until brown on all sides; add water. Cover and cook, breast side up, over low heat until chicken is done, 30 to 40 min-

utes. Remove chicken; keep warm. Prepare Gravy; serve with chicken.

Gravy

Milk
½ cup milk
¼ cup all-purpose flour
½ teaspoon salt
⅛ teaspoon ground allspice
1 can (4 ounces) mushroom stems and pieces, drained
1 teaspoon currant jelly

Pour drippings into measuring cup; skim off any excess fat. Add enough milk to drippings to measure 1½ cups; return to Dutch oven. Shake ½ cup milk, the flour, salt and allspice in tightly covered container; gradually stir into drippings mixture. Stir in mushrooms and jelly. Heat to boiling, stirring constantly. Boil and stir 1 minute.

7 servings; 210 calories per serving.

☐ Pressure Cooker Directions: Prepare chicken as directed. Heat 1 tablespoon margarine in 6-quart pressure cooker until melted. Cook chicken until brown on all sides. Place chicken on rack; add water. Following manufacturer's directions, cover and cook at 15 pounds pressure 12 to 15 minutes. Cool 5 minutes; reduce pressure. Remove chicken; keep warm. Prepare Gravy; serve with chicken.

☆ ☆ ☆ ☆ ☆

bone area of chicken with stuffing first. Fasten neck skin to back with skewer. Fold wings across back with tips touching. Fill body cavity lightly. (Place any remaining stuffing in small ungreased baking dish; cover and refrigerate. Place in oven with chicken the last 30 minutes of roasting.) Tie or skewer drumsticks to tail. Place chicken, breast side up, on rack in shallow roasting pan. Mix 2 tablespoons margarine and the paprika; brush over chicken. Roast uncovered in 375° oven until thickest parts are done and drumstick meat feels very soft, 1¼ to 1¾ hours.

7 servings; 395 calories per serving.

☆ ☆ ☆ ☆ ☆

Wine Sauced Chicken

Good source of protein and niacin

3 - *to 4-pound whole broiler-fryer chicken*
1 *tablespoon margarine or butter, melted*
1 *cup dry red wine*
1 *can (8 ounces) tomato sauce*
1 *medium onion, finely chopped*
2 *large cloves garlic, finely chopped*
1 *teaspoon dried basil leaves*
½ *teaspoon salt*

Fold wings of chicken across back with tips touching. Tie or skewer drumsticks to tail. Place chicken, breast side up, on rack in shallow roasting pan; brush with margarine. Roast uncovered in 375° oven until thickest parts are done, 1¾ to 2¼ hours. Mix remaining ingredients in 1½-quart saucepan. Heat to boiling, stirring occasionally; reduce heat. Cover and simmer 30 minutes. Serve sauce with chicken.

7 servings; 185 calories per serving.

☆ ☆ ☆ ☆ ☆

Rice Stuffed Chicken

Rice Stuffed Chicken

Good source of protein, niacin and vitamin A

⅓ *cup margarine or butter, melted*
1 *teaspoon salt*
1 *teaspoon ground ginger*
½ *teaspoon finely shredded lemon peel*
¼ *teaspoon garlic powder*
1½ *cups cooked brown or regular rice*
1 *medium apple, chopped (about 1 cup)*
½ *cup chopped nuts*
½ *cup cut-up prunes*
½ *cup cut-up dried apricots*
¼ *cup chopped celery*
2½ - *to 3-pound whole broiler-fryer chicken*
2 *tablespoons margarine or butter, melted*
¼ *teaspoon paprika*

Mix ⅓ cup margarine, the salt, ginger, lemon peel and garlic powder; toss with rice, apple, nuts, prunes, apricots and celery. Fill wish-

Broiled Pepper Chicken

Good source of protein and niacin

2½ - to 3-pound broiler-fryer chicken
1   tablespoon vegetable oil
2   teaspoons dried marjoram leaves
1   to 1½ teaspoons red pepper flakes
2   teaspoons margarine or butter, melted
½   teaspoon salt

Cut chicken into pieces; cut each breast half into halves. Mix oil, marjoram, red pepper, margarine and salt; brush chicken on both sides with margarine mixture. Place chicken, skin sides down, on rack in broiler pan. Set oven control to broil and/or 550°. Broil chicken with tops 7 to 9 inches from heat 30 minutes; turn. Broil until brown and thickest pieces are done, 20 to 30 minutes longer.

7 servings; 150 calories per serving.

☆ ☆ ☆ ☆ ☆

Oven Barbecued Chicken

Good source of protein and niacin

2½ - to 3-pound broiler-fryer chicken
¾   cup chili sauce
2   tablespoons honey
2   tablespoons soy sauce
1   teaspoon dry mustard
½   teaspoon prepared horseradish
½   teaspoon red pepper sauce

Cut chicken into pieces; cut each breast half into halves. Place chicken pieces, skin sides up, in ungreased rectangular pan, 13 × 9 × 2 inches. Mix remaining ingredients; pour over chicken. Cover and cook in 375° oven 30 minutes. Spoon sauce over chicken; cook uncovered until thickest pieces are done, about 30 minutes longer.

7 servings; 175 calories per serving.

□ *Microwave Directions:* Arrange chicken pieces, skin sides up, with meatiest parts to outside edges in microwavable dish, 12 × 7½ × 2 inches. Mix remaining ingredients; pour over chicken. Cover with waxed paper and microwave on high (100%) 10 minutes. Spoon sauce over chicken; rotate dish ½ turn. Cover and microwave until thickest pieces are done, 6 to 10 minutes longer.

☆ ☆ ☆ ☆ ☆

Herbed Chicken

Good source of protein and niacin

2½ - to 3-pound broiler-fryer chicken
2   tablespoons margarine or butter
2   tablespoons olive or vegetable oil
¼   cup finely chopped onion
¼   cup lemon juice
2   tablespoons Worcestershire sauce
½   teaspoon dried basil leaves
¼   teaspoon dried marjoram leaves
¼   teaspoon dried oregano leaves
2   large cloves garlic, finely chopped

Cut chicken into pieces; cut each breast half into halves and remove skin. Heat margarine and oil in rectangular pan, 13 × 9 × 2 inches, in 375° oven until margarine is melted. Stir in remaining ingredients except chicken. Place chicken, meaty sides down, in pan, turning to coat with herb mixture. Cook uncovered 30 minutes. Turn chicken; cook until thickest pieces are done, about 30 minutes longer.

7 servings; 200 calories per serving.

□ *Microwave Directions:* Prepare chicken as directed. Place margarine and oil in microwavable dish, 12 × 7½ × 2 inches. Microwave uncovered on high (100%) until margarine is melted, 45 to 60 seconds. Stir in remaining ingredients except chicken. Place chicken in dish, turning to coat with herb mixture. Arrange with thickest pieces to outside edges in dish. Cover with waxed paper and microwave on high (100%) 10 minutes; rotate dish ½ turn. Microwave until thickest pieces are done, 6 to 10 minutes longer.

☆ ☆ ☆ ☆ ☆

Chicken with Apricots

Good source of protein and niacin

2½ - to 3-pound broiler-fryer chicken
2 tablespoons soy sauce
2 tablespoons honey
1 tablespoon vegetable oil
1 tablespoon chili sauce
½ teaspoon ground ginger
⅛ teaspoon cayenne pepper
1 can (16 ounces) apricot halves in juice,
   drained

Cut chicken into pieces; cut each breast half into halves and remove skin. Place chicken in rectangular pan, 13 × 9 × 2 inches. Mix remaining ingredients except apricots; brush over chicken, turning pieces to coat. Cook uncovered in 375° oven, brushing with soy mixture occasionally, until thickest pieces are done, 50 to 60 minutes. About 5 minutes before chicken is done, arrange apricots around chicken; brush chicken and apricots with soy mixture. Cook until apricots are hot, about 5 minutes. Spoon liquid from pan over chicken and apricots.

7 servings; 205 calories per serving.

☐ *Microwave Directions:* Prepare chicken as directed. Arrange with thickest parts to outside edges in microwavable dish, 12 × 7½ × 2 inches. Brush chicken with soy mixture, turning pieces to coat. Cover tightly and microwave on high (100%) 10 minutes. Brush with soy mixture; rotate dish ½ turn. Cover and microwave until thickest pieces are done, 6 to 10 minutes longer. Arrange apricots around chicken; brush chicken and apricots with soy mixture. Microwave uncovered until apricots are hot, about 1 minute.

☆ ☆ ☆ ☆ ☆

Cornmeal Chicken

Good source of protein and niacin

2½ - to 3-pound broiler-fryer chicken
2 tablespoons yellow cornmeal
⅛ teaspoon salt
½ teaspoon chili powder
¼ teaspoon dried oregano leaves
2 tablespoons margarine or butter
2 tablespoons vegetable oil
   Casera Sauce (below)

Cut chicken into pieces; cut each breast half into halves and remove skin. Mix cornmeal, salt, chili powder and oregano. Coat chicken with cornmeal mixture. Heat margarine and oil in rectangular pan, 13 × 9 × 2 inches, in 375° oven until margarine is melted. Place chicken, meaty sides down, in pan. Cook uncovered 30 minutes. Turn chicken; cook until brown and thickest pieces are done, 20 to 30 minutes longer. Prepare Casera Sauce; serve with chicken.

Casera Sauce

1 medium tomato, finely chopped
1 small onion, chopped (about ¼ cup)
1 small clove garlic, crushed
1 canned green chili or jalapeño pepper,
   seeded and finely chopped
2 teaspoons finely snipped cilantro or parsley
2 teaspoons lemon juice
¼ teaspoon dried oregano leaves

Mix all ingredients.

7 servings; 200 calories per serving.

☆ ☆ ☆ ☆ ☆

Chicken with Artichokes and Grapes

Good source of protein and niacin

2¹/₂ - to 3-pound broiler-fryer chicken
  6 slices bacon, cut up
  ¹/₂ teaspoon salt
  ¹/₂ teaspoon paprika
  ¹/₂ teaspoon dried tarragon leaves
  ¹/₂ cup dry white wine or apple juice
  4 ounces mushrooms, sliced (about 1¹/₂ cups) or
        1 can (4 ounces) mushroom stems
        and pieces, drained
  1 can (14 ounces) artichoke hearts, drained
        and cut into halves
  2 cups seedless green or red grapes
  1 tablespoon cornstarch
  2 tablespoons cold water

Cut chicken into pieces; cut each breast half into halves and remove skin. Fry bacon in 4-quart Dutch oven until crisp. Remove with slotted spoon and drain; reserve. Pour off all but 2 tablespoons bacon fat. Mix salt, paprika and tarragon; sprinkle over chicken. Cook chicken in bacon fat until light brown on all sides; add wine and mushrooms. Heat to boiling; reduce heat. Cover and simmer until thickest pieces are done, about 40 minutes. Remove chicken; keep warm. Add artichokes and grapes to Dutch oven; heat to boiling. Mix cornstarch and cold water; stir into artichoke mixture. Heat to boiling, stirring constantly. Boil and stir 1 minute. Pour over chicken; sprinkle with bacon.

7 servings; 230 calories per serving.

☐ *Microwave Directions:* Prepare chicken as directed. Place bacon in microwavable dish, 12 × 7¹/₂ × 2 inches. Cover loosely and microwave on high (100%) until crisp, 6 to 9 minutes. Remove with slotted spoon and drain; reserve. Drain bacon fat from dish. Arrange chicken pieces with thickest parts to outside edges in dish. Mix salt, paprika and tarragon; sprinkle over chicken. Place mushrooms on chicken. Pour wine over chicken and mushrooms. Cover tightly and microwave on high (100%) 10 minutes; rotate dish ¹/₂ turn. Microwave until thickest pieces are done, 6 to 10 minutes longer. Remove chicken; keep warm. Mix cornstarch and cold water; stir into liquid in dish. Microwave uncovered, stirring every minute, until slightly thickened, 3 to 4 minutes. Stir in artichokes and grapes. Microwave uncovered 2 minutes. Pour over chicken; sprinkle with bacon.

☆ ☆ ☆ ☆ ☆

Chicken Mozzarella

Good source of protein and niacin

2½ - to 3-pound broiler-fryer chicken
2 eggs, beaten
½ cup dry bread crumbs
¼ cup margarine or butter
1 can (8 ounces) tomato sauce
½ teaspoon dried basil leaves
Mozzarella Sauce (below)
½ cup shredded mozzarella cheese
¼ teaspoon paprika

Cut chicken into serving pieces; cut each breast half into halves and remove skin. Dip chicken into eggs; coat with bread crumbs. Heat margarine in 12-inch skillet until melted. Cook chicken over medium heat until brown on all sides. Stir in tomato sauce and basil; reduce heat. Cover and cook over low heat until done, about 30 minutes. Prepare Mozzarella Sauce. Arrange chicken pieces in ungreased square pan, 9×9×2 inches. Spoon Mozzarella Sauce over chicken; sprinkle with cheese and paprika. Set oven control to broil and/or 550°. Broil chicken with tops 6 to 7 inches from heat until cheese is melted and sauce is bubbly around edges.

Mozzarella Sauce

1 tablespoon margarine or butter
1 tablespoon all-purpose flour
⅛ teaspoon salt
⅛ teaspoon cayenne pepper
½ cup chicken broth (page 56)
½ cup half-and-half
½ cup shredded mozzarella cheese

Heat margarine in 1-quart saucepan until melted. Blend in flour, salt and cayenne pepper. Cook over low heat, stirring constantly, until smooth and bubbly; remove from heat. Stir in chicken broth and half-and-half. Heat to boiling, stirring constantly. Boil and stir 1 minute. Stir in cheese until melted.

7 servings; 335 calories per serving.

☐ *Microwave Directions:* Place margarine in 4-cup microwavable measure. Microwave un-covered on high (100%) until melted, about 45 seconds. Blend in flour, salt, cayenne pepper, chicken broth and half-and-half. Microwave, stirring every minute, until sauce is thickened, 3 to 4 minutes; stir in mozzarella cheese. Prepare chicken as directed. Dip chicken into eggs; coat with bread crumbs mixed with 1 teaspoon paprika. Place margarine in micro-wavable dish, 12×7½×2 inches. Microwave uncovered on high (100%) until melted, about 1 minute. Place chicken pieces, skin sides down, in dish; turn pieces over. Mix tomato sauce and basil; pour over chicken. Microwave uncovered 14 minutes. Pour Mozzarella Sauce over chicken. Sprinkle with cheese and papri-ka; rotate dish ½ turn. Microwave until thickest pieces are done, 4 to 8 minutes longer.

☆ ☆ ☆ ☆ ☆

Chicken with Vegetables

Good source of protein and niacin

2½ - to 3-pound broiler-fryer chicken
1 teaspoon salt
1 teaspoon paprika
2 tablespoons vegetable oil
1 can (16½ ounces) whole kernel corn, drained
3 medium tomatoes, cut into wedges
2 cloves garlic, finely chopped
1 medium zucchini, cut into ¼-inch slices
1 medium onion, chopped (about ½ cup)
1 teaspoon dried oregano leaves
1 teaspoon chili powder
½ teaspoon ground cumin

Cut chicken into pieces; cut each breast half into halves and remove skin. Sprinkle chicken with salt and paprika. Cook chicken in oil in 4-quart Dutch oven or 12-inch skillet over medium heat until light brown, 15 to 20 minutes; reduce heat. Cover and cook 20 minutes. Stir in remaining ingredients. Heat to boiling; reduce heat. Cover and cook until zucchini is crisp-tender and vegetables are heated through, 5 to 10 minutes. Remove vegetables with slotted spoon; serve with chicken.

7 servings; 230 calories per serving.

☆ ☆ ☆ ☆ ☆

Chicken Provençal

Good source of protein, niacin and vitamin A

2½ - to 3-pound broiler-fryer chicken
⅓ cup all-purpose flour
1 teaspoon paprika
1 teaspoon dried basil leaves
½ teaspoon salt
½ teaspoon dried oregano leaves
¼ teaspoon pepper
¼ teaspoon dried marjoram leaves
3 tablespoons vegetable oil
16 small pitted ripe olives
8 medium carrots, cut into fourths
8 small whole onions
4 medium potatoes, cut into fourths
1 cup chicken broth (page 56)
1 tablespoon cornstarch
1 tablespoon cold water

Cut chicken into pieces; cut each breast half into halves and remove skin. Mix flour, paprika, basil, salt, oregano, pepper and marjoram. Coat chicken with flour mixture. Heat oil in 4-quart Dutch oven until hot. Cook chicken until brown on all sides, about 15 minutes. Add olives, carrots, onions and potatoes; pour chicken broth over vegetables. Heat to boiling; reduce heat. Cover and cook until chicken is done, about 45 minutes. Remove chicken and vegetables; keep warm. Mix cornstarch and cold water; stir into liquid in Dutch oven. Heat to boiling, stirring constantly. Boil and stir 1 minute. Serve sauce with chicken.

7 servings; 340 calories per serving.

☐ *Pressure Cooker Directions:* Prepare chicken as directed. Heat oil in 6-quart pressure cooker until hot. Cook chicken until brown on all sides. Add olives, carrots, onions, potatoes and chicken broth. Following manufacturer's directions, cover and cook at 15 pounds pressure 10 to 15 minutes. Cool 5 minutes; reduce pressure. Continue as directed except — remove all but 1 cup liquid from pressure cooker before making sauce.

☆ ☆ ☆ ☆ ☆

Chicken Provençal

Chicken-Rice Soup

Chicken-Rice Soup

Good source of protein and niacin

    Chicken Broth (below)
2   *cups cooked rice*
2   *medium tomatoes, cut into wedges*
1   *medium green pepper, chopped (about 1 cup)*
1   *medium onion, chopped (about ½ cup)*
1   *cup frozen green peas*
¼   *cup sliced pimiento-stuffed green olives*
1   *tablespoon capers*

Prepare Chicken Broth. Remove skin from reserved chicken; remove chicken from bones. Cut chicken into pieces. Stir chicken and remaining ingredients into broth. Heat uncovered until hot, about 10 minutes.

Chicken Broth

2½ - *to 3-pound broiler-fryer chicken*
4   *cups water*
4   *medium carrots, cut into ½-inch slices (about 2 cups)*
2   *medium stalks celery, cut into ½-inch slices (about 1 cup)*
2   *cloves garlic, crushed*
1   *tablespoon instant chicken bouillon*
1   *teaspoon salt*
½   *teaspoon dried marjoram leaves*

Cut chicken into pieces. Heat all ingredients to boiling in 4-quart Dutch oven; reduce heat. Cover and simmer until chicken is done, about 45 minutes. Skim off fat if necessary. Remove chicken from broth; reserve chicken. Cool broth slightly and strain.

7 servings (about 1¼ cups); 200 calories each.

☐ *Pressure Cooker Directions:* Place chicken, water, carrots, celery, garlic, instant bouillon, salt and marjoram in 4-quart pressure cooker. Following manufacturer's directions, cover and cook at 15 pounds pressure 10 to 15 minutes. Cool 5 minutes; reduce pressure. Remove chicken from broth; cool slightly. Strain broth. Remove chicken from bones and skin; cut into pieces. Add chicken, rice, tomatoes, green pepper, onion, peas, olives and capers to chicken broth. Heat uncovered until hot, about 10 minutes.

NOTE: Cut-up cooked chicken and broth can be covered and refrigerated separately; use within 24 hours. For longer storage, freeze chicken and broth together no longer than 6 months. About 3 cups cut-up cooked chicken and 4 cups broth.

☆ ☆ ☆ ☆ ☆

Chicken-Cabbage Soup

Good source of protein, niacin and vitamin A

3	cups cocktail vegetable juice
2	cups water
5	cups finely chopped cabbage
1	medium onion, sliced
4	medium carrots, cut into 1/4-inch slices
2	medium stalks celery, chopped (about 1 cup)
2	tablespoons instant chicken bouillon
1/4	teaspoon pepper
2 1/2 -	to 3-pound broiler-fryer chicken
1/2	teaspoon salt
1/2	teaspoon paprika
3	tablespoons margarine or butter

Heat vegetable juice, water, cabbage, onion, carrots, celery, bouillon and pepper to boiling in 4-quart Dutch oven; reduce heat. Cover and simmer 30 minutes. Cut chicken into pieces; cut each breast half into halves and remove skin. Sprinkle chicken with salt and paprika. Cook chicken in margarine until light brown on all sides, 15 to 20 minutes. Add chicken pieces to soup mixture. Heat to boiling; reduce heat.

Cover and simmer until chicken is done, about 30 minutes longer. Serve chicken pieces in soup bowls; pour soup over chicken.

8 servings (about 1 cup); 240 calories each.

☆ ☆ ☆ ☆ ☆

Chicken with Lentils

Good source of protein and niacin

4	slices bacon, cut into 2-inch pieces
2 1/2 -	to 3-pound broiler-fryer chicken
1	cup lentils
1	large stalk celery, sliced (about 3/4 cup)
1	medium onion, chopped (about 1/2 cup)
1	large clove garlic, finely chopped
1/2	cup dry white wine
1	can (16 ounces) whole tomatoes
1	teaspoon salt
1/2	teaspoon dried thyme leaves
1	tablespoon snipped parsley

Fry bacon in 12-inch skillet or 4-quart Dutch oven until crisp. Remove with slotted spoon and drain; reserve. Cut chicken into pieces; cut each breast half into halves and remove skin. Cook chicken in bacon fat over medium heat until light brown on all sides; remove chicken from skillet. Add lentils, celery, onion, garlic, wine, tomatoes (with liquid), salt, thyme and reserved bacon to skillet. Break up tomatoes with fork. Place chicken on mixture. Heat to boiling; reduce heat. Cover and cook until chicken is done and lentils are tender, about 45 minutes; sprinkle with parsley.

7 servings; 275 calories per serving.

☆ ☆ ☆ ☆ ☆

COOKING LEAN

Did you know that skinning chicken before you cook it subtracts about 70 calories for a 3-ounce serving? Skinning fish and trimming fat from meat saves additional calories. And when you make a soup or stew, chill it, skim congealed fat from the top and discard the fat before reheating. Depending on the recipe, you can also reduce calories by stewing, poaching, baking and steaming foods. Keep in mind the method of steaming that your mother or grandmother used — the old, reliable pressure cooker, which is again popular. The tightly sealed cooker traps steam from the boiling liquid (as in Chicken-Rice Soup, page 56). Under pressure, the cooking temperature can be raised higher than is possible with normal cooking, and the hot steam cooks foods evenly, quickly, safely and with fewer calories than other methods, such as frying. As a special bonus, you'll be saving time, too.

Italian Chicken Salad

Good source of protein and niacin

1 whole chicken breast (about 1 pound)
  Garlic Dressing (below)
4 cups bite-size pieces salad greens
1 cup cherry tomato halves
1 small red onion, sliced and separated into rings
1/2 cup small pitted ripe olives
1/4 pound salami, cut into julienne strips
1/4 pound mozzarella or Monterey Jack cheese,
  cut into julienne strips
1 can (2 ounces) anchovies, drained

Place chicken breast, skin side up, in ungreased square pan, 9×9×2 inches; cover tightly. Cook in 350° oven until done, about 1 hour. Carefully remove skin and bone; cover and refrigerate chicken until cold. Cut into julienne strips.

Prepare Garlic Dressing. Toss with greens, tomatoes, onion and olives. Arrange chicken, salami and cheese on greens mixture; garnish with anchovies.

Garlic Dressing

2 tablespoons grated Parmesan cheese
3 tablespoons olive or vegetable oil
2 tablespoons red wine vinegar
1 teaspoon dry mustard
1/4 teaspoon pepper
2 large cloves garlic, crushed

Shake all ingredients in tightly covered jar.

6 servings (about 1 1/3 cups); 295 calories each.

☆ ☆ ☆ ☆ ☆

Chicken with Plums

Good source of protein, niacin and vitamin C

  Fennel Seed Dressing (below)
2 whole chicken breasts (about 2 pounds)
2 tablespoons margarine or butter
1 tablespoon vegetable oil
4 plums, sliced
2 stalks celery, sliced (about 1 cup)
2 cups small cauliflowerets
  Lettuce leaves
1/2 cup cashew halves

Prepare Fennel Seed Dressing. Remove skin and bones from chicken. Cook chicken in 10-inch skillet in margarine and oil until done, about 6 minutes on each side. Cool slightly; cut into thin slices. Toss plums, celery and cauliflowerets with dressing in 4-quart bowl. Carefully stir in chicken. Cover and refrigerate at least 4 hours. Spoon onto lettuce leaves with slotted spoon; garnish with cashews.

Fennel Seed Dressing

1/3 cup olive or vegetable oil
1/4 cup dry white wine
1 teaspoon fennel seed
1 teaspoon sugar
1/2 teaspoon salt
1/4 teaspoon dried rosemary leaves
1/4 teaspoon dried tarragon leaves
  Dash of cayenne pepper

Shake all ingredients in tightly covered jar.

6 servings (about 1 cup); 305 calories each.

☆ ☆ ☆ ☆ ☆

SAFE HANDLING OF RAW OR COOKED FOODS

The most perishable foods are those containing poultry, seafood, meat, eggs and milk. Remember, neither raw nor cooked foods should be left at room temperature for more than an hour or two; bacteria thrive in lukewarm food. A good rule is to keep cold foods cold (below 40°) and hot foods hot (about 140°).

Be sure to keep your hands, utensils and countertops hot soap-and-water clean. For cutting raw poultry or meats, use a hard plastic cutting surface which is less porous and safer than wood. When cleaning up after working with raw foods, use disposable paper towels.

Once poultry and other perishable foods are cooked, refrigerate as quickly as possible. Leftover cooked poultry, stuffing and giblets should be refrigerated in separate containers as soon as possible; use within a few days, or freeze.

Stir-Fried Chicken

Good source of protein and niacin

2   whole chicken breasts (about 2 pounds)
1   egg white
1   teaspoon cornstarch
1   teaspoon soy sauce
½   teaspoon salt
3   medium zucchini
2   tablespoons cornstarch
2   tablespoons cold water
3   tablespoons vegetable oil
1   medium onion, thinly sliced
2   large cloves garlic, finely chopped
1   teaspoon finely chopped gingerroot
8   ounces mushrooms, sliced (about 3 cups)
½   cup chicken broth (page 56)
2   tablespoons soy sauce

Remove skin and bones from chicken; cut chicken into strips, 2 × 1 inch. Mix egg white, 1 teaspoon cornstarch, 1 teaspoon soy sauce and the salt in 1½-quart bowl; stir in chicken. Cover and refrigerate 20 minutes.

Cut zucchini lengthwise into halves; cut each half diagonally into ¼-inch slices. Mix 2 tablespoons cornstarch and the water; reserve.

Heat oil in 12-inch skillet or wok over high heat until hot. Add chicken; cook and stir until chicken turns white, about 3 minutes. Remove chicken from skillet. Add onion, garlic and gingerroot; cook and stir until garlic is brown. Add zucchini and mushrooms; cook and stir 2 minutes. Stir in chicken, chicken broth and 2 tablespoons soy sauce; heat to boiling. Stir in cornstarch mixture. Boil and stir 1 minute.

6 servings (about 1 cup); 200 calories each.

☆ ☆ ☆ ☆ ☆

Tarragon Chicken

Tarragon Chicken

Good source of protein, niacin and vitamin A

6   small chicken breast halves (about 2 pounds)
½   teaspoon paprika
6   small zucchini, cut lengthwise into halves,
      then into 2-inch pieces
4   medium carrots, cut into ¼-inch slices
4   ounces small mushrooms
⅓   cup margarine or butter, melted
1   tablespoon lemon juice
1   teaspoon dried tarragon leaves
½   teaspoon salt
⅛   teaspoon pepper

Remove skin from chicken breasts. Place chicken, meaty sides up, in ungreased rectangular baking dish, 13 × 9 × 2 inches; sprinkle with paprika. Place zucchini, carrots and mushrooms around and over chicken. Mix remaining ingredients; drizzle over chicken and vegetables. Cover and cook in 350° oven until chicken is done, 50 to 60 minutes.

6 servings; 250 calories per serving.

☆ ☆ ☆ ☆ ☆

Garlic Chicken Breasts, and Asparagus with Bacon (page 148)

Preparing Chicken Breast

Place 1 piece of margarine mixture on center of each flattened chicken breast. Fold sides up and secure with wooden picks.

Garlic Chicken Breasts

Good source of protein and niacin

¹/₄	cup margarine or butter, softened
1	tablespoon snipped chives or parsley
¹/₈	teaspoon garlic powder
6	small chicken breast halves (about 2 pounds)
3	cups cornflakes cereal, crushed (about 1¹/₂ cups)
2	tablespoons snipped parsley
¹/₂	teaspoon paprika
¹/₄	cup buttermilk or milk

Mix margarine, chives and garlic powder; shape into rectangle, 3 × 2 inches. Cover and freeze until firm, about 30 minutes. Remove skin and bones from chicken breasts. Flatten each chicken breast to ¹/₄-inch thickness between waxed paper or plastic wrap. Cut margarine mixture crosswise into 6 pieces. Place 1 piece on center of each chicken breast. Fold long sides over margarine; fold ends up and secure with wooden pick. Mix cereal, parsley and paprika. Dip chicken into buttermilk; coat evenly with cereal mixture. Place chicken breasts, seam sides down, in greased square pan, 9 × 9 × 2 inches. Cook uncovered in 425° oven until chicken is done, about 35 minutes.

6 servings; 265 calories per serving.

☐ *Microwave Directions:* Prepare chicken as directed. Arrange coated chicken breasts, seam sides down, on microwavable rack in microwavable dish. Microwave uncovered on high (100%) 4 minutes; rotate dish ¹/₂ turn. Microwave until chicken is done, 4 to 6 minutes longer. Let stand 5 minutes.

☆ ☆ ☆ ☆ ☆

Lemon-Dill Chicken

Good source of protein and niacin

6   small chicken breast halves (about 2 pounds)
1/4 cup margarine or butter
1/2 cup dry white wine
1   tablespoon lemon juice
1/4 teaspoon salt
1/8 teaspoon dried dill weed
1/2 lemon, thinly sliced
2   tablespoons sliced green onions (with tops)

Remove skin and bones from chicken breasts. Cook chicken in margarine in 10-inch skillet until light brown, turning once, about 5 minutes on each side. Mix wine, lemon juice, salt and dill weed; pour over chicken. Place lemon slices on chicken. Heat to boiling; reduce heat. Cover and simmer until chicken is done, 10 to 15 minutes. Remove chicken; keep warm. Heat wine mixture to boiling; cook until reduced to about half, about 3 minutes. Pour over chicken; sprinkle with onions.

6 servings; 220 calories per serving.

☐ *Microwave Directions:* Prepare chicken as directed. Decrease margarine to 2 tablespoons and wine to 1/4 cup. Place margarine in 3-quart microwavable casserole. Microwave uncovered on high (100%) until melted, about 1 1/2 minutes. Arrange chicken in margarine with thickest pieces to outside edge. Cover tightly and microwave on high (100%) 4 minutes. Mix wine, lemon juice, salt and dill weed; pour over chicken. Place lemon slices on chicken; rotate casserole 1/2 turn. Cover and microwave until chicken is done, 4 to 6 minutes longer. Let stand 5 minutes; sprinkle with onions.

☆ ☆ ☆ ☆ ☆

Curried Chicken Breasts

Good source of protein and niacin

6   small chicken breast halves (about 2 pounds)
2/3 cup plain yogurt
4   cloves garlic, crushed
1   teaspoon ground coriander
1   teaspoon ground ginger
1   teaspoon sesame seed
1/4 teaspoon cayenne pepper
1/8 teaspoon ground turmeric
3   large onions, thinly sliced
2   tablespoons margarine or butter
    Paprika
1   small cucumber

Remove skin from chicken breasts. Place chicken, meaty sides up, in ungreased rectangular baking dish, 12 × 7 1/2 × 2 inches. Mix yogurt, garlic, coriander, ginger, sesame seed, pepper and turmeric; pour over chicken. Turn chicken to coat both sides. Cover and refrigerate at least 4 hours.

Cook and stir onions in margarine in 10-inch skillet over medium heat until onions are tender, about 10 minutes. Remove chicken from baking dish; stir onions into yogurt in dish. Place chicken on onion mixture; sprinkle with paprika. Cook uncovered in 350° oven until chicken is done, about 1 hour. Cut cucumber lengthwise into halves; remove seeds. Chop cucumber; sprinkle over chicken.

6 servings; 230 calories per serving.

☆ ☆ ☆ ☆ ☆

Chicken Parmesan

Good source of protein and niacin

Tomato Sauce (below)
6 large chicken thighs (about 1½ pounds)
⅓ cup all-purpose flour
¼ teaspoon salt
⅛ teaspoon pepper
½ cup milk
1 egg, slightly beaten
½ cup dry bread crumbs
2 tablespoons olive or vegetable oil
1 cup shredded mozzarella cheese
¼ cup grated Parmesan cheese

Prepare Tomato Sauce. Remove skin and bones from chicken thighs. Pound chicken thighs between waxed paper or plastic wrap to about ¼-inch thickness. Mix flour, salt and pepper. Coat chicken with flour mixture. Mix milk and egg. Dip chicken into milk mixture; coat with bread crumbs. Heat oil in 10-inch skillet over medium heat until hot. Cook chicken, turning once, until golden brown (add oil to skillet if necessary). Place chicken in rectangular pan, 13 × 9 × 2 inches. Sprinkle with mozzarella cheese. Pour Tomato Sauce over cheese; sprinkle with Parmesan cheese. Cook uncovered in 375° oven until hot and bubbly, about 20 minutes.

Tomato Sauce

1 medium onion, chopped
2 large cloves garlic, crushed
1 tablespoon olive or vegetable oil
1 can (16 ounces) whole tomatoes, undrained
1 can (4 ounces) mushroom stems and pieces, drained and chopped
2 tablespoons red wine vinegar
½ teaspoon dried oregano leaves
½ teaspoon dried basil leaves
¼ teaspoon dried marjoram leaves

Cook and stir onion and garlic in oil in 2-quart saucepan until onion is tender, about 5 minutes. Add remaining ingredients. Break up tomatoes with fork. Heat to boiling; reduce heat. Simmer uncovered, stirring occasionally, until thickened, about 10 minutes.

6 servings; 390 calories per serving.

☆ ☆ ☆ ☆ ☆

Chicken with Yogurt

Good source of protein and niacin

¼ cup sliced almonds
1 tablespoon margarine or butter
8 chicken drumsticks (about 2 pounds)
1 tablespoon margarine or butter
½ teaspoon paprika
¼ teaspoon salt
¼ teaspoon dried dill weed
⅓ cup water
1 teaspoon instant chicken bouillon
1 medium onion, sliced
½ cup plain yogurt
1½ teaspoons cornstarch
¼ cup cold water

Cook and stir almonds in 1 tablespoon margarine in 10-inch skillet over medium heat until golden brown. Remove with slotted spoon and drain; reserve. Remove skin from drumsticks. Brown drumsticks on all sides in 1 tablespoon margarine over medium heat; reduce heat. Sprinkle with paprika, salt and dill weed. Mix ⅓ cup water and the bouillon; pour over chicken. Add onion. Cover and simmer until drumsticks are done, about 30 minutes. Remove drumsticks; keep warm. Stir yogurt into liquid in skillet. Mix cornstarch and ¼ cup cold water; gradually stir into yogurt mixture. Heat to boiling, stirring constantly. Boil and stir 1 minute. Pour yogurt sauce over drumsticks; sprinkle with sliced almonds.

4 servings; 360 calories per serving.

☆ ☆ ☆ ☆ ☆

Wheat-Stuffed Drumsticks

Wheat-Stuffed Drumsticks

Good source of protein and niacin

³/₄	cup cracked wheat (bulgur)
³/₄	cup cold water
¹/₃	cup chopped green onions (with tops)
¹/₄	teaspoon salt
¹/₄	teaspoon ground sage
¹/₈	teaspoon pepper
8	chicken drumsticks (about 2 pounds)
2	tablespoons margarine or butter
2	tablespoons vegetable oil
¹/₂	cup whole wheat or all-purpose flour
1	teaspoon paprika
¹/₂	teaspoon salt
¹/₄	teaspoon ground sage
¹/₄	teaspoon pepper

Cover cracked wheat with cold water. Let stand 1 hour. Mix cracked wheat, onions, ¼ teaspoon salt, ¼ teaspoon sage and ⅛ teaspoon pepper. Carefully separate skin from meat all around each drumstick, beginning at wide end. Fill opening with wheat mixture. Wipe off excess filling on outside of drumstick. Heat margarine and oil in 375° oven in rectangular pan, 13 × 9 × 2 inches, until margarine is melted. Mix flour, paprika, ½ teaspoon salt, ¼ teaspoon sage and ¼ teaspoon pepper. Coat drumsticks with flour mixture; place in pan. Cook uncovered 30 minutes. Turn drumsticks; cook until done, about 30 minutes longer.

4 servings; 505 calories per serving.

☆ ☆ ☆ ☆ ☆

Chicken with Duchess Potatoes

Good source of protein, niacin and vitamin A

	Duchess Potatoes (below)
1/4	cup all-purpose flour
1	teaspoon salt
1/2	teaspoon paprika
1/8	teaspoon pepper
8	chicken drumsticks (about 2 pounds)
2	tablespoons vegetable oil
1/2	cup dry white wine
1/4	cup water
3/4	cup peeled pearl onions (about 4 ounces)
2	medium carrots, cut into thin strips about 2 inches long
1/4	teaspoon dried thyme leaves
1/4	teaspoon salt
1	tablespoon margarine or butter, melted

Prepare Duchess Potatoes. Mix flour, 1 teaspoon salt, the paprika and pepper. Coat drumsticks with flour mixture. Heat oil in 10-inch skillet over medium heat until hot. Cook drumsticks in oil until light brown on all sides, about 15 minutes; remove from skillet. Stir in wine, water, onions, carrots, thyme and 1/4 teaspoon salt. Heat to boiling; reduce heat. Cover and simmer 10 minutes. Add drumsticks; cover and simmer until drumsticks are done and vegetables are tender, about 30 minutes longer.

Brush Duchess Potatoes with margarine. Heat in 425° oven until light brown, about 15 minutes. Serve Duchess Potatoes with drumsticks and vegetables. Skim excess fat from pan juices if necessary; serve juices with chicken.

Duchess Potatoes

3	medium potatoes (about 1 pound)
2	tablespoons milk
2	tablespoons margarine or butter, softened
1/4	teaspoon salt
	Dash of pepper
1	egg yolk, beaten

Pare potatoes; cut into large pieces. Heat 1 inch salted water (1/2 teaspoon salt to 1 cup water) to boiling. Add potatoes. Cover and heat to boiling; reduce heat. Simmer until tender, 20 to 25 minutes; drain. Shake pan gently over low heat to dry potatoes. Mash potatoes until no lumps remain. Gradually beat in milk. Add margarine, salt and pepper; beat until potatoes are light and fluffy. Beat in egg yolk. (Add more milk if necessary; potatoes should be smooth and fluffy.) Drop mixture by spoonfuls or form rosettes with decorators' tube on ungreased cookie sheet; refrigerate.

4 servings (2 drumsticks and about 1/2 cup potatoes); 525 calories each.

☆ ☆ ☆ ☆ ☆

Chicken Livers with Yogurt

Good source of protein, niacin, riboflavin, iron and vitamin A

1	pound chicken livers, cut into 1-inch pieces
3	tablespoons margarine or butter
1	can (8 ounces) sliced water chestnuts, drained
4	ounces mushrooms, cut into halves (about 1 1/2 cups)
1	small onion, sliced
1	clove garlic, finely chopped
1 1/2	teaspoons Worcestershire sauce
1/4	teaspoon salt
1/4	teaspoon ground sage
1/4	teaspoon dried basil leaves
1/2	cup plain yogurt
1	tablespoon all-purpose flour
1	tablespoon snipped parsley

Cook and stir chicken livers in margarine in 10-inch skillet over medium heat 5 minutes. Stir in water chestnuts, mushrooms, onion, garlic, Worcestershire sauce, salt, sage and basil. Heat to boiling; reduce heat. Cover and simmer 5 minutes. Mix yogurt and flour; stir into chicken livers. Heat, stirring constantly, just until hot. Sprinkle with parsley.

4 servings (about 1 cup); 295 calories each.

☆ ☆ ☆ ☆ ☆

Chili Chicken Salad

Chicken Casserole

Good source of protein, riboflavin and vitamin A

- 3   cups soft bread cubes
- 1   cup cut-up cooked chicken or turkey
- 1   package (10 ounces) frozen chopped spinach, thawed and very well drained
- ³/₄ cup dairy sour cream
- 1   can (4 ounces) mushroom stems and pieces, drained
- 2   tablespoons finely chopped onion
- 1   medium clove garlic, finely chopped
- ³/₄ teaspoon salt
- ¹/₄ teaspoon dry mustard
- 3   eggs, separated
- 3   tablespoons margarine or butter, melted
- ¹/₂ teaspoon poppy seed

Heat oven to 350°. Mix 1½ cups of the bread cubes, the chicken, spinach, sour cream, mushrooms, onion, garlic, salt, mustard and egg yolks. Beat egg whites until stiff but not dry; fold into chicken mixture. Pour into greased 1½-quart casserole. Toss remaining bread cubes, the margarine and poppy seed; sprinkle over chicken mixture. Cook uncovered in 350° oven until center is set and top is golden, about 45 minutes.

5 servings; 405 calories per serving.

═══════════ ☆ ☆ ☆ ☆ ☆ ═══════════

Chili Chicken Salad

Good source of protein and vitamin C

  Salad Dressing (below)
- 3   cups cut-up cooked chicken or turkey
- ¹/₂ teaspoon salt
- 1   can (4 ounces) chopped green chilies, drained
- 2   tablespoons finely chopped onion
- 1   medium head lettuce, torn into bite-size pieces (about 6 cups)
- 2   medium tomatoes, cut into thin wedges

Prepare Salad Dressing. Mix chicken, salt, chilies, onion and Salad Dressing. Toss with lettuce and tomatoes.

Salad Dressing

- 1   tablespoon sugar
- 2   tablespoons vinegar
- 1   tablespoon vegetable oil
- ¹/₂ teaspoon salt
- ¹/₄ teaspoon ground cumin

Shake all ingredients in tightly covered jar.

8 servings (about 1¼ cups); 125 calories each.

═══════════ ☆ ☆ ☆ ☆ ☆ ═══════════

Chicken-Rice Salad

Good source of protein, niacin and vitamin C

  Ginger-Lemon Dressing (below)
3 cups cut-up cooked chicken or turkey
2 cups cold cooked rice
2 cups cut-up fresh pineapple or 1 can (20 ounces)
    pineapple chunks in juice, drained
1 medium stalk celery, chopped (about 1/3 cup)
1 medium carrot, shredded (about 1/2 cup)
1 small onion, chopped (about 1/4 cup)
  Lettuce leaves
1 cup alfalfa sprouts
2 tablespoons salted sunflower nuts

Prepare Ginger-Lemon Dressing. Mix chicken, rice, pineapple, celery, carrot and onion; toss with Ginger-Lemon Dressing. Cover and refrigerate until cold, at least 4 hours. Serve on lettuce leaves; top with alfalfa sprouts. Sprinkle with sunflower nuts.

Ginger-Lemon Dressing

1/3 cup vegetable oil
3 tablespoons lemon juice
1 tablespoon honey
1/4 to 1/2 teaspoon ground ginger
1/8 teaspoon garlic powder
4 to 6 drops red pepper sauce

Shake all ingredients in tightly covered jar.

6 servings (about 1 cup); 365 calories each.

☆ ☆ ☆ ☆ ☆

Chicken-Rice Salad

Chicken-Broccoli Soup

Good source of protein, niacin and vitamin A

1	cup water
12	ounces broccoli, cut up
1	medium stalk celery, chopped (about ½ cup)
1	small onion, chopped (about ¼ cup)
1	tablespoon lemon juice
1	tablespoon margarine or butter
1	tablespoon all-purpose flour
1¼	cups water
1½	teaspoons instant chicken bouillon
1	teaspoon salt
	Dash of ground nutmeg
1½	cups cut-up cooked chicken or turkey
¾	cup half-and-half

Heat 1 cup water to boiling in 3-quart saucepan. Add broccoli, celery, onion and lemon juice. Cover and heat to boiling; reduce heat. Simmer until vegetables are tender, about 15 minutes; do not drain. Place broccoli mixture in blender container. Cover and blend on medium speed, stopping blender frequently to scrape sides, until mixture is of uniform consistency, about 45 seconds.

Heat margarine in same saucepan over low heat until melted. Blend in flour. Cook, stirring constantly, until mixture is smooth and bubbly; remove from heat. Stir in 1¼ cups water. Heat to boiling, stirring constantly. Boil and stir 1 minute. Stir in broccoli mixture, bouillon, salt and nutmeg. Heat just to boiling. Stir in chicken and half-and-half. Heat just to boiling. Garnish each serving with yogurt, sour cream or lemon slice if desired.

4 servings (about 1 cup); 220 calories each.

□ *Food Processor Directions:* Place broccoli mixture in workbowl fitted with steel blade. Cover and process until mixture is of uniform consistency, about 15 seconds.

☆ ☆ ☆ ☆ ☆

Turkey with Stuffing

Good source of protein and niacin

2	stalks celery, sliced (about 1 cup)
1	medium onion, chopped (about ½ cup)
½	cup margarine or butter
¼	cup snipped parsley
1¼	teaspoons salt
1	teaspoon dried sage leaves
½	teaspoon dried marjoram leaves
¼	teaspoon dried tarragon leaves
7	cups soft bread cubes
2	medium carrots, shredded (about 1⅓ cups)
1	medium zucchini, shredded (about 1 cup)
1	can (8 ounces) mushroom stems and pieces, drained and chopped
12 -	pound turkey
	Margarine or butter, softened

Cook and stir celery and onion in ½ cup margarine until onion is tender. Stir in parsley, salt, sage, marjoram and tarragon. Toss celery mixture with bread cubes, carrots, zucchini and mushrooms. Fill wishbone area of turkey with stuffing first. Fasten neck skin to back with skewer. Fold wings across back with tips touching. Fill body cavity lightly. (Place any remaining stuffing in small ungreased baking dish; cover and refrigerate. Place in oven with turkey the last 30 minutes of roasting.) Tuck drumsticks under band of skin at tail, or tie together with heavy string, then tie to tail.

Place turkey, breast side up, on rack in shallow roasting pan. Brush with margarine. Insert meat thermometer so tip is in thickest part of inside thigh muscle or thickest part of breast meat and does not touch bone. Roast uncovered in 325° oven until drumstick meat feels very soft or meat thermometer registers 185°, 3½ to 4½ hours. Place a tent of aluminum foil loosely over turkey when it begins to turn golden brown. When ⅔ done, cut band of skin or string holding legs.

24 servings; 245 calories per serving.

☆ ☆ ☆ ☆ ☆

Turkey with Pineapple

Good source of protein and niacin

4½ - to 5-pound turkey breast
1   pineapple
½   cup dry white wine
2   tablespoons honey
2   tablespoons soy sauce
1   large clove garlic, finely chopped
1   teaspoon finely chopped gingerroot or
*   ½ teaspoon ground ginger*
2   teaspoons cornstarch
2   tablespoons cold water

Place turkey breast, skin side up, on rack in shallow roasting pan. Insert meat thermometer so tip is in thickest part of meat and does not touch bone. Roast uncovered in 325° oven 1 hour.

Pare pineapple; cut lengthwise into halves. Remove core; cut each half crosswise into 8 slices. Mix wine, honey, soy sauce, garlic and gingerroot. Arrange pineapple on rack around turkey. Brush turkey and pineapple with wine mixture. Roast uncovered, brushing turkey and pineapple frequently with wine mixture, until thermometer registers 185°, about 1 hour longer. Remove turkey and pineapple; keep warm.

Pour drippings into measuring cup; skim off any excess fat. Add enough water to drippings to measure 1 cup. Heat drippings to boiling in 1-quart saucepan. Mix cornstarch and cold water; stir into drippings. Boil and stir 1 minute. Serve with turkey.

16 servings (about 3 ounces turkey and 1 slice pineapple each); 190 calories per serving.

☆ ☆ ☆ ☆ ☆

Braised Turkey Breast

Good source of protein and niacin

4½ - to 5-pound turkey breast
¼   cup all-purpose flour
3   tablespoons vegetable oil
1   medium onion, chopped (about ½ cup)
1   medium carrot, chopped (about ½ cup)
1   medium stalk celery, chopped (about ½ cup)
1   clove garlic, finely chopped
1   bay leaf
1   cup water
½   cup dry white wine
1   teaspoon instant chicken bouillon
½   teaspoon dried marjoram leaves
½   teaspoon salt
¼   teaspoon pepper
2   tablespoons snipped parsley
1   clove garlic, finely chopped
1   teaspoon grated lemon peel
1   tablespoon plus 1 teaspoon cornstarch
¼   cup cold water

Coat turkey breast with flour. Heat oil in 5-quart Dutch oven until hot. Cook turkey over medium heat until light brown on all sides, about 20 minutes. Add onion, carrot, celery, 1 clove garlic, the bay leaf, water, wine, bouillon, marjoram, salt and pepper. Heat to boiling; reduce heat. Cover and simmer until turkey is done, 2 to 2½ hours. Mix parsley, 1 clove garlic and the lemon peel; reserve. Remove turkey and vegetables; keep warm. Sprinkle turkey with parsley mixture. Measure broth; skim off any excess fat. Add enough water to broth, if necessary, to measure 2 cups; return to Dutch oven. Heat to boiling. Mix cornstarch and cold water; stir into broth. Boil and stir 1 minute. Serve with turkey.

16 servings; 195 calories per serving.

☆ ☆ ☆ ☆ ☆

Turkey with Peppers

Good source of protein

2   *turkey thighs (about 2 pounds)*
2   *tablespoons margarine or butter*
1   *tablespoon vegetable oil*
½   *cup water*
2   *tablespoons soy sauce*
2   *tablespoons snipped parsley*
½   *teaspoon dried thyme leaves*
¼   *teaspoon dried rosemary leaves*
2   *medium green peppers, cut into ¼-inch strips*
¼   *cup sliced green onions (with tops)*
1   *teaspoon cornstarch*
1   *tablespoon cold water*
2   *tablespoons grated Parmesan cheese*

Remove skin and bones from turkey; cut turkey into strips, 2 × 1 inch. Cook turkey in margarine and oil in 10-inch skillet, stirring occasionally, until light brown, about 6 minutes. Add ½ cup water, the soy sauce, parsley, thyme and rosemary. Heat to boiling; reduce heat. Cover and simmer until turkey is tender, about 30 minutes. Add green peppers and onions. Cover and simmer just until peppers are crisp-tender, about 5 minutes. Mix cornstarch and 1 tablespoon cold water; stir into turkey mixture. Heat to boiling, stirring constantly. Boil and stir 1 minute. Sprinkle with Parmesan cheese.

6 servings (about ¾ cup); 290 calories each.

☆ ☆ ☆ ☆ ☆

Braised Turkey Breast, and Turkey with Peppers

Brunswick-Style Stew

Good source of protein and niacin

1   pound bulk pork sausage
2   turkey legs (about 3 pounds)
1   cup water
1   large onion, sliced
2   medium stalks celery, sliced (about 1 cup)
1   bay leaf
1   teaspoon dried basil leaves
1/2   teaspoon salt
1/2   teaspoon red pepper sauce
1   can (16 ounces) whole tomatoes
1   package (10 ounces) frozen whole kernel corn
1   package (10 ounces) frozen baby lima beans
2   tablespoons snipped parsley

Cook and stir sausage in 4-quart Dutch oven until brown. Remove with slotted spoon; reserve. Pour off all but 1 tablespoon fat. Cook turkey legs in fat, turning occasionally, until golden brown. Add water, onion, celery, bay leaf, basil, salt, pepper sauce and reserved sausage. Heat to boiling; reduce heat. Cover and simmer until turkey is tender, 2 to 2½ hours. Remove turkey; cool slightly. Remove meat from skin and bones; cut meat into bite-size pieces. Return meat to Dutch oven; add tomatoes (with liquid), corn and lima beans. Break tomatoes up with fork. Heat to boiling; reduce heat. Cover and simmer until vegetables are tender, about 10 minutes. Sprinkle with parsley.

8 servings (about 1 cup); 265 calories per serving.

□ *Pressure Cooker Directions:* Cook and stir sausage in 6-quart pressure cooker until brown. Remove with slotted spoon; reserve. Pour off all but 1 tablespoon fat. Cook turkey legs in fat, turning occasionally, until golden brown. Add water, onion, celery, bay leaf, basil, salt, pepper sauce and reserved sausage. Following manufacturer's directions, cover and cook at 15 pounds pressure 20 minutes. Cool 5 minutes; reduce pressure. Remove turkey; cool slightly. Remove meat from skin and bones; cut meat into bite-size pieces. Return meat to pressure cooker. Drain tomatoes; add tomatoes, corn and lima beans. Break up tomatoes with fork. Heat to boiling; reduce heat. Simmer uncovered until vegetables are tender, about 15 minutes. Sprinkle with parsley.

☆ ☆ ☆ ☆ ☆

Turkey with Cheese Fondue Sauce

Good source of protein and calcium

1   pound cooked turkey breast, cut into ¼-inch slices
1   jar (6 ounces) marinated artichoke hearts, drained and cut into fourths
1   clove garlic, finely chopped
2   tablespoons margarine or butter
2   tablespoons all-purpose flour
¼   teaspoon salt
    Dash of pepper
    Dash of ground nutmeg
1   cup milk
¼   cup dry white wine
1   cup shredded Swiss cheese (about 4 ounces)
1   tablespoon cherry brandy
    Paprika

Overlap turkey in ungreased rectangular baking dish, 12 × 7½ × 2 inches. Place artichokes on turkey. Cook garlic in margarine in 1½-quart saucepan over medium heat until garlic is light brown, about 3 minutes; reduce heat. Blend in flour, salt, pepper and nutmeg. Cook over low heat, stirring constantly, until smooth and bubbly; remove from heat. Stir in milk and wine. Heat to boiling, stirring constantly. Boil and stir 1 minute; remove from heat. Stir in cheese and brandy until cheese is melted. Pour sauce over turkey and artichokes. Sprinkle with paprika. Cook in 350° oven until hot and bubbly, about 20 minutes.

6 servings; 330 calories per serving.

☆ ☆ ☆ ☆ ☆

Turkey Kabobs

Good source of protein and niacin

12	slices bacon
1	can (16 ounces) whole new potatoes, drained
24	1-inch cubes cooked turkey
18	1-inch squares green pepper
6	cherry tomatoes
	Gingered Wine Sauce (below)

Fry bacon until cooked but not crisp; drain. For each kabob, thread 1 potato on metal skewer. Push end of 1 slice bacon next to potato. Thread bacon around 1 turkey cube, 1 green pepper square and 1 turkey cube. Add 1 green pepper square. Thread another slice bacon around 1 turkey cube, 1 green pepper square and 1 turkey cube. Add 1 potato and 1 cherry tomato. Prepare Gingered Wine Sauce. Place kabobs on rack in broiler pan; brush all sides with sauce. Set oven control to broil and/ or 550°. Broil kabobs with tops about 4 inches from heat until hot, about 5 minutes; turn. Brush with sauce. Broil 3 minutes longer.

Gingered Wine Sauce

½	cup dry white wine
2	tablespoons packed brown sugar
2	tablespoons soy sauce
½	teaspoon ground ginger
1	clove garlic, crushed
1	teaspoon cornstarch

Cook all ingredients over medium heat, stirring constantly, until sauce is thickened, 3 to 4 minutes.

6 servings; 270 calories per serving.

☆ ☆ ☆ ☆ ☆

Turkey Kabobs

Turkey-Rice Casserole

Good source of protein, riboflavin and calcium

3	cups hot cooked rice
2	cups cut-up turkey or chicken
1	medium green pepper, chopped (about 1 cup)
1	medium onion, chopped (about ½ cup)
1	cup shredded Monterey Jack or mozzarella cheese (about 4 ounces)
4	eggs, slightly beaten
2½	cups milk
1	teaspoon salt
1	teaspoon dry mustard
½	teaspoon dried basil leaves
½	teaspoon red pepper sauce
⅛	teaspoon pepper
¼	cup grated Parmesan cheese

Mix rice, turkey, green pepper, onion and Monterey Jack cheese; spread in greased square pan, 9 × 9 × 2 inches. Mix eggs, milk, salt, mustard, basil, pepper sauce and pepper; pour over rice mixture. Sprinkle with Parmesan cheese. Cook uncovered in 325° oven until set, 45 to 50 minutes. Let stand 10 minutes; cut into squares.

6 servings; 405 calories per serving.

☆ ☆ ☆ ☆ ☆

Turkey in a Bread Basket

Preparing Bread Basket

Cut into bread ½ inch from outside edge.

Remove bread within cuts, leaving a ½-inch base.

Spoon hot turkey mixture into toasted bread.

Turkey in a Bread Basket

Good source of protein, niacin, riboflavin and vitamin A

  Bread Basket (below)
8 ounces broccoli
1 medium onion, thinly sliced
4 ounces mushrooms, sliced (about 1½ cups) or
     1 can (4 ounces) mushroom stems
     and pieces, drained
2 tablespoons margarine or butter
2 tablespoons all-purpose flour
½ teaspoon salt
⅛ teaspoon pepper
⅛ teaspoon ground sage
1 cup milk
2½ cups cut-up cooked turkey or chicken
4 slices bacon, crisply fried and crumbled

Prepare Bread Basket. Remove flowerets from broccoli; reserve. Cut stalks into 1-inch pieces (about 2½ cups). Place steamer basket in ½ inch water in saucepan or skillet (water should not touch bottom of basket). Place broccoli pieces in basket. Cover tightly and heat to boiling; reduce heat. Steam 5 minutes. Add reserved flowerets. Cover and steam until crisp-tender, about 5 minutes longer.

Cook and stir onion and mushrooms in margarine in 3-quart saucepan until onion is tender, about 5 minutes. Blend in flour, salt, pepper and sage. Cook over low heat, stirring constantly, until bubbly; remove from heat. Stir in milk. Heat to boiling, stirring constantly. Boil and stir 1 minute. Stir in turkey and broccoli; heat just until turkey is hot, about 5 minutes. Stir in bacon. Spoon turkey mixture into Bread Basket.

Bread Basket

1 loaf (about 1½ pounds) unsliced sandwich
     bread
½ cup margarine or butter, melted
1 large clove garlic, crushed

Remove crust from bread. Make cuts down into bread ½ inch from outside edges. Remove bread within cuts, leaving a base at least ½ inch thick. (Removed bread can be used for bread crumbs or stuffing.) Remove any loose crumbs from bread. Place bread on rack in jelly roll pan, 15½ × 10½ × 1 inch. Mix margarine and garlic; brush inside, outside and bottom of bread with margarine mixture. Cook uncovered in 325° oven until all sides are golden brown and crisp, 25 to 30 minutes; cool.

6 servings; 460 calories per serving.

☆ ☆ ☆ ☆ ☆

Turkey-Leek Casserole

Good source of protein

5 medium leeks or 2 medium onions, sliced
2 tablespoons margarine or butter
2 tablespoons all-purpose flour
½ teaspoon salt
¼ teaspoon ground nutmeg
⅛ teaspoon pepper
1 cup chicken broth (page 56)
1 cup milk
3 cups cut-up cooked turkey or chicken
½ cup finely chopped fully cooked smoked ham
1 jar (2 ounces) diced pimiento, drained
3 cups hot cooked noodles
1 cup shredded Swiss cheese (about 4 ounces)

Cook and stir leeks in margarine in 3-quart saucepan over medium heat until tender, about 5 minutes. Blend in flour, salt, nutmeg and pepper. Cook over low heat, stirring constantly, until bubbly; remove from heat. Stir in chicken broth and milk. Heat to boiling, stirring constantly. Boil and stir 1 minute. Stir in turkey, ham and pimiento. Spread about half of the turkey mixture in ungreased square pan, 9 × 9 × 2 inches, or 2½-quart casserole. Spoon noodles over turkey mixture; top with remaining turkey mixture. Sprinkle with cheese. Cook uncovered in 350° oven until cheese is light brown, 25 to 30 minutes.

8 servings (about 1 cup); 300 calories each.

☆ ☆ ☆ ☆ ☆

Tossed Turkey Salad

Good source of protein

    Onion Dressing (below)
3   *cups cut-up cooked turkey or chicken*
1   *medium head lettuce, torn into bite-size pieces (about 9 cups)*
5   *radishes, sliced*
1   *small cucumber, sliced*
12 *pitted ripe olives*
1/4 *cup crumbled blue or feta cheese*

Prepare Onion Dressing. Toss with turkey, lettuce, radishes, cucumber and olives. Sprinkle with cheese.

Onion Dressing

1/2 *cup vegetable oil*
1/3 *cup red wine vinegar*
3   *green onions (with tops), cut into 1/2-inch pieces*
1   *teaspoon dried oregano leaves*
1/2 *teaspoon salt*

Shake all ingredients in tightly covered jar.

6 servings (about 2 cups); 350 calories each.

☆ ☆ ☆ ☆ ☆

Turkey-Fruit Salad

Good source of protein and vitamin C

    Honey Dressing (below)
3   *cups cut-up cooked turkey or chicken*
1 1/2 *cups seedless green or red grapes*
1   *can (8 ounces) water chestnuts, drained and chopped*
1/4 *cup sliced green onions (with tops)*
1/4 *cup chopped green pepper*
2   *oranges, pared and sectioned*
1/4 *head lettuce, torn into bite-size pieces (about 3 cups)*
1/4 *cup toasted slivered almonds*

Prepare Honey Dressing. Toss with turkey, grapes, water chestnuts, onions and green pepper. Cover and refrigerate until cold,

about 2 hours. Toss turkey mixture with orange sections and lettuce. Spoon into lettuce cups if desired. Sprinkle with almonds.

Honey Dressing

1/4 *cup vegetable oil*
2   *tablespoons vinegar*
1   *tablespoon honey*
3/4 *teaspoon salt*
    Dash of pepper
4   *to 6 drops red pepper sauce*

Shake all ingredients in tightly covered jar.

6 servings (about 1 1/2 cups); 325 calories each.

☆ ☆ ☆ ☆ ☆

Turkey-Bacon Salad

Good source of protein, niacin and vitamin C

3   *cups cut-up cooked turkey or chicken*
8   *slices bacon, crisply fried and crumbled*
1/2 *small head cauliflower, separated into tiny flowerets (about 2 cups)*
1/4 *cup sliced radishes*
1/3 *cup plain yogurt*
2   *tablespoons mayonnaise or salad dressing*
1   *green onion (with top), sliced*
1/4 *teaspoon dried dill weed*
1/8 *teaspoon salt*
    Dash of pepper
    Lettuce cups or leaves
1   *medium avocado, cut into 12 slices*

Mix turkey, bacon, cauliflower and radishes in 2 1/2-quart bowl. Mix yogurt, mayonnaise, onion, dill weed, salt and pepper; toss with turkey mixture. Spoon into lettuce cups; arrange 2 avocado slices on each salad.

6 servings (about 1 cup); 320 calories each.

☆ ☆ ☆ ☆ ☆

Turkey-Bacon Salad, Tossed Turkey Salad, and Turkey Fruit Salad

Turkey-Pasta Salad

Good source of protein, niacin, iron, vitamins A and C

Spinach Sauce (below)
2   *packages (5 ounces each) spiral macaroni*
3   *cups cut-up cooked turkey or chicken*
1/2   *cup sliced ripe olives*
1   *tablespoon olive or vegetable oil*
1   *teaspoon vinegar*
1   *tablespoon pine nuts or slivered almonds*

Prepare Spinach Sauce. Cook macaroni as directed on package; drain. Rinse in cold water; drain. Toss macaroni with 1/2 cup Spinach Sauce. Toss turkey, olives, oil and vinegar; spoon into center of macaroni mixture. Sprinkle with pine nuts. Serve with remaining Spinach Sauce.

Spinach Sauce

4   *cups spinach leaves*
1   *cup parsley sprigs*
3   *large cloves garlic, cut into halves*
1/4   *cup lemon juice*
1/2   *cup grated Parmesan cheese*
2   *tablespoons olive or vegetable oil*
1   *teaspoon dried basil leaves*
1/2   *teaspoon pepper*

Place half of the spinach, parsley, garlic and lemon juice in blender container. Cover and blend on medium speed, stopping blender frequently to scrape sides, until spinach leaves are finely chopped, about 3 minutes. Repeat with remaining spinach, parsley, garlic and lemon juice. Place all spinach mixture in blender container. Add cheese, oil, basil and pepper. Cover and blend on medium speed, stopping blender frequently to scrape sides, until mixture is smooth, about 2 minutes.

6 servings (about 1 1/2 cups); 410 calories each.

□ *Food Processor Directions:* Place spinach, parsley, garlic and lemon juice in workbowl fitted with steel blade. Cover and process until leaves are finely chopped, about 20 seconds. Add cheese, oil, basil and pepper. Cover and process until smooth, about 5 seconds longer.

☆ ☆ ☆ ☆ ☆

Cornish Hens with Glazed Oranges

Good source of protein and niacin

3   *Rock Cornish hens (about 1 1/2 pounds each)*
2   *tablespoons margarine or butter, melted*
    Glazed Oranges (below)
1/2   *cup orange juice*
1   *tablespoon honey*
1/2   *teaspoon salt*
1/4   *teaspoon dry mustard*
1/8   *teaspoon paprika*

Place hens, breast sides up, on rack in shallow roasting pan; brush with margarine. Roast uncovered in 350° oven 30 minutes. Prepare Glazed Oranges. Mix remaining ingredients; brush half of the orange juice mixture over hens. Roast uncovered, brushing with remaining orange juice mixture, until hens are done, about 45 minutes. Cut each hen along backbone from tail to neck into halves with kitchen scissors. Serve with Glazed Oranges.

Glazed Oranges

3   *medium oranges*
2   *tablespoons margarine or butter*
1/4   *cup light corn syrup*
1   *tablespoon honey*

Cut off ends of oranges; cut each orange into 1/8-inch slices. Heat margarine over medium heat in 12-inch skillet until melted. Stir in corn syrup and honey. Heat to boiling; add oranges and reduce heat. Simmer, spooning sauce frequently over oranges, until oranges are tender and glazed, about 25 minutes.

6 servings; 325 calories per serving.

☆ ☆ ☆ ☆ ☆

Duckling with Sauerkraut Stuffing

Good source of protein, niacin, riboflavin, thiamin and iron

4 - to 5-pound duckling
1   can (27 ounces) sauerkraut, rinsed and drained
2   medium stalks celery, chopped (about 1 cup)
1   medium onion, chopped (about ½ cup)
1   small green pepper, chopped (about ½ cup)
2   tablespoons packed brown sugar
⅛   teaspoon caraway seed

Fasten neck skin of duckling to back with skewer. Lift wing tips up and over back for natural brace. Mix remaining ingredients. Fill body cavity lightly with sauerkraut mixture. Fasten opening with skewer. (Place remaining sauerkraut mixture in greased casserole; cover and refrigerate. Place in oven with duckling the last 30 minutes of roasting.) Place duckling, breast side up, on rack in shallow roasting pan. Prick skin with fork. Roast uncovered in 350° oven until drumstick meat feels very soft, about 3 hours, removing excess fat from pan occasionally. (If duckling becomes too brown, place piece of aluminum foil lightly over breast.) Remove duckling; let stand 10 minutes. Cut into quarters with kitchen scissors. Serve with sauerkraut mixture.

4 servings; 325 calories per serving.

☆ ☆ ☆ ☆ ☆

THINK LESS PROTEIN

Americans today consume about twice the amount of protein they need daily. To correct this, serving portions of meat, poultry and seafood in this cookbook have been adjusted. While they may be smaller than what you are accustomed to, all are nutritionally adequate for protein. For heartier appetites, count on fewer servings per recipe, or serve a greater variety of other foods. Check the Nutrition Information Chart at the end of each chapter to determine how much protein each recipe provides per serving.

Stewed Rabbit

Good source of protein, niacin and vitamin A

2½ - to 3-pound domestic rabbit
⅓   cup all-purpose flour
½   teaspoon salt
¼   teaspoon pepper
6   slices bacon, cut up
1   large onion, sliced
2   medium carrots, cut crosswise
        into ½-inch slices
2   medium cloves garlic, crushed
1   bay leaf
1¼ cups water
¾   cup dry red wine
1   tablespoon packed brown sugar
½   teaspoon salt
½   teaspoon dried rosemary leaves
½   teaspoon paprika
1   tablespoon cornstarch
2   tablespoons cold water

Cut rabbit into pieces. Mix flour, ½ teaspoon salt and the pepper. Coat rabbit with flour mixture. Fry bacon in 4-quart Dutch oven over medium heat until crisp. Remove with slotted spoon and drain; reserve. Pour off all but 2 tablespoons bacon fat. Cook rabbit in bacon fat over medium heat, turning occasionally, until brown. Add onion, carrots, garlic, reserved bacon and bay leaf. Mix 1¼ cups water, the wine, brown sugar, ½ teaspoon salt, the rosemary and paprika; pour over rabbit. Heat to boiling; reduce heat. Cover and simmer until rabbit is tender, 1 to 1½ hours. Remove rabbit and vegetables; keep warm. Mix cornstarch and 2 tablespoons cold water; stir into liquid in Dutch oven. Heat to boiling, stirring constantly. Boil and stir 1 minute. Pour sauce over rabbit and vegetables.

6 servings; 380 calories per serving.

☆ ☆ ☆ ☆ ☆

Nutrition Information Per Serving or Unit

Recipe and Page Number	Protein	Carbo-hydrates	Fat	Sodium	Potas-sium	Protein	Calcium	Iron
		Grams		Milligrams		Percent U.S. Recommended Daily Allowance		
CHICKEN								
Broiled Pepper Chicken, 51	19	1	8	225	180	42	0	6
Chicken-Broccoli Soup, 67	18	10	12	915	585	40	16	10
Chicken-Cabbage Soup, 57	22	13	11	1095	790	50	8	12
Chicken Casserole, 65	21	17	28	825	490	42	20	22
Chicken Livers with Yogurt, 64	23	19	14	380	725	52	6	58
Chicken Mozzarella, 54	26	10	21	540	350	58	14	12
Chicken Parmesan, 62	25	18	24	460	420	50	20	14
Chicken Potato Roast, 49	22	21	18	375	590	42	2	10
Chicken Provençal, 55	24	32	13	420	870	48	8	16
Chicken-Rice Salad, 66	21	30	18	325	400	38	4	12
Chicken-Rice Soup, 56	19	19	5	530	430	36	4	12
Chicken with Apricots, 52	20	16	7	380	350	44	2	8
Chicken with Artichokes and Grapes, 53	23	14	9	305	480	52	2	10
Chicken with Duchess Potatoes, 64	34	30	30	1040	780	64	8	18
Chicken with Gravy, 49	22	7	10	440	275	48	8	6
Chicken with Lentils, 57	28	22	8	515	410	54	4	20
Chicken with Plums, 58	21	10	20	205	425	48	4	10
Chicken with Vegetables, 54	21	14	10	485	445	48	4	10
Chicken with Yogurt, 62	32	6	23	470	365	70	8	12
Chili Chicken Salad, 65	14	6	5	320	320	32	2	8
Cornmeal Chicken, 52	20	3	12	170	210	44	2	6
Curried Chicken Breasts, 61	29	11	8	135	465	66	8	8
Garlic Chicken Breasts, 60	28	13	11	320	265	62	2	10
Gingered Chicken with Vegetables, 48	22	8	15	495	505	50	2	10
Herbed Chicken, 51	19	2	12	140	240	42	2	8
Herbed Lemon Chicken, 48	20	7	18	515	245	38	2	8

Nutrition Information Per Serving or Unit

Recipe and Page Number	Protein	Carbo-hydrates	Fat	Sodium	Potas-sium	Protein	Calcium	Iron
	Grams			Milligrams		Percent U.S. Recommended Daily Allowance		
Italian Chicken Salad, 58	20	5	22	565	320	44	16	8
Lemon-Dill Chicken, 61	27	2	11	450	260	60	2	6
Oven Barbecued Chicken, 51	20	12	5	695	295	44	2	8
Rice-Stuffed Chicken, 50	22	28	22	640	445	44	4	14
Stir-Fried Chicken, 59	21	9	9	705	485	48	4	8
Tarragon Chicken, 59	25	11	12	345	670	56	8	12
Wheat-Stuffed Drumsticks, 63	34	36	25	565	325	66	4	18
Wine Sauced Chicken, 50	20	5	7	380	335	44	2	10
TURKEY Braised Turkey Breast, 68	25	3	9	170	295	56	2	8
Brunswick-Style Stew, 70	28	20	8	510	685	62	6	18
Tossed Turkey Salad, 74	23	6	26	420	470	52	10	12
Turkey-Bacon Salad, 74	26	7	21	240	690	58	6	14
Turkey-Fruit Salad, 74	23	23	16	335	630	52	6	12
Turkey in a Bread Basket, 73	26	28	27	730	545	50	14	16
Turkey Kabobs, 71	24	19	11	545	570	54	4	14
Turkey-Leek Casserole, 73	26	21	12	440	380	50	22	16
Turkey-Pasta Salad, 76	30	37	16	290	585	56	20	26
Turkey-Rice Casserole, 71	30	33	17	1415	475	56	36	18
Turkey with Cheese Fondue Sauce, 70	30	10	18	260	330	66	26	14
Turkey with Peppers, 69	34	4	15	520	490	76	8	20
Turkey with Pineapple, 68	25	9	6	185	325	56	2	8
Turkey with Stuffing, 67	32	6	10	300	380	60	4	12
CORNISH HENS/ DUCKLING Cornish Hens with Glazed Oranges, 76	29	25	12	360	490	64	2	16
Duckling with Sauerkraut Stuffing, 77	32	18	14	1395	755	70	10	26
GAME Stewed Rabbit, 77	39	14	16	505	625	88	4	16

Eggs, Cheese
& Dried Beans
★★★

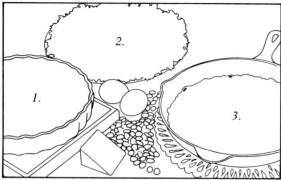

1. Three Cheese Pie, 2. Italian Bean Salad,
3. Egg-Spaghetti Skillet

Green Chili Omelet

Good source of protein

4 eggs
1 tablespoon margarine or butter
2 whole canned mild green chilies, seeded
1/4 cup shredded Monterey Jack cheese
  Salt

Mix eggs with fork just until whites and yolks are blended. Heat margarine in 10-inch skillet over medium-high heat just until hot enough to sizzle a drop of water. Tilt skillet in all directions to coat side thoroughly. Quickly pour eggs all at once into skillet. Start sliding skillet back and forth rapidly over heat. At the same time, stir quickly with fork to spread eggs continuously over bottom of skillet as they thicken. Let stand over heat a few seconds to lightly brown bottom of omelet. (Do not overcook; omelet will continue to cook after folding.) Tilt skillet; run fork under edge of omelet, then jerk skillet sharply to loosen eggs from bottom of skillet. Place green chilies on one half of omelet; sprinkle with cheese. Fold portion of omelet nearest you just to center. (Allow for portion of omelet to slide up side of skillet.)

Grasp skillet handle; turn omelet onto warm plate, flipping folded portion of omelet over so far side is on bottom. Sprinkle with salt. Tuck sides of omelet under if necessary. Garnish with sliced tomatoes if desired.

2 servings; 245 calories per serving.

☆ ☆ ☆ ☆ ☆

Mushroom-Alfalfa Omelet

Good source of protein and riboflavin

2 thin slices onion
1/2 cup sliced mushrooms
1 teaspoon margarine or butter
2 eggs
2 teaspoons margarine or butter
  Salt
1/4 cup alfalfa sprouts
1 teaspoon salted sunflower nuts

Cook and stir onion and mushrooms in 1 teaspoon margarine in 8- or 9-inch skillet or omelet pan over medium heat until onion is tender, about 5 minutes. Remove from skillet; keep warm.

Mix eggs with fork just until whites and yolks are blended. Heat 2 teaspoons margarine in same skillet over medium-high heat just until hot enough to sizzle a drop of water. Tilt skillet in all directions to coat side thoroughly. Quickly pour eggs all at once into skillet. Start sliding skillet back and forth rapidly over heat. At the same time, stir quickly with fork to spread eggs continuously over bottom of skillet as they thicken. Let stand over heat a few seconds to lightly brown bottom of omelet. (Do not overcook; omelet will continue to cook after folding.) Tilt skillet; run fork under edge of omelet, then jerk pan sharply to loosen eggs from bottom of skillet. Fold portion of omelet nearest you just to center. (Allow for portion of omelet to slide up side of skillet.)

Grasp skillet handle; turn omelet onto warm plate, flipping folded portion of omelet over so far side is on bottom. Sprinkle with salt. Tuck sides of omelet under if necessary. Spoon warm mushrooms and onion over omelet; top with alfalfa sprouts and sprinkle with sunflower nuts.

1 serving; 320 calories per serving.

☆ ☆ ☆ ☆ ☆

Broccoli Oven Omelet

Cheesy Oven Omelet

Good source of protein and calcium

2 tablespoons margarine or butter
9 eggs
½ cup dairy sour cream
½ cup milk
½ teaspoon salt
¼ teaspoon dry mustard
   Dash of ground thyme
5 slices bacon, crisply fried and crumbled
1 cup shredded Swiss cheese (about 4 ounces)
1 tablespoon chopped green onion (with top)

Heat margarine in square baking dish, 8 × 8 × 2 inches, in 325° oven until melted. Tilt dish to coat bottom of dish. Beat eggs, sour cream, milk, salt, mustard and thyme. Stir in bacon, cheese and onion. Pour into dish. Cook uncovered until puffed and center is set, about 35 minutes.

6 servings; 330 calories per serving.

☆ ☆ ☆ ☆ ☆

Broccoli Oven Omelet

Good source of protein and vitamin A

9 eggs
1 package (10 ounces) frozen chopped broccoli, thawed and drained
⅓ cup finely chopped onion
¼ cup grated Parmesan cheese
2 tablespoons milk
½ teaspoon salt
½ teaspoon dried basil leaves
¼ teaspoon garlic powder
1 medium tomato, cut into 6 slices
¼ cup grated Parmesan cheese

Beat eggs with hand beater in 2½-quart bowl until light and fluffy. Stir in broccoli, onion, ¼ cup Parmesan cheese, the milk, salt, basil and garlic powder. Pour into ungreased rectangular baking dish, 11 × 7½ × 2 inches. Arrange tomato slices on top; sprinkle with ¼ cup Parmesan cheese. Cook uncovered in 325° oven until set, 25 to 30 minutes.

6 servings; 190 calories per serving.

☆ ☆ ☆ ☆ ☆

Egg Soufflé Roll

Good source of protein, riboflavin and vitamin A

¹/₄   cup margarine or butter
¹/₂   cup all-purpose flour
¹/₂   teaspoon salt
      Dash of cayenne pepper
2   cups milk
4   eggs, separated
¹/₄   teaspoon cream of tartar
¹/₃   cup grated Parmesan cheese
      Egg Filling (below)

Grease jelly roll pan, 15¹/₂ × 10¹/₂ × 1 inch. Line bottom of pan with waxed paper; grease lightly and flour. Heat margarine in 2-quart saucepan over low heat until melted. Blend in flour, salt and pepper. Cook over low heat, stirring constantly, until smooth and bubbly; remove from heat. Stir in milk. Heat to boiling, stirring constantly. Boil and stir 1 minute; remove from heat. Beat in egg yolks, one at a time.

Heat oven to 350°. Beat egg whites and cream of tartar in large bowl on high speed until stiff but not dry. Stir about ¹/₄ of the egg whites into egg yolk mixture. Fold egg yolk mixture and cheese into remaining egg whites. Spread evenly in pan.

Bake until puffed and golden brown, 35 to 40 minutes. Prepare Egg Filling. Immediately loosen soufflé from edges of pan; invert on cloth-covered wire rack. Carefully peel off waxed paper. Spread soufflé with Egg Filling; roll up from narrow end. Cut into about 1¹/₂-inch slices.

Egg Filling

8   hard-cooked eggs, chopped
1   can (4 ounces) mushroom stems and pieces, drained and chopped
¹/₃   cup mayonnaise or salad dressing
¹/₄   cup sliced green onions (with tops)
1   jar (2 ounces) diced pimiento, drained
2   tablespoons Dijon-style mustard
¹/₂   teaspoon salt
¹/₈   teaspoon pepper
      Pinch of dried dill weed

Mix all ingredients. Heat over low heat, stirring occasionally, just until hot.

6 servings; 445 calories per serving.

☆ ☆ ☆ ☆ ☆

Egg Soufflé Roll

Egg-Creole Casserole

Good source of protein and vitamin A

1   medium green pepper, chopped (about 1 cup)
1   medium onion, sliced
1   medium stalk celery, sliced (about 1/2 cup)
2   tablespoons margarine or butter
2   tablespoons all-purpose flour
1   teaspoon salt
1   can (16 ounces) whole tomatoes
1/4 teaspoon red pepper sauce
8   hard-cooked eggs, coarsely chopped
2   cups hot cooked rice
1   cup shredded mozzarella cheese

Cook and stir green pepper, onion and celery in margarine in 3-quart saucepan over medium heat until onion is tender, about 5 minutes. Blend in flour and salt. Cook, stirring constantly, until mixture is bubbly. Stir in tomatoes (with liquid) and pepper sauce. Break up tomatoes with fork. Heat to boiling; reduce heat. Simmer uncovered until thickened, about 10 minutes. Carefully fold in eggs. Spread rice in ungreased 2-quart casserole. Pour egg mixture over rice; sprinkle with cheese. Cook uncovered in 350° oven until hot and cheese is melted, 25 to 30 minutes.

6 servings (about 1 cup); 305 calories each.

☆ ☆ ☆ ☆ ☆

Deviled Egg Salads

Good source of protein, vitamins A and C

9   hard-cooked eggs
1/3 cup mayonnaise or salad dressing
1/2 teaspoon Dijon-style mustard
1/4 teaspoon salt
1/4 teaspoon pepper
18 capers
6   medium tomatoes
    Leaf lettuce
1/2 cup shredded Cheddar cheese (about 2 ounces)
3   green onions (with tops), sliced

Cut peeled eggs lengthwise into halves. Slip out yolks; mash with fork. Stir in mayonnaise, mustard, salt and pepper. Fill whites with egg yolk mixture, heaping it slightly. Place a caper on each. Cut stem ends from tomatoes. Cut each tomato into sixths to within 1 inch of bottom. Place tomatoes on lettuce on each of 6 plates. Carefully spread out sections, forming a flower. Sprinkle inside of each tomato with cheese and onion. Arrange egg halves around each tomato.

6 servings; 295 calories per serving.

☆ ☆ ☆ ☆ ☆

Egg-Spaghetti Skillet

Good source of protein and vitamin A

2   cups hot cooked spaghetti (about 4 ounces uncooked)
3   tablespoons margarine or butter, melted
1/4 cup grated Parmesan cheese
6   eggs, beaten
1   can (4 ounces) mushroom stems and pieces, drained
1   small onion, chopped (about 1/4 cup)
2   tablespoons snipped parsley
1/2 teaspoon salt
1/8 teaspoon pepper
3   tablespoons margarine or butter

Toss spaghetti with 3 tablespoons melted margarine and the Parmesan cheese. Let stand 15 minutes. Mix in eggs, mushrooms, onion, parsley, salt and pepper. Heat 3 tablespoons margarine in 10-inch skillet until melted. Tilt skillet to coat bottom. Pour egg mixture into skillet. Cook uncovered, without stirring, over low heat until set around edge and golden brown on bottom, about 15 minutes. Set oven control to broil and/or 550°. Broil with top about 4 inches from heat until set, about 2 minutes. Invert; cut into wedges.

4 servings; 390 calories per serving.

☆ ☆ ☆ ☆ ☆

Scrambled Eggs in Buns

Good source of protein

6   unsliced hamburger buns
1/4 cup margarine or butter, melted
6   tablespoons shredded Cheddar cheese
8   eggs
1/2 cup milk
1   teaspoon salt
1/4 teaspoon pepper
2   tablespoons margarine or butter

Cut a hole about 2 inches in diameter in top of each bun; scoop out the inside, leaving about a 1/4-inch wall. Place on ungreased cookie sheet. Brush insides of buns with 1/4 cup melted margarine; spoon 1 tablespoon shredded cheese into each. Cook in 350° oven until buns are slightly crisp, 10 to 15 minutes.

Mix eggs, milk, salt and pepper with fork until uniform in color. Heat 2 tablespoons margarine in 10-inch skillet just until hot enough to sizzle a drop of water. Pour egg mixture into skillet. As mixture begins to set at bottom and side, gently lift cooked portions with spatula so that thin uncooked portions can flow to bottom. Avoid constant stirring. Cook until eggs are thickened throughout but still moist. Spoon eggs into warm buns. Garnish with olives if desired.

6 servings; 380 calories per serving.

☆ ☆ ☆ ☆ ☆

Scrambled Eggs in Buns

Preparing Buns

Cut a 2-inch hole in top of each bun; scoop out inside, leaving 1/4-inch wall.

Filling Buns

Spoon hot scrambled egg mixture into warm, toasted buns.

Eggs in Toast Cups

Good source of protein, riboflavin and vitamin A

4   slices whole wheat bread
8   teaspoons margarine or butter, softened
½   cup shredded Cheddar cheese (about 2 ounces)
2   green onions (with tops), sliced
    Dried marjoram leaves
8   eggs
4   teaspoons milk
    Salt
    Pepper
2   tablespoons toasted sliced almonds

Spread 1 side of each slice of bread with margarine. Press each slice, margarine side down, in 10-ounce individual casserole or custard cup. Divide cheese and onions among casseroles; sprinkle each with marjoram. Break 2 eggs into each casserole. Pour 1 teaspoon milk over each egg; sprinkle with salt, pepper and almonds. Place casseroles in jelly roll pan, 15½ × 10½ × 1 inch. Cook uncovered in 350° oven until egg whites are set, 20 to 25 minutes.

4 servings; 395 calories per serving.

☆ ☆ ☆ ☆ ☆

Italian-Style Eggs

Good source of protein, thiamin, vitamins A and C

1   pound Italian sausage
1   medium onion, chopped (about ½ cup)
1   can (16 ounces) whole tomatoes
2   tablespoons margarine or butter, melted
⅛   teaspoon garlic powder
4   slices (¾ inch thick) diagonally cut French
        bread, toasted
4   eggs
2   tablespoons grated Parmesan cheese

Remove sausage from casing. Cook and stir sausage and onion in 2-quart saucepan until sausage is done, 10 to 15 minutes; drain. Stir in tomatoes (with liquid). Break up tomatoes with fork. Heat to boiling; reduce heat. Simmer uncovered until sausage mixture thickens, about 30 minutes.

Mix margarine and garlic powder; brush each piece of toast with garlic mixture. Place toast in 4 individual serving dishes. Heat water (1½ to 2 inches) to boiling; reduce to simmer. Break each egg into measuring cup or saucer; holding cup close to water's surface, slip 1 egg at a time into water. Cook until desired doneness, 3 to 5 minutes. Remove eggs from water with slotted spoon. Place 1 egg on each piece of toast; spoon sausage mixture over egg. Sprinkle with cheese.

4 servings; 395 calories per serving.

☆ ☆ ☆ ☆ ☆

Egg-Bean Sandwiches

Good source of protein

1   can (16 ounces) refried beans
3   English muffins, split and toasted
¾   cup shredded Cheddar cheese (about 6 ounces)
2   medium tomatoes, thinly sliced
6   eggs
¼   cup chopped green onions (with tops)

Heat beans until hot; spread muffin halves with beans. Sprinkle cheese over beans; arrange tomatoes on cheese. Heat water (1½ to 2 inches) to boiling; reduce to simmer. Break each egg into measuring cup or saucer; holding cup close to water's surface, slip 1 egg at a time into water. Cook until desired doneness, 3 to 5 minutes. Remove eggs from water with slotted spoon. Place eggs on tomatoes; sprinkle with onions.

6 servings; 230 calories per serving.

☆ ☆ ☆ ☆ ☆

Eggs with Wine Sauce

Eggs with Wine Sauce

Good source of protein, thiamin and riboflavin

¼	cup sliced green onions (with tops)
3	tablespoons margarine or butter
3	tablespoons all-purpose flour
½	teaspoon dry mustard
¼	teaspoon dried tarragon leaves
⅛	teaspoon white pepper
¾	cup dry white wine
¾	cup chicken broth (page 56)
6	slices bacon, crisply fried and crumbled
8	eggs
4	croissants, split*

Cook and stir onions in margarine in 1-quart saucepan over medium heat 3 minutes. Blend in flour, mustard, tarragon and pepper. Cook over low heat, stirring constantly, until bubbly; remove from heat. Stir in wine and chicken broth. Heat to boiling, stirring constantly. Boil and stir 1 minute. Stir in bacon.

Heat water (1½ to 2 inches) to boiling; reduce to simmer. Break each egg into measuring cup or saucer; holding cup close to water's surface, slip 1 egg at a time into water. Cook until desired doneness, 3 to 5 minutes. Remove eggs with slotted spoon. Place 2 eggs on bottom half of each croissant; spoon wine mixture over eggs. Serve with top half of croissant.

4 servings; 430 calories per serving.

*Four English muffins, split and toasted, can be substituted for the croissants. Place 1 egg on each muffin half; spoon wine mixture over eggs.

☆ ☆ ☆ ☆ ☆

Chili-Cheese Soufflé

Good source of protein, riboflavin, calcium, vitamins A and C

Guacamole Sauce (page 98)
1/4 cup margarine or butter
1/4 cup all-purpose flour
1/2 teaspoon salt
1/4 teaspoon dry mustard
Dash of cayenne pepper
1 cup milk
1 cup shredded Cheddar cheese (about 4 ounces)
1 cup shredded Monterey Jack cheese (about 4 ounces)
1 can (4 ounces) chopped green chilies, drained
3 eggs, separated
1/4 teaspoon cream of tartar

Prepare Guacamole Sauce. Heat oven to 350°. Butter 6-cup soufflé dish or 1½-quart casserole. Heat margarine in 2-quart saucepan over low heat until melted. Blend in flour, salt, mustard and cayenne pepper. Cook over low heat, stirring constantly, until smooth and bubbly; remove from heat. Stir in milk. Heat to boiling, stirring constantly. Boil and stir 1 minute. Stir in cheeses and chilies; stir until cheese is melted.

Beat egg whites and cream of tartar in large bowl on high speed until stiff but not dry. Beat egg yolks in small bowl until very thick and lemon colored, about 5 minutes; stir into cheese mixture. Stir about 1/4 of the egg whites into cheese mixture. Fold cheese mixture into remaining egg whites. Carefully pour into soufflé dish. Cook uncovered until knife inserted halfway between center and edge comes out clean, 50 to 60 minutes. Divide soufflé into sections with 2 forks. Serve immediately with Guacamole Sauce.

4 servings; 600 calories per serving.

✩ ✩ ✩ ✩ ✩

Cabbage-Cheese Soufflé

Good source of protein and calcium

1/4 cup margarine or butter
1/4 cup all-purpose flour
3/4 teaspoon salt
1/2 teaspoon dry mustard
1/2 teaspoon dried rosemary leaves
Dash of cayenne pepper
1 cup milk
1 cup shredded Cheddar cheese (about 4 ounces)
1 cup finely shredded green cabbage
3 eggs, separated
1/4 teaspoon cream of tartar

Heat oven to 350°. Butter 5-cup soufflé dish or 1½-quart casserole. Heat margarine in 2-quart saucepan over low heat until melted. Blend in flour, salt, mustard, rosemary and cayenne pepper. Cook over medium heat, stirring constantly, until smooth and bubbly; remove from heat. Stir in milk. Heat to boiling, stirring constantly. Boil and stir 1 minute. Stir in cheese until melted; remove from heat. Stir in cabbage.

Beat egg whites and cream of tartar in large bowl on high speed until eggs are stiff but not dry. Beat egg yolks in small bowl until very thick and lemon colored, about 5 minutes; stir into cheese mixture. Stir about 1/4 of the egg whites into cheese mixture. Fold cheese mixture into remaining egg whites. Carefully pour into soufflé dish. Cook uncovered until knife inserted halfway between center and edge comes out clean, 50 to 60 minutes. Divide soufflé into sections with 2 forks. Serve immediately.

4 servings; 350 calories per serving.

✩ ✩ ✩ ✩ ✩

Gouda Strata

Good source of protein and calcium

2   tablespoons margarine or butter, softened
6   slices whole wheat bread
1   cup shredded Monterey Jack cheese (about 4 ounces)
1   cup shredded Gouda cheese (about 4 ounces)
1/4 cup finely chopped onion
1   large clove garlic, crushed
1   teaspoon dry mustard
1/2 teaspoon salt
4   eggs, slightly beaten
1 1/2 cups milk
1/2 cup dry white wine
1/4 teaspoon red pepper sauce

Spread margarine on 1 side of each slice of bread. Cut each slice diagonally into 4 triangles. Place 8 triangles with buttered sides upright against sides of ungreased square baking dish, 8 × 8 × 2 inches. Arrange 8 triangles, buttered sides down, on bottom of dish. Mix cheeses, onion, garlic, mustard and salt; spread over bread. Arrange remaining 8 triangles, buttered sides up, on cheese mixture. Mix remaining ingredients; pour over bread. Cook uncovered in 325° oven until knife inserted in center comes out clean, about 1 hour 10 minutes. Let stand about 10 minutes before serving.

6 servings; 340 calories per serving.

═══════ ☆ ☆ ☆ ☆ ☆ ═══════

Fettuccine with Cheese

Good source of protein, riboflavin, calcium, iron and vitamin A

    Green Fettuccine (page 220)*
8   slices bacon, cut into 1/2-inch pieces
3   eggs, beaten
1/2 cup grated Parmesan cheese
1/2 cup half-and-half
1/8 teaspoon freshly ground pepper
1/2 cup grated Parmesan cheese

Prepare Green Fettuccine as directed. Let dry at least 30 minutes. Fry bacon over medium heat until crisp; remove with slotted spoon and drain. Reserve 2 tablespoons bacon fat. Cook fettuccine as directed; drain. Return to pan. Immediately add bacon, reserved bacon fat, the eggs, 1/2 cup Parmesan cheese and the half-and-half. Toss over low heat until egg coats noodles and appears cooked, about 1 minute. Sprinkle with pepper; serve with 1/2 cup Parmesan cheese.

5 servings (about 1 cup); 465 calories each.

*10 ounces packaged fettuccine can be substituted for Green Fettuccine. Cook as directed on package; drain but do not rinse.

═══════ ☆ ☆ ☆ ☆ ☆ ═══════

Three-Cheese Pie

Good source of protein and calcium

1   cup shredded Cheddar cheese (about 4 ounces)
1   cup shredded mozzarella cheese (about 4 ounces)
1   cup shredded Monterey Jack cheese (about 4 ounces)
1   medium onion, chopped (about 1/2 cup)
2   tablespoons all-purpose flour
4   eggs
1   cup milk
1/2 teaspoon salt
1/2 teaspoon dry mustard
1/2 teaspoon Worcestershire sauce
2   medium tomatoes, sliced

Mix cheeses, onion and flour. Spread in greased pie plate, 10 × 1 1/2 inches, or quiche dish, 9 × 2 inches. Beat eggs slightly; beat in milk, salt, mustard and Worcestershire sauce. Pour over cheese mixture. Cook uncovered in 350° oven until set, 35 to 40 minutes. Let stand 10 minutes; arrange tomato slices around edge of pie, overlapping slices slightly.

8 servings; 230 calories per serving.

═══════ ☆ ☆ ☆ ☆ ☆ ═══════

Eggplant Parmigiana

Good source of protein, calcium and vitamin A

> Italian Sauce (below)
> 2   small eggplant (about 1 pound each)
> 1   egg
> 2   tablespoons water
> ½   cup wheat germ or dry bread crumbs
> ¼   cup olive or vegetable oil
> 2   cups shredded mozzarella cheese
> ¼   cup grated Parmesan cheese

Prepare Italian Sauce. Cut each eggplant crosswise into ¼-inch slices. Mix egg and water. Dip eggplant into egg mixture; coat with wheat germ. Heat oil in 10-inch skillet over medium heat until hot. Cook 3 or 4 slices at a time, turning once, until light brown; drain. Repeat with remaining slices, adding 1 or 2 tablespoons oil if necessary. Place half of the eggplant in ungreased rectangular baking dish, $12 \times 7\frac{1}{2} \times 2$ inches, overlapping slices slightly. Spoon half of the Italian Sauce over eggplant; sprinkle with 1 cup of the mozzarella cheese. Repeat; sprinkle with Parmesan cheese. Cook uncovered in 350° oven until sauce is bubbly and cheese is light brown, about 25 minutes.

Italian Sauce

> 1   medium onion, chopped (about ½ cup)
> 1   small green pepper, chopped (about ½ cup)
> 1   large clove garlic, finely chopped
> 2   tablespoons olive or vegetable oil
> 1   can (16 ounces) whole tomatoes, undrained
> 1   can (8 ounces) tomato sauce
> 1   teaspoon dried basil leaves
> ½   teaspoon salt
> ½   teaspoon dried oregano leaves
> ¼   teaspoon fennel seed
> ⅛   teaspoon pepper

Cook and stir onion, green pepper and garlic in oil in 3-quart saucepan until onion is tender. Stir in remaining ingredients. Break up tomatoes with fork. Heat to boiling; reduce heat. Cover and simmer 45 minutes.

6 servings; 365 calories per serving.

☆ ☆ ☆ ☆ ☆

Eggplant Parmigiana

Cheese Enchiladas

Cheese Enchiladas

Good source of protein, calcium and vitamin A

1	large onion, chopped (about 1 cup)
2	large cloves garlic, crushed
1	tablespoon chili powder
2	tablespoons vegetable oil
1	can (28 ounces) whole tomatoes
1	teaspoon ground cumin
1	teaspoon dried oregano leaves
1/2	teaspoon salt
1/8	teaspoon pepper
1 1/2	cups shredded Cheddar cheese (about 6 ounces)
1 1/2	cups shredded Monterey Jack cheese (about 6 ounces)
1/2	cup vegetable oil
1	package (9 ounces) 6- or 7-inch corn tortillas (12 tortillas)
1 1/2	cups shredded lettuce
1/3	cup sliced radishes
1/4	cup sliced ripe olives

Cook and stir onion, garlic and chili powder in 2 tablespoons oil in 3-quart saucepan until onion is tender, about 5 minutes. Stir in tomatoes (with liquid), cumin, oregano, salt and pepper. Break up tomatoes with fork. Heat to boiling; reduce heat. Simmer uncovered until sauce thickens, about 30 minutes.

Mix Cheddar and Monterey Jack cheese. Heat 1/2 cup oil in 8-inch skillet until hot. Dip each tortilla lightly into hot oil to soften; drain. Dip each tortilla into tomato sauce to coat both sides. Spoon about 2 tablespoons cheese on each tortilla; roll tortilla around cheese. Place seam side down in ungreased rectangular baking dish, $13 \times 9 \times 2$ inches. Pour remaining tomato sauce over enchiladas; sprinkle with remaining cheese. Cook uncovered in 350° oven until cheese is melted and enchiladas are hot, about 20 minutes. Top each serving with lettuce, radishes and olives. Serve with sour cream if desired.

6 servings (2 enchiladas); 490 calories each.

☆ ☆ ☆ ☆ ☆

Cheese Broil

Good source of protein and calcium

12 slices (³/₄ inch thick) diagonally cut French bread
1 can (12 ounces) beer
6 slices bacon, cut into halves and crisply fried
2 packages (8 ounces each) Swiss cheese slices (7 × 4 inches)

Set oven control to broil and/or 550°. Place bread in ungreased jelly roll pan, 15½ × 10½ × 1 inch. Broil 5 inches from heat until light brown, about 3 minutes; turn bread. Broil about 2 minutes longer. Pour beer evenly over toast. Place bacon on top of each piece of toast. Cut each cheese slice crosswise into fourths. Place 4 pieces of cheese on each piece of toast, covering surface of toast completely. Broil until cheese is melted and bubbly, 2 to 3 minutes.

6 servings; 480 calories per serving.

☆ ☆ ☆ ☆ ☆

Cheesy Lasagne

Good source of protein and calcium

Egg Noodles (page 221) or 12 uncooked lasagne noodles
½ cup margarine or butter
½ cup all-purpose flour
½ teaspoon salt
4 cups milk
1 cup shredded Swiss cheese
1 cup shredded mozzarella cheese
½ cup grated Parmesan cheese
2 cups creamed cottage cheese
¼ cup snipped parsley
1 teaspoon dried basil leaves
½ teaspoon salt
½ teaspoon dried oregano leaves
2 cloves garlic, crushed
½ cup grated Parmesan cheese

Prepare Egg Noodles as directed except — divide dough into halves. Roll one half into rectangle, 13 × 12 inches; cut rectangle lengthwise into 6 strips, 13 × 2 inches. Repeat with other half. Spread strips on wire rack; let stand until dry, at least 1 hour.

Heat margarine in 2-quart saucepan over low heat until melted. Blend in flour and ½ teaspoon salt. Cook over low heat, stirring constantly, until smooth and bubbly; remove from heat. Stir in milk. Heat to boiling, stirring constantly. Boil and stir 1 minute. Stir in Swiss cheese, mozzarella cheese and ½ cup Parmesan cheese. Stir over low heat until cheeses are melted. Mix cottage cheese, parsley, basil, ½ teaspoon salt, the oregano and garlic.

Spread ¼ of the cheese sauce mixture in ungreased rectangular baking dish, 13 × 9 × 2 inches; top with 4 uncooked noodles. Spread 1 cup of the cottage cheese mixture over noodles; spread with ¼ of the cheese sauce mixture. Repeat with 4 noodles, the remaining cottage cheese mixture, ¼ of the cheese sauce mixture, the remaining noodles and the remaining cheese sauce mixture. Sprinkle with ½ cup Parmesan cheese. Cook uncovered in 350° oven until noodles are done, 35 to 40 minutes. Let stand 10 minutes before cutting.

12 servings; 360 calories per serving.

☆ ☆ ☆ ☆ ☆

EASY-STEP PASTA DISHES

The most difficult part of preparing lasagne is cooking and draining the lasagne noodles and then preventing them from sticking together. Filling cooked manicotti tubes isn't any easier. Now, both Cheesy Lasagne (left) and Manicotti (page 124) are assembled using uncooked pasta.

For success, two easy steps must be followed. First, sauce must be spooned into the pan so that the uncooked pasta can steam and become tender between layers of sauce. Second, it is very important that the pasta be completely covered with sauce; if not, the pasta will remain uncooked and hard. However, these two steps are easier to handle than cooked pasta!

Baked Soy Beans

Good source of protein, thiamin and iron

  4   cups water
 12   ounces dried soy beans (about 2 cups)
  1   medium onion, sliced
 ¼   cup packed brown sugar
  3   tablespoons molasses
  2   tablespoons vegetable oil
  2   teaspoons salt
 ¾   teaspoon dry mustard
 ⅛   teaspoon pepper

Heat water and beans to boiling in 3-quart saucepan. Boil 2 minutes; remove from heat. Skim off loose bean skins. Cover and let stand 1 hour. Add enough water, if necessary, to cover beans. Heat to boiling; reduce heat. Cover and simmer until beans are tender, 1 to 1½ hours (do not boil or beans will burst). Drain beans, reserving liquid. Layer beans and onion in ungreased 2½-quart casserole. Mix brown sugar, molasses, oil, salt, mustard, pepper and reserved bean liquid; pour over beans. Add enough water to almost cover beans. Cover and cook in 350° oven, stirring occasionally, 3 hours. Uncover and cook 30 minutes longer.

4 servings (about 1 cup); 430 calories each.

☆ ☆ ☆ ☆ ☆

1. Three Bean Casserole
2. Baby Lima Beans
3. Pinto Beans
4. Soy Beans
5. Baked Soy Beans
6. Split Peas

Baked Pinto Beans

Good source of thiamin

  4   cups water
  1   pound dried pinto beans (about 2½ cups)
 ½   cup packed brown sugar
  1   teaspoon salt
 ¼   teaspoon ground cloves
 ¼   teaspoon pepper
 ¼   teaspoon celery seed
 ¼   cup water
  1   tablespoon vinegar
 ½   cup strong black coffee
  2   tablespoons brandy
  1   medium onion, sliced
  4   slices bacon

Heat 4 cups water and the beans to boiling in 3-quart saucepan. Boil 2 minutes; remove from heat. Cover and let stand 1 hour. Add enough water, if necessary, to cover beans. Heat to boiling; reduce heat. Cover and simmer until beans are tender, about 1½ hours (do not boil or beans will burst). Drain beans, reserving liquid. Heat brown sugar, salt, cloves, pepper, celery seed, ¼ cup water and the vinegar to boiling, stirring occasionally. Stir in coffee and brandy.

Place half of the beans in ungreased 2-quart casserole; arrange onion on top. Pour half of the coffee mixture over onion; top with remaining beans. Pour remaining coffee mixture and the reserved bean liquid over beans. Cover and cook in 350° oven 1½ hours. Stir beans; arrange bacon on top. Cook uncovered 30 minutes longer.

6 servings (about 1 cup); 285 calories each.

☆ ☆ ☆ ☆ ☆

Country Baked Limas

Good source of iron

4	cups water
1	pound dried baby lima beans (about 2½ cups)
1	medium onion, sliced
6	slices bacon, cut up
1	cup tomato juice
¼	cup molasses
¼	cup chili sauce
2	tablespoons packed brown sugar
1	teaspoon salt
1	tablespoon prepared mustard

Heat water and beans to boiling in 3-quart saucepan. Boil 2 minutes; remove from heat. Cover and let stand 1 hour. Add enough water, if necessary, to cover beans. Heat to boiling; reduce heat. Simmer uncovered until tender, about 30 minutes (do not boil or beans will burst). Drain beans, reserving liquid. Layer beans, onion and bacon in ungreased 2-quart casserole. Mix remaining ingredients; pour over beans. Add enough reserved bean liquid to cover. Cover and cook in 300° oven 1 hour; stir. Cook uncovered 30 minutes longer.

5 servings (about 1¼ cups); 330 calories each.

☆ ☆ ☆ ☆ ☆

Split Pea-Vegetable Soup

Good source of protein, thiamin, niacin and iron

8	cups water
1	pound dried split peas (about 2¼ cups)
1	pound fully cooked smoked Polish sausages or kielbasa
1	large onion, chopped (about 1 cup)
2	stalks celery, sliced (about 1 cup)
2	large potatoes, cut into ½-inch pieces
1	small rutabaga, cut into ½-inch pieces
1	teaspoon salt
¼	teaspoon pepper
2	medium tomatoes, cut into ½-inch pieces

Heat water and peas to boiling in 4-quart Dutch oven. Boil 2 minutes; remove from heat. Cover and let stand 1 hour. Heat to boiling; reduce heat. Cover and simmer until peas are tender, about 1 hour. Skim off foam if necessary.

Cut sausages into ½-inch thick slices; cut each slice into halves. Cook and stir sausages, onion and celery until sausage is hot, about 15 minutes. Remove sausage mixture from skillet with slotted spoon. Stir sausage mixture, potatoes, rutabaga, salt and pepper into peas. Heat to boiling; reduce heat. Cover and simmer until vegetables are tender, about 30 minutes. Stir in tomatoes; cook uncovered 5 minutes.

8 servings (about 1½ cups); 495 calories each.

☆ ☆ ☆ ☆ ☆

Chili-Bean Soup

Good source of protein, calcium and vitamin A

1	medium onion, sliced
1	large clove garlic, crushed
2	tablespoons margarine or butter
1	can (28 ounces) whole tomatoes
1	can (20 ounces) kidney beans, drained
1	can (16 ounces) pinto beans, drained
1	can (4 ounces) chopped green chilies, drained
1	tablespoon chili powder
¼	teaspoon ground coriander
½	cup shredded Cheddar cheese (about 2 ounces)
1	cup shredded Monterey Jack cheese (about 4 ounces)

Cook and stir onion and garlic in margarine in 3-quart saucepan until onion is tender, about 5 minutes. Stir in tomatoes (with liquid), kidney beans, pinto beans, chilies, chili powder and coriander. Break up tomatoes with fork. Heat to boiling; reduce heat. Cover and simmer 30 minutes. Stir in Cheddar cheese and ½ cup of the Monterey Jack cheese; stir over low heat until cheese is melted. Sprinkle each serving with remaining cheese.

6 servings (about 1 cup); 345 calories each.

☆ ☆ ☆ ☆ ☆

Bean-Pasta Soup

Good source of protein and thiamin

1	medium onion, sliced
2	cloves garlic, crushed
4	ounces fully cooked smoked ham, chopped (about 1 cup)
2	tablespoons olive or vegetable oil
1	can (16 ounces) whole tomatoes
3	cups water
1	teaspoon dried oregano leaves
1/2	teaspoon dried thyme leaves
1/4	teaspoon pepper
1	cup uncooked spiral macaroni
2	medium potatoes, cut into 1/2-inch pieces
1	can (20 ounces) cannellini or red kidney beans, drained
1	small zucchini, thinly sliced
1/3	cup grated Parmesan cheese

Cook and stir onion, garlic and ham in oil in 4-quart Dutch oven over medium heat until onion is tender, about 5 minutes. Stir in tomatoes (with liquid), water, oregano, thyme and pepper. Break up tomatoes with fork. Heat to boiling. Stir in macaroni and potatoes; reduce heat. Cook uncovered until macaroni is tender, about 10 minutes. Stir in beans and zucchini. Cook just until zucchini is crisp-tender, about 3 minutes. Sprinkle each serving with Parmesan cheese.

6 servings (about 1 1/3 cups); 310 calories each.

☆ ☆ ☆ ☆ ☆

Bean-Nut Burgers

Good source of protein, iron and thiamin

2	cans (15 ounces each) Great Northern beans, drained and mashed
3/4	cup finely chopped walnuts
1/4	cup roasted salted sunflower nuts
1/4	cup grated Parmesan cheese
1/4	cup snipped parsley
1	tablespoon prepared horseradish
1	egg, slightly beaten
3	tablespoons vegetable oil
6	hamburger buns, split and toasted
2	tablespoons prepared mustard
6	lettuce leaves
2	medium tomatoes, sliced
1/3	cup chopped onion

Mix beans, walnuts, sunflower nuts, Parmesan cheese, parsley, horseradish and egg. Heat oil in 12-inch skillet over medium heat until hot. Drop bean mixture into 6 equal mounds in skillet; flatten and shape into patties 3 1/2 inches in diameter. Cook patties until light brown, about 5 minutes; turn. Cook until hot and light brown, about 5 minutes longer.

Spread buns with mustard. Place patty on bottom half of each bun; top with lettuce leaf. Arrange tomato slice on lettuce leaf; sprinkle with onion and top with remaining bun half.

6 servings; 510 calories per serving.

☆ ☆ ☆ ☆ ☆

Bean Patties

1-inch thickness; push in sides to form patties. Cook over medium heat until brown, about 5 minutes on each side. Top each patty with Guacamole Sauce.

Guacamole Sauce

1   *large ripe avocado, mashed*
1   *medium tomato, finely chopped*
1   *clove garlic, crushed*
2   *tablespoons finely chopped onion*
1   *tablespoon finely snipped cilantro, if desired*
1   *tablespoon lemon juice*
1/4   *teaspoon salt*
4   *drops red pepper sauce*

Mix all ingredients. Cover and refrigerate at least 1 hour.

4 servings; 475 calories per serving.

☆ ☆ ☆ ☆ ☆

Bean and Rice Casserole

Good source of protein and thiamin

1   *pound pork sausage*
2   *medium stalks celery, sliced (about 1 cup)*
1   *medium onion, chopped (about 1/2 cup)*
2   *cups cooked brown or regular rice*
1   *can (15 ounces) kidney beans, drained*
1   *can (16 ounces) whole tomatoes, undrained*
1   *teaspoon dried oregano leaves*
1   *teaspoon salt*
1/2   *teaspoon dried savory leaves*
1/4   *teaspoon pepper*
1/2   *teaspoon red pepper sauce*
1   *cup shredded Monterey Jack cheese*

Cook and stir sausage, celery and onion in 10-inch skillet over medium heat until sausage is brown, 10 to 15 minutes; drain. Stir in remaining ingredients except cheese. Break up tomatoes with fork. Pour mixture into ungreased 2-quart casserole. Cook uncovered in 350° oven 30 minutes; sprinkle with cheese. Cook uncovered until cheese is melted, about 5 minutes longer.

6 servings (about 1 1/4 cups); 340 calories each.

☆ ☆ ☆ ☆ ☆

Bean Patties

Good source of vitamin C

Guacamole Sauce (below)
1   *can (17 ounces) refried beans*
1   *can (4 ounces) chopped green chilies, drained*
1   *egg, slightly beaten*
1/2   *cup dry bread crumbs*
1   *small onion, chopped (about 1/4 cup)*
1/2   *cup shredded cheese (about 2 ounces)*
1/2   *teaspoon salt*
2   *tablespoons margarine or butter*
2   *tablespoons vegetable oil*

Prepare Guacamole Sauce. Mix beans, chilies, egg, bread crumbs, onion, cheese and salt. Heat margarine and oil in 10-inch skillet until margarine is melted. Drop bean mixture by 4 spoonfuls into skillet. Flatten with spatula to

Three-Bean Casserole

Good source of protein, thiamin and iron

1   pound pork sausage
2   medium stalks celery, sliced (about 1 cup)
1   medium onion, chopped (about ½ cup)
1   large clove garlic, crushed
2   cans (21 ounces each) baked beans in tomato
     sauce
1   can (17 ounces) lima beans, drained
1   can (15 ounces) kidney beans, drained
1   can (8 ounces) tomato sauce
2   tablespoons honey
1   tablespoon vinegar
1   tablespoon dry mustard
1   teaspoon salt
¼   teaspoon red pepper sauce

Cook and stir sausage, celery, onion and garlic until sausage is done, about 10 minutes; drain. Mix sausage mixture with remaining ingredients in ungreased 3-quart casserole. Cook uncovered in 400° oven, stirring once, until hot and bubbly, about 45 minutes.

8 servings (about 1¼ cups); 525 calories each.

===== ☆ ☆ ☆ ☆ ☆ =====

Italian-Style Beans

Good source of protein

1½   pounds Italian sausage
3   stalks celery, sliced (about 1½ cups)
1   medium green pepper, chopped (about 1 cup)
1   medium onion, chopped (about ½ cup)
1   can (16 ounces) lima beans, drained
1   can (16 ounces) pork and beans
1   can (15 ounces) chili with beans

Remove sausage from casing. Cook and stir sausage, celery, green pepper and onion in 4-quart Dutch oven over medium heat until sausage is done, about 15 minutes; drain. Stir in remaining ingredients. Heat to boiling; reduce heat. Simmer uncovered, stirring occasionally, until hot, 10 to 15 minutes.

8 servings (about 1⅓ cups); 330 calories each.

===== ☆ ☆ ☆ ☆ ☆ =====

Bean-Cheese Pie

Good source of protein, thiamin, calcium and iron

¾   cup all-purpose flour
½   cup shredded Cheddar cheese (about 2 ounces)
1½   teaspoons baking powder
½   teaspoon salt
⅓   cup milk
1   egg, slightly beaten
1   can (15½ ounces) garbanzo beans, drained
1   can (15 ounces) kidney beans, drained
1   can (8 ounces) tomato sauce
½   cup shredded Cheddar cheese (about 2 ounces)
1   small green pepper, chopped (about ½ cup)
1   small onion, chopped (about ¼ cup)
2   teaspoons chili powder
½   teaspoon dried oregano leaves
¼   teaspoon garlic powder
½   cup shredded Cheddar cheese (about 2 ounces)

Mix flour, ½ cup cheese, the baking powder and salt in 1½-quart bowl. Stir in milk and egg until blended. Spread over bottom and up side of greased pie plate, 10 × 1½ inches. Mix garbanzo beans, kidney beans, tomato sauce, ½ cup cheese, the green pepper, onion, chili powder, oregano and garlic powder. Spoon into pie plate; sprinkle with ½ cup cheese. Bake in 375° oven until edges are puffy and light brown, about 25 minutes. Let stand 10 minutes before cutting.

8 servings; 385 calories per serving.

===== ☆ ☆ ☆ ☆ ☆ =====

Italian Bean Salad

Good source of protein, niacin, iron and vitamin C

2   cans (20 ounces each) canellini beans, drained
1   jar (2 ounces) diced pimiento, drained
1   large green pepper, chopped (about 1 cup)
1   medium onion, chopped (about ½ cup)
¼   cup snipped parsley
¼   cup olive or vegetable oil
2   tablespoons lemon juice
2   tablespoons capers
½   teaspoon salt
¼   teaspoon red pepper sauce
    Lettuce leaves
1   can (6½ ounces) tuna in water, drained

Mix beans, pimiento, green pepper, onion and parsley. Shake oil, lemon juice, capers, salt and pepper sauce in tightly covered container; toss with bean mixture. Spoon bean mixture on lettuce; top with tuna. Serve with lemon wedges if desired.

5 servings (about 1¼ cups); 344 calories each.

☆ ☆ ☆ ☆ ☆

Walnut-Wheat Casserole

Good source of protein, iron, calcium and vitamin A

1½   cups cracked wheat (bulgur)
1½   cups cold water
1½   cups coarsely chopped walnuts
1   medium onion, chopped (about ½ cup)
1   small green pepper, chopped (about ½ cup)
2   eggs, slightly beaten
1   can (8 ounces) tomato sauce
1   jar (2 ounces) diced pimiento, drained
¼   cup snipped parsley
1   teaspoon salt
1   teaspoon dried basil leaves
¼   teaspoon ground coriander
⅛   teaspoon pepper
     Cheese Sauce (below)

Cover cracked wheat with cold water. Let stand 1 hour. Mix cracked wheat, walnuts, onion, green pepper, eggs, tomato sauce, pimiento, parsley, salt, basil, coriander and pepper. Spread mixture in ungreased 1½-quart casserole. Cook uncovered in 350° oven until light brown, about 35 minutes. Prepare Cheese Sauce; serve with casserole.

Cheese Sauce

2   tablespoons margarine or butter
2   tablespoons all-purpose flour
¼   teaspoon salt
    Dash of cayenne pepper
1   cup milk
1   cup shredded Cheddar cheese (about 4 ounces)

Heat margarine in 1-quart saucepan over low heat until melted. Blend in flour, salt and cayenne pepper. Cook over low heat, stirring constantly, until smooth and bubbly; remove from heat. Stir in milk. Heat to boiling, stirring constantly. Boil and stir 1 minute. Stir in cheese until melted.

5 servings (about 1 cup); 625 calories each.

☆ ☆ ☆ ☆ ☆

Chili-Tofu Casserole

Good source of protein and calcium

1   can (8 ounces) tomato sauce
1   medium onion, chopped (about ½ cup)
1   large clove garlic, crushed
½   teaspoon salt
½   teaspoon dried oregano leaves
¼   teaspoon ground cumin
2   pounds firm tofu, cut into ½-inch slices
1   can (4 ounces) whole green chilies
1   cup shredded Cheddar cheese (about 4 ounces)

Mix tomato sauce, onion, garlic, salt, oregano and cumin. Spread half of the tomato mixture in greased baking dish, 8 × 8 × 2 inches. Arrange tofu on tomato sauce, overlapping slices. Split and flatten chilies; remove seeds and membranes. Arrange chilies on tofu; spread with remaining tomato mixture. Sprinkle with cheese. Cook uncovered in 350° oven until sauce is hot, about 15 minutes.

6 servings; 220 calories per serving.

☆ ☆ ☆ ☆ ☆

Tofu-Vegetable Salad

Tofu-Vegetable Salad

Good source of vitamin C

    Ginger Dressing (below)
1½   *pounds firm tofu, cut into ½-inch cubes (about 4½ cups)*
1   *tablespoon toasted sesame seed*
1   *tablespoon sliced green onion (with top)*
8   *ounces medium mushrooms, sliced*
1   *package (6 ounces) frozen pea pods, thawed and drained*
1   *small cucumber, sliced*
12   *radishes, sliced*

Prepare Ginger Dressing; pour over tofu. Cover and refrigerate at least 2 hours. Remove tofu with slotted spoon; reserve dressing. Place tofu in center of serving platter or 6 plates. Sprinkle with sesame seed and green onion. Arrange mushrooms, pea pods, cucumber and radishes around tofu. Drizzle reserved dressing over vegetables. Serve with rice crackers if desired.

Ginger Dressing

⅔   *cup vegetable oil*
¼   *cup lemon juice*
2   *tablespoons soy sauce*
2   *teaspoons dry mustard*
½   *teaspoon salt*
½   *teaspoon garlic powder*
½   *teaspoon ground ginger*
¼   *teaspoon ground coriander*

Shake all ingredients in tightly covered jar.

6 servings; 365 calories per serving.

☆ ☆ ☆ ☆ ☆

Nutrition Information Per Serving or Unit

Recipe and Page Number	Protein	Carbo-hydrates	Fat	Sodium	Potas-sium	Protein	Calcium	Iron
	Grams			Milligrams		Percent U.S. Recommended Daily Allowance		
EGGS								
Broccoli Oven Omelet, 83	15	6	12	435	300	34	18	14
Cheesy Oven Omelet, 83	19	4	26	480	210	42	28	12
Deviled Egg Salads, 85	15	9	22	345	475	32	14	16
Egg-Bean Sandwiches, 87	14	14	13	380	225	26	18	12
Egg-Creole Casserole, 85	16	23	17	705	415	30	18	16
Eggs in Toast Cups, 87	21	15	28	735	295	40	22	18
Egg Soufflé Roll, 84	20	15	34	870	335	44	24	18
Egg-Spaghetti Skillet, 85	15	19	28	695	195	30	14	16
Eggs with Wine Sauce, 88	19	25	25	825	365	44	4	10
Green Chili Omelet, 82	15	4	19	380	150	32	8	14
Italian-Style Eggs, 87	21	17	27	925	535	48	10	16
Mushroom-Alfalfa Omelet, 82	16	5	26	585	350	36	8	18
Scrambled Eggs in Buns, 86	15	23	25	865	180	30	16	14
CHEESE								
Cabbage-Cheese Soufflé, 89	15	10	28	815	265	34	32	8
Cheese Broil, 93	29	30	27	550	160	54	76	8
Cheese Enchiladas, 92	18	29	34	785	474	40	54	18
Cheesy Lasagne, 93	19	24	21	1025	290	36	38	8
Chili-Cheese Soufflé, 89	24	18	49	970	795	44	54	12
Eggplant Parmigiana, 91	15	20	25	665	715	30	30	18
Fettuccine with Cheese, 90	24	40	23	980	410	54	34	26
Gouda Strata, 90	19	16	22	690	280	36	40	10
Three-Cheese Pie, 90	15	6	16	410	215	34	34	6
DRIED BEANS								
Baked Pinto Beans, 95	13	51	3	430	600	20	10	22
Baked Soy Beans, 95	22	46	18	1110	1315	34	22	38
Bean and Rice Casserole, 98	16	35	15	1185	640	30	14	16
Bean-Cheese Pie, 99	22	48	12	510	750	40	28	32

Nutrition Information Per Serving or Unit

Recipe and Page Number	Protein	Carbo-hydrates	Fat	Sodium	Potas-sium	Protein	Calcium	Iron
	Grams			Milligrams		Percent U.S. Recommended Daily Allowance		
Bean-Nut Burgers, 97	20	56	23	360	870	30	18	32
Bean-Pasta Soup, 97	17	42	8	365	710	30	12	22
Bean Patties, 98	12	28	35	860	755	22	16	14
Chili-Bean Soup, 96	18	37	14	400	810	28	28	24
Country Baked Limas, 96	14	58	5	1290	825	22	12	38
Italian Bean Salad, 100	21	38	12	530	765	38	8	26
Italian-Style Beans, 99	19	30	15	1070	615	36	8	22
Split Pea-Vegetable Soup, 96	25	63	16	935	1350	45	10	26
Three-Bean Casserole, 99	27	55	22	1970	935	46	14	34
TOFU AND NUTS Chili-Tofu Casserole, 100	17	9	13	475	160	30	38	20
Tofu-Vegetable Salad, 101	13	11	30	540	375	20	20	18
Walnut-Wheat Casserole, 100	22	54	36	985	610	40	32	28

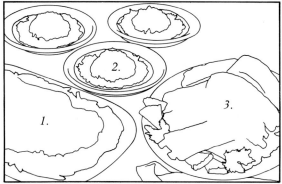

1. Roast with Peppers, 2. Hamburgers Ranchero,
3. Sweet'n Pungent Spareribs

French-Style Beef Roast

Good source of protein and vitamin A

3 - pound beef boneless chuck or rolled rump roast
1   teaspoon salt
1   teaspoon dried thyme leaves
1   bay leaf
1   large clove garlic, cut into fourths
6   whole cloves
5   peppercorns
4   cups water
4   medium carrots, cut crosswise into halves
2   medium onions, cut into fourths
2   medium turnips, cut into fourths
2   medium stalks celery, cut into 1-inch pieces

Place beef, salt, thyme, bay leaf, garlic, cloves and peppercorns in 4-quart Dutch oven; add water. Heat to boiling; reduce heat. Cover and simmer 2½ hours. Add remaining ingredients. Cover and simmer until beef and vegetables are tender, about 30 minutes. Remove beef; cut into ¼-inch slices. Serve vegetables with beef. Strain broth; serve with beef and vegetables.

8 servings; 300 calories per serving.

☐ *Pressure Cooker Directions:* Decrease water to 2 cups. Place beef, salt, thyme, bay leaf, garlic, cloves and peppercorns in 6-quart pressure cooker; add water. Following manufacturer's directions, cover and cook at 15 pounds pressure 1 hour. Cool 5 minutes; reduce pressure. Add remaining ingredients. Cover and cook at 15 pounds pressure 8 minutes. Cool 5 minutes; reduce pressure. Remove beef; cut into ¼-inch slices. Serve vegetables with beef. Strain broth; serve with beef and vegetables.

☆ ☆ ☆ ☆ ☆

Roast with Peppers

Good source of protein, niacin and iron

3 - to 4-pound beef arm, blade or cross rib pot roast
2   large cloves garlic, crushed
½   cup dry red wine
¼   cup red wine vinegar
2   tablespoons olive or vegetable oil
1   tablespoon soy sauce
1   teaspoon dried rosemary leaves
1   teaspoon dry mustard
2   tablespoons olive or vegetable oil
2   large green peppers, cut into ¼-inch strips
1   large red onion, cut into halves and thinly sliced
2   tablespoons olive or vegetable oil
1   tablespoon red wine vinegar
1   teaspoon dried oregano leaves
¼   teaspoon salt
⅛   teaspoon pepper

Pierce surface of beef with fork. Place beef in rectangular baking dish, 13 × 9 × 2 inches, or glass bowl. Mix garlic, wine, ¼ cup vinegar, 2 tablespoons oil, the soy sauce, rosemary and mustard. Pour over beef. Cover and refrigerate at least 12 hours but no longer than 24 hours.

Remove beef from wine mixture; reserve wine mixture. Cook beef in 4-quart Dutch oven in 2 tablespoons oil until brown; add reserved wine mixture. Heat to boiling; reduce heat. Cover and simmer until beef is tender, about 2 hours. Cook and stir green peppers and onion in 2 tablespoons oil until crisp-tender, 3 to 5 minutes. Stir in 1 tablespoon vinegar, the oregano, salt and pepper; serve with beef.

8 servings; 440 calories per serving.

☐ *Pressure Cooker Directions:* Prepare beef as directed. Cook in oil in 6-quart pressure cooker until brown; add reserved wine mixture. Following manufacturer's directions, cover and cook at 15 pounds pressure 35 to 45 minutes. Cool 5 minutes; reduce pressure. Cook and stir green peppers and onion in 2 tablespoons oil until crisp-tender, 3 to 5 minutes. Stir in 1 tablespoon vinegar, the oregano, salt and pepper; serve with beef.

☆ ☆ ☆ ☆ ☆

Oriental Pot Roast

Good source of protein, niacin, iron and vitamin A

4 - *pound beef arm, blade or cross rib pot roast*
1 *can (15¼ ounces) pineapple chunks in juice*
1 *large onion, sliced*
3 *tablespoons soy sauce*
1 *teaspoon ground ginger*
1 *large clove garlic, crushed*
2 *medium stalks celery, diagonally sliced (about 1 cup)*
1 *package (10 ounces) frozen spinach leaves, thawed*
1 *can (4 ounces) mushroom stems and pieces, drained*

Cook beef in 4-quart Dutch oven over medium heat until brown. Drain pineapple; reserve juice. Place onion on beef. Mix pineapple juice, soy sauce, ginger and garlic; pour over beef. Heat to boiling; reduce heat. Cover and simmer until tender, about 2½ hours. Add celery. Cover and simmer 20 minutes. Add pineapple chunks, spinach and mushrooms. Cover and simmer 5 minutes. Remove beef, pineapple and vegetables. Skim fat from broth; serve broth with beef.

8 servings; 390 calories per serving.

□ *Pressure Cooker Directions:* Cook beef in 6-quart pressure cooker over medium heat until brown. Drain pineapple; reserve juice. Place onion on beef. Mix pineapple juice, soy sauce, ginger and garlic; pour over beef. Following manufacturer's directions, cover and cook at 15 pounds pressure 35 to 45 minutes. Cool 5 minutes; reduce pressure. Add celery. Cover and cook at 15 pounds pressure 5 minutes. Cool 5 minutes; reduce pressure. Add pineapple chunks, spinach and mushrooms. Uncover and cook until pineapple chunks are hot, about 5 minutes. Remove beef, pineapple and vegetables. Skim fat from broth; serve broth with beef.

☆ ☆ ☆ ☆ ☆

Fruited Beef Roast

Good source of protein, niacin, iron and vitamin A

4 - *pound beef arm, blade or cross rib pot roast*
½ *teaspoon salt*
¼ *teaspoon pepper*
2 *medium onions, sliced*
2 *medium tomatoes, chopped (about 1½ cups)*
1 *cup dry white wine*
2 *medium yams or sweet potatoes, cut into ¼-inch slices*
1 *can (16 ounces) sliced peaches in juice, drained*
1 *can (16 ounces) sliced pears in juice, drained*
1 *tablespoon cornstarch*
2 *tablespoons cold water*

Cook beef in 4-quart Dutch oven over medium heat until brown; reduce heat. Sprinkle with salt and pepper. Add onions, tomatoes and wine. Heat to boiling; reduce heat. Cover and simmer 3 hours.

Add yams, peaches and pears. Cover and cook until yams are tender, about 30 minutes. Remove beef, fruit and vegetables; keep warm. Skim excess fat from broth. If necessary, add enough water to measure 2 cups. Mix cornstarch and cold water; gradually stir into broth. Heat to boiling, stirring constantly. Boil and stir 1 minute. Serve with beef. Garnish with snipped parsley if desired.

8 servings; 500 calories per serving.

□ *Pressure Cooker Directions:* Cook beef in 6-quart pressure cooker until brown. Sprinkle with salt and pepper. Add onions, tomatoes and wine. Following manufacturer's directions, cover and cook at 15 pounds pressure 40 minutes. Cool 5 minutes; reduce pressure. Add yams. Cover and cook at 15 pounds pressure 5 minutes. Cool 5 minutes; reduce pressure. Add peaches and pears. Uncover and cook just until fruit is hot, about 5 minutes. Remove beef, fruit and vegetables; keep warm. Skim excess fat from broth. Mix cornstarch and cold water; gradually stir into broth. Heat to boiling, stirring constantly. Boil and stir 1 minute. Serve with beef.

☆ ☆ ☆ ☆ ☆

Beef with Tomatoes and Rice

Good source of protein, niacin and iron

Marinated Tomatoes (below)
4 - pound beef tip, heel of round or rolled
      rump roast
2⅓   cups uncooked regular rice
4⅔   cups water
2   teaspoons salt
1   teaspoon ground turmeric
½   cup snipped parsley

Prepare Marinated Tomatoes. Place beef, fat side up, on rack in shallow roasting pan. Insert meat thermometer so tip is in center of thickest part of beef and does not rest in fat. Roast uncovered in 325° oven until thermometer registers 160°, about 3 hours.

About 30 minutes before beef is done, heat rice, water, salt and turmeric to boiling, stirring once or twice; reduce heat. Cover and simmer 14 minutes (do not lift cover or stir). Remove from heat; fluff rice lightly with fork. Cover and let steam 5 to 10 minutes. Stir parsley into rice. Cut beef into ¼-inch slices. Arrange beef and tomato slices on rice; spoon remaining marinade over beef.

Marinated Tomatoes

4   medium tomatoes, cut into ¼-inch slices
¼   cup olive or vegetable oil
2   tablespoons red wine vinegar
⅛   teaspoon salt
3   drops red pepper sauce
2   large cloves garlic, finely chopped

Place tomatoes in glass or plastic dish. Mix remaining ingredients; pour over tomatoes. Cover and let stand at room temperature about 3 hours.

14 servings; 400 calories per serving.

☆ ☆ ☆ ☆ ☆

Beef with Tomatoes and Rice

Garlic Beef Roast

Good source of protein

4 - pound beef tip, heel of round or rolled
    rump roast
4 large cloves garlic, cut into slivers
1½ cups beer or apple cider
2 tablespoons vegetable oil
¼ teaspoon pepper
2 tablespoons toasted sesame seed
1 tablespoon sugar
3 tablespoons soy sauce
1 teaspoon ground ginger
1 tablespoon cornstarch
2 tablespoons cold water

Cut slits in beef with small sharp knife. Insert 1 sliver of garlic into each slit. Pierce beef thoroughly with fork. Place beef in deep glass bowl. Mix beer, oil and pepper; pour over beef. Cover and refrigerate, turning occasionally, at least 12 hours.

Remove beef from beer mixture; reserve 1¼ cups of the beer mixture. Place beef, fat side up, on rack in shallow roasting pan. Insert meat thermometer so tip is in center of thickest part of beef and does not rest in fat. Mix reserved beer mixture, the sesame seed, sugar, soy sauce and ginger; brush over beef. Roast uncovered, brushing occasionally with beer mixture, in 325° oven until thermometer registers 160°, about 3 hours.

Remove beef; keep warm. Heat remaining beer mixture over medium heat until hot. Mix cornstarch and cold water; gradually stir into beer mixture. Heat to boiling, stirring constantly. Boil and stir 1 minute. Serve with beef.

14 servings; 390 calories per serving.

☆ ☆ ☆ ☆ ☆

Vegetable-Chili Steak

Good source of protein, niacin and iron

2 tablespoons all-purpose flour
1 tablespoon chili powder
½ teaspoon salt
¼ teaspoon pepper
1½ - pound beef bone-in round or chuck steak,
    about ½ inch thick
1 tablespoon vegetable oil
2 medium stalks celery, sliced (about 2 cups)
1 large onion, coarsely chopped
½ cup chili sauce
½ cup water
1 medium green pepper, cut into ¼-inch strips
2 medium zucchini, sliced
1 can (15 ounces) red kidney beans

Mix flour, chili powder, salt and pepper. Sprinkle 1 side of beef with half of the flour mixture; pound in. Turn beef and pound in remaining flour mixture. Cut beef into 6 serving pieces. Heat oil in 4-quart Dutch oven. Cook beef over medium heat until brown, about 15 minutes. Add celery, onion, chili sauce and water. Heat to boiling; reduce heat. Cover and simmer until beef is tender, about 1 hour. Add green pepper, zucchini and beans (with liquid). Cover and simmer until green pepper is crisp-tender, about 8 minutes.

6 servings; 285 calories per serving.

☐ *Pressure Cooker Directions:* Prepare beef as directed. Heat oil in 4-quart pressure cooker. Cook beef over medium heat until brown, about 15 minutes. Add celery, onion, chili sauce and water. Following manufacturer's directions, cover and cook at 15 pounds pressure 25 minutes. Cool 5 minutes; reduce pressure. Add green pepper, zucchini and beans (with liquid). Heat to boiling; reduce heat. Uncover and simmer until green pepper is crisp-tender, about 8 minutes.

☆ ☆ ☆ ☆ ☆

Dilled Steak

Good source of protein and niacin

  2   *tablespoons all-purpose flour*
 ½   *teaspoon salt*
 ⅛   *teaspoon pepper*
1½ - *pound beef bone-in round or chuck steak,*
       about ½ inch thick
  1   *tablespoon vegetable oil*
 ½   *cup water*
  2   *teaspoons vinegar*
 ½   *teaspoon dried dill weed*
 12 *small new potatoes (about 1½ pounds)*
  3   *medium zucchini, cut into 1-inch pieces*
 ¼   *cup cold water*
  2   *tablespoons all-purpose flour*
 ½   *cup plain yogurt or dairy sour cream*

Mix 2 tablespoons flour, the salt and pepper. Sprinkle 1 side of beef with half of the flour mixture; pound in. Turn beef and pound in remaining flour mixture. Cut beef into 6 serving pieces. Heat oil in 4-quart Dutch oven. Cook beef over medium heat until brown, about 15 minutes. Mix ½ cup water, the vinegar and dill weed; pour over beef. Heat to boiling; reduce heat. Cover and simmer until beef is just tender, about 45 minutes. Add potatoes. Cover and simmer 15 minutes. Add zucchini. Cover and simmer until vegetables are tender, 10 to 15 minutes. Remove beef and vegetables; keep warm.

Add enough water to broth to measure 1 cup. Shake ¼ cup water and 2 tablespoons flour in tightly covered container; gradually stir into broth. Heat to boiling, stirring constantly. Boil and stir 1 minute. Stir in yogurt; heat just until hot. Serve with beef and vegetables.

6 servings; 270 calories per serving.

☐ *Pressure Cooker Directions:* Prepare beef as directed. Heat oil in 4-quart pressure cooker. Cook beef over medium heat until brown, about 15 minutes. Mix ½ cup water, the vinegar and dill weed; pour over beef. Following manufacturer's directions, cover and cook at 15 pounds pressure 15 minutes. Cool 5 minutes; reduce pressure. Add potatoes and zucchini. Cover and cook at 15 pounds pressure 8 to 10 minutes. Cool 5 minutes; reduce pressure. Remove beef and vegetables; keep warm. Add enough water to broth, if necessary, to measure 1 cup. Shake ¼ cup water and 2 tablespoons flour in tightly covered container; gradually stir into broth. Heat to boiling, stirring constantly. Boil and stir 1 minute. Stir in yogurt; heat just until hot. Serve with beef and vegetables.

☆ ☆ ☆ ☆ ☆

Broiled Herb Steak

Good source of protein

2 - *pound beef bone-in round steak, about 1 inch*
    thick
2 *tablespoons soy sauce*
2 *tablespoons vegetable oil*
1 *tablespoon catsup*
1 *teaspoon dried basil leaves*
½ *teaspoon salt*
½ *teaspoon coarsely ground pepper*
½ *teaspoon dried oregano leaves*
1 *large clove garlic, crushed*

Place beef on large piece of plastic wrap. Mix remaining ingredients; brush both sides of beef with soy mixture. Fold plastic wrap over beef and secure tightly. Refrigerate at least 5 hours but no longer than 24 hours.

Place beef on rack in broiler pan. Set oven control to broil and/or 550°. Broil beef with top about 3 inches from heat until medium doneness, 8 to 10 minutes on each side. Cut into ¼-inch slices.

8 servings; 175 calories per serving.

☆ ☆ ☆ ☆ ☆

Beef Roll-Ups

Good source of protein, niacin and vitamin A

1½ - pound beef boneless round steak, about ½ inch
     thick
¼   teaspoon pepper
2   tablespoons Dijon-style mustard
1   medium onion, finely chopped
2   medium carrots, cut into 3 × ½-inch pieces
1   medium stalk celery, cut into 3 × ½-inch
     pieces
2   tablespoons vegetable oil
1   can (10½ ounces) condensed beef broth
1   can (7½ ounces) whole tomatoes
1   bay leaf
½   teaspoon dried thyme leaves
1   tablespoon plus 1 teaspoon cornstarch
2   tablespoons cold water
     Snipped parsley

Pound beef until at least ¼ inch thick; sprinkle with pepper. Cut beef into 6 pieces. Spread each piece with 1 teaspoon mustard; sprinkle with onion. Divide carrots and celery among beef pieces. Roll up; secure with wooden picks or tie with string.

Cook rolls in oil in 10-inch skillet over medium heat, turning occasionally, until light brown on all sides. Add beef broth, tomatoes (with liquid), bay leaf and thyme.

Break up tomatoes with fork. Heat to boiling; reduce heat. Cover and simmer until rolls are tender, about 1¼ hours.

Remove rolls; keep warm. Remove wooden picks or string. If necessary, add enough water to broth to measure 2 cups. Mix cornstarch and cold water; gradually stir into broth. Heat to boiling, stirring constantly. Boil and stir 1 minute. Pour over rolls; sprinkle with parsley.

6 servings; 235 calories per serving.

☐ *Pressure Cooker Directions:* Prepare rolls as directed. Cook in oil in 4-quart pressure cooker until light brown on all sides. Add beef broth, tomatoes (with liquid), bay leaf and thyme. Break up tomatoes with fork. Following manufacturer's directions, cover and cook at 15 pounds pressure 15 minutes. Cool 5 minutes; reduce pressure. Remove rolls; keep warm. Remove wooden picks or string. Remove all but 2 cups broth from pressure cooker. Mix cornstarch and cold water; gradually stir into broth. Heat to boiling, stirring constantly. Boil and stir 1 minute. Pour over rolls; sprinkle with parsley.

☆ ☆ ☆ ☆ ☆

Sausage-Stuffed Steak

Good source of protein

$1\frac{1}{2}$ - pound beef flank steak
  1 teaspoon finely chopped garlic
  1 pound chorizo sausage
  1 medium onion, chopped (about $\frac{1}{2}$ cup)
 $\frac{1}{3}$ cup snipped parsley
  1 egg, slightly beaten
 $\frac{1}{4}$ cup all-purpose flour
 $\frac{1}{2}$ teaspoon salt
 $\frac{1}{4}$ teaspoon pepper
  2 tablespoons vegetable oil
  1 can ($10\frac{1}{2}$ ounces) condensed beef broth
  1 can (8 ounces) whole tomatoes
  1 can (4 ounces) chopped green chilies
  1 tablespoon cornstarch
  2 tablespoons cold water

Cut beef lengthwise almost into halves; open flat with cut side up. Sprinkle evenly with garlic. Remove sausage from casing; mix sausage, onion, parsley and egg. Spread sausage mixture over beef to within 1 inch of edges. Roll up, beginning at narrow end; secure with wooden picks.

Mix flour, salt and pepper; coat roll-up with flour mixture. Heat oil in 4-quart Dutch oven. Cook roll-up over medium heat, turning occasionally, until brown; drain. Add beef broth, tomatoes (with liquid) and chilies (with liquid). Break up tomatoes with fork. Heat to boiling; reduce heat. Cover and simmer until roll-up is tender, about 2 hours. Remove roll-up; remove wooden picks and keep warm. Skim fat from broth. Mix cornstarch and cold water; stir into broth. Heat to boiling, stirring constantly. Boil and stir 1 minute. Cut roll-up into slices; serve with sauce.

8 servings; 275 calories per serving.

☆ ☆ ☆ ☆ ☆

Sausage-Stuffed Steak

Cutting Steak

Cut beef lengthwise almost into halves.

Rolling Steak

Roll up beef, beginning at narrow end.

Mustard-Marinated Steak

Good source of protein

2 - pound beef bone-in chuck steak, about ¾ inch
    thick
2 tablespoons lemon juice
2 tablespoons olive or vegetable oil
1 tablespoon Dijon-style mustard
¼ teaspoon pepper
2 tablespoons water

Pierce beef on both sides with fork. Place beef in glass or plastic dish. Mix lemon juice, oil, mustard and pepper; pour over beef. Cover and refrigerate, turning occasionally, at least 4 hours. Place beef on rack in broiler pan; reserve marinade.

Set oven control to broil and/or 550°. Broil beef with top about 3 inches from heat until medium doneness, about 10 minutes on each side. Heat reserved marinade and water to boiling in 1-quart saucepan, stirring occasionally; pour over beef.

8 servings; 315 calories per serving.

☆ ☆ ☆ ☆ ☆

Lemon-Honey Beef Ribs

Good source of protein

½ cup lemon juice
¼ cup honey
2 tablespoons vegetable oil
1 tablespoon catsup
½ teaspoon salt
¼ teaspoon dried oregano leaves
6 drops red pepper sauce
2 cloves garlic, finely chopped
4 pounds beef ribs

Mix lemon juice, honey, oil, catsup, salt, oregano, pepper sauce and garlic in 1½-quart saucepan. Heat to boiling; reduce heat. Cover and simmer 10 minutes. Place beef on rack in shallow roasting pan. Cook in 325° oven, turning and brushing with sauce occasionally, until beef is tender, about 1½ hours.

4 servings; 505 calories per serving.

☆ ☆ ☆ ☆ ☆

Tangy Short Ribs

Good source of protein

    Barbecue Sauce (below)
4 pounds beef short ribs, cut into pieces
1 tablespoon chili powder
1 teaspoon salt
1 teaspoon dried oregano leaves
1 teaspoon dry mustard
⅛ teaspoon cayenne pepper
2 large cloves garlic, crushed
2 medium onions, sliced

Prepare Barbecue Sauce. Cook beef in 4-quart Dutch oven over medium heat until brown, about 10 minutes; drain. Mix chili powder, salt, oregano, mustard, cayenne pepper and garlic; sprinkle over beef. Place onions on beef; pour Barbecue Sauce over onions and beef. Cover and cook in 350° oven until beef is tender, about 2 hours. Skim fat from sauce. Serve sauce with beef.

Barbecue Sauce

¾ cup catsup
⅓ cup water
¼ cup vinegar
1 tablespoon packed brown sugar
2 teaspoons Worcestershire sauce
½ teaspoon salt

Mix all ingredients.

8 servings; 455 calories per serving.

☐ *Pressure Cooker Directions:* Prepare Barbecue Sauce. Cook beef in 6-quart pressure cooker over medium heat until brown, about 10 minutes; drain. Mix chili powder, salt, oregano, mustard, cayenne pepper and garlic; sprinkle over beef. Place onions on beef; pour Barbecue Sauce over onions and beef. Following manufacturer's directions, cover and cook at 15 pounds pressure 30 to 35 minutes. Cool 5 minutes; reduce pressure. Skim fat from sauce. Serve sauce with beef.

☆ ☆ ☆ ☆ ☆

Italian-Style Liver

Good source of protein, riboflavin, niacin, iron and vitamin A

1   medium onion, sliced
2   tablespoons olive or vegetable oil
1   pound beef liver, about ½ inch thick
2   tablespoons water
1   teaspoon ground coriander
1   teaspoon fennel seed
½   teaspoon salt
½   teaspoon ground cumin
1   medium zucchini or yellow summer squash,
        cut into ¼-inch slices

Cook and stir onion in oil in 10-inch skillet over medium heat until onion is tender, about 5 minutes. Remove onion with slotted spoon; reserve. Cut liver into 6 serving pieces if necessary. Cook liver in same skillet over medium-high heat until brown, 2 to 3 minutes on each side. Drizzle water over liver. Mix coriander, fennel seed, salt and cumin; sprinkle over liver. Arrange onion and zucchini over liver. Cover and cook over low heat until zucchini is crisp-tender, 6 to 8 minutes.

6 servings; 170 calories per serving.

☆ ☆ ☆ ☆ ☆

STIR-FRYING TECHNIQUES

Stir-frying is a Chinese method of cooking food quickly in a small amount of oil over high heat. Vegetable and peanut oils are used because they are tolerant to high heat. Margarine and butter are not used because they burn too easily.

It is important to measure and prepare all ingredients before beginning to cook. Assemble ingredients in the order in which they will be used.

Stir-fried food is done when it changes in color: pork and chicken turn white, beef loses its redness and vegetables become brighter in color while remaining crisp.

Stir-Fried Beef

Good source of protein and niacin

1   pound beef flank or boneless sirloin steak
1   tablespoon vegetable oil
1   teaspoon cornstarch
1   teaspoon salt
1   teaspoon soy sauce
⅛   teaspoon pepper
4   large stalks bok choy
1   medium onion
2   tablespoons cornstarch
2   tablespoons cold water
2   tablespoons vegetable oil
1   teaspoon finely chopped gingerroot
1   teaspoon finely chopped garlic
4   ounces pea pods (about 1½ cups)
4   ounces mushrooms, sliced (about 2 cups)
½   cup chicken broth (page 56)
1   tablespoon soy sauce

Trim fat from beef. Cut beef with grain into 2-inch strips. Cut strips across grain into ⅛-inch slices. (Beef is easier to slice if partially frozen.) Toss beef, 1 tablespoon oil, 1 teaspoon cornstarch, the salt, 1 teaspoon soy sauce and the pepper. Cover and refrigerate 30 minutes.

Separate bok choy leaves from stems. Cut leaves into 2-inch pieces; cut stems diagonally into ¼-inch slices. (Do not combine leaves and stems.) Cut onion into halves. Place each half cut side down; cut into thin slices. Mix 2 tablespoons cornstarch and the cold water.

Heat 2 tablespoons oil in 10-inch skillet or wok over high heat until hot. Add beef mixture, gingerroot and garlic; cook and stir until beef is brown, about 3 minutes. Remove beef from skillet with slotted spoon.

Add bok choy stems and onion; cook and stir 3 minutes. Add bok choy leaves, pea pods and mushrooms; cook and stir 2 minutes. Stir in chicken broth and 1 tablespoon soy sauce; heat to boiling. Stir in cornstarch mixture; cook and stir 1 minute. Stir in beef; heat just until beef is hot.

5 servings (about 1 cup); 255 calories each.

☆ ☆ ☆ ☆ ☆

Spicy Stir-Fried Beef

Good source of protein, niacin and vitamin A

$1^1/_2$ pounds boneless beef sirloin steak
1   tablespoon cornstarch
1   tablespoon vegetable oil
1   tablespoon soy sauce
1   teaspoon sugar
$^1/_4$ teaspoon salt
$^1/_4$ teaspoon pepper
1   tablespoon soy sauce
$^1/_4$ to $^1/_2$ teaspoon finely crushed dried red pepper
2   tablespoons vegetable oil
1   teaspoon finely chopped gingerroot
2   large cloves garlic, finely chopped
1   large green pepper, cut into $^1/_4$-inch strips
2   medium carrots, shredded (about 1 cup)
1   can ($8^1/_2$ ounces) bamboo shoots, drained
1   can (8 ounces) sliced water chestnuts
4   green onions (with tops), cut into 2-inch pieces

Trim fat from beef. Cut beef into 2-inch wide strips. Cut strips into $^1/_8$-inch slices. Stack slices and cut into thin strips. (Beef is easier to slice if partially frozen.) Toss beef, cornstarch, 1 tablespoon oil, 1 tablespoon soy sauce, the sugar, salt and pepper in glass or plastic bowl. Cover and refrigerate 30 minutes. Mix 1 tablespoon soy sauce and the red pepper; let stand at room temperature.

Heat 2 tablespoons oil in 12-inch skillet or wok over high heat until hot. Add beef mixture, gingerroot and garlic; cook and stir until beef is brown, about 5 minutes. Add green pepper, carrots, bamboo shoots and water chestnuts; cook and stir 3 minutes. Add onions and red pepper mixture; cook and stir 1 minute.

6 servings; 300 calories per serving.

Spicy Stir-Fried Beef

Cutting Beef Strips

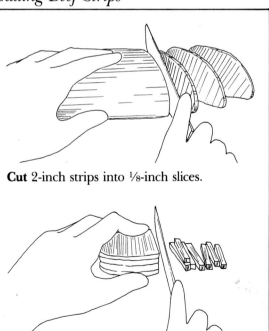

Cut 2-inch strips into $^1/_8$-inch slices.

Stack slices and cut into thin strips.

Chile con Carne

Good source of protein, thiamin, niacin and iron

1½	pounds beef round steak, cut into ½-inch cubes
2	tablespoons vegetable oil
1	large green pepper, chopped (about 1½ cups)
1	large onion, chopped (about 1 cup)
⅓	cup snipped parsley
1	large clove garlic, crushed
1	large bay leaf, finely crushed
2	teaspoons paprika
1	teaspoon salt
1	teaspoon ground cumin
1	teaspoon dried oregano leaves
½	to 1 teaspoon crushed dried red pepper
½	teaspoon ground coriander
1½	cups water
1	can (10½ ounces) condensed beef broth
3	cups cooked rice
1	can (15½ ounces) garbanzo beans

Cook beef in oil in 4-quart Dutch oven over medium heat until light brown. Stir in remaining ingredients except rice and beans. Heat to boiling; reduce heat. Cover and simmer, stirring occasionally, 1 hour. Uncover and cook until mixture is thickened and beef is tender, stirring occasionally, about 30 minutes longer. Mix rice and beans (with liquid). Heat over low heat just until hot, stirring occasionally. Divide rice mixture among 8 serving bowls; spoon beef mixture over rice.

8 servings; 415 calories per serving.

☆ ☆ ☆ ☆ ☆

Easy Burgundy Stew

Good source of protein, niacin and vitamin A

2	pounds beef boneless bottom or top round, tip or chuck steak, cut into 1-inch cubes
4	medium carrots, sliced (about 2 cups)
2	medium stalks celery, sliced (about 1 cup)
2	medium onions, sliced
1	can (8 ounces) water chestnuts, sliced
1	can (8 ounces) mushroom stems and pieces, drained
3	tablespoons all-purpose flour
1	teaspoon salt
1	teaspoon dried thyme leaves
1	teaspoon dry mustard
¼	teaspoon pepper
1	can (16 ounces) whole tomatoes, undrained
1	cup water
1	cup dry red wine

Mix beef, carrots, celery, onions, water chestnuts and mushrooms in 4-quart Dutch oven or casserole. Mix flour, salt, thyme, mustard and pepper; stir into beef mixture. Stir in remaining ingredients. Break up tomatoes with fork. Cover and cook in 325° oven until beef is tender and stew is thickened, about 4 hours.

8 servings (about 1 cup); 225 calories each.

NOTE: 1 cup water and 1 teaspoon instant beef bouillon can be substituted for the wine.

☐ *Pressure Cooker Directions:* Increase flour to ⅓ cup and omit 1 cup water. Mix all ingredients in 6-quart pressure cooker. Following manufacturer's directions, cover and cook at 15 pounds pressure 30 minutes. Cool 5 minutes; reduce pressure. Uncover and cook, stirring occasionally, until stew is thickened, about 10 minutes.

☆ ☆ ☆ ☆ ☆

Beef and Eggplant Salad

Beef and Eggplant Salad

Good source of protein

1	medium eggplant (about 1½ pounds)
1	cup water
½	teaspoon salt
¼	cup olive or vegetable oil
2	tablespoons lemon juice
1	teaspoon dried oregano leaves
½	teaspoon salt
¼	teaspoon pepper
1	pound cold cooked roast beef, cut into julienne strips
1	tablespoon snipped parsley
1	medium tomato, cut into 8 wedges
8	Greek or large ripe olives

Cut eggplant into ¾-inch cubes. Heat water and ½ teaspoon salt to boiling in 3-quart saucepan. Add eggplant. Cover and heat to boiling; reduce heat. Simmer until tender, about 10 minutes; drain.

Place eggplant in glass or plastic bowl. Mix oil, lemon juice, oregano, ½ teaspoon salt and the pepper; pour over eggplant and toss. Cover and refrigerate at least 5 hours. Arrange beef strips on platter or individual plates on lettuce leaves if desired; top with eggplant. Sprinkle eggplant with parsley. Garnish with tomato wedges and olives.

8 servings (about ¾ cup); 295 calories each.

☆ ☆ ☆ ☆ ☆

Beef and Beer Stew

Good source of protein

4	medium onions, sliced
2	tablespoons vegetable oil
2	pounds beef boneless chuck, tip or round, cut into 1-inch cubes
2	cans (12 ounces each) beer
1	cup water
1	tablespoon corn syrup
1¼	teaspoons salt
½	teaspoon dried thyme leaves
½	teaspoon dried marjoram leaves
¼	teaspoon pepper
2	tablespoons cornstarch
¼	cup cold water

Cook and stir onions in oil in 4-quart Dutch oven over medium heat until tender, about 10 minutes. Remove onions with slotted spoon; reserve. Cook and stir beef in Dutch oven until brown, about 10 minutes. Add reserved onions, beer, 1 cup water, the corn syrup, salt, thyme, marjoram and pepper. Heat to boiling, scraping particles from bottom of Dutch oven. Mix cornstarch and ¼ cup cold water; gradually stir into beef mixture. Boil and stir 1 minute. Cover and cook in 350° oven 2 hours. Uncover and cook until beef is tender, about 45 minutes longer.

8 servings (about ¾ cup); 220 calories each.

☆ ☆ ☆ ☆ ☆

Beef-Baguette Slices

Good source of protein

    Garlic Sauce (below)
1 *baguette*
1 *cup shredded lettuce*
1 *pound cooked roast beef, thinly sliced*
1 *small red onion, thinly sliced*

Prepare Garlic Sauce. Cut baguette lengthwise into halves. Place lettuce on bottom half. Arrange beef on lettuce; arrange onion slices on beef. Spoon Garlic Sauce over onion and beef; top with remaining baguette half. Cut diagonally into 12 slices.

Garlic Sauce

1 *hard-cooked egg*
2 *cloves garlic, finely chopped*
1 *tablespoon snipped parsley*
1 *tablespoon Dijon-style mustard*
2 *teaspoons lemon juice*
1 *teaspoon water*
2 *drops red pepper sauce*
    Dash of salt
1/4 *cup olive or vegetable oil*

Place egg, garlic, parsley, mustard, lemon juice, water, pepper sauce and salt in blender container. Cover and blend on low speed, stopping blender occasionally to scrape sides, until smooth, about 45 seconds. Add oil, 1 tablespoon at a time; blend after each addition until smooth.

6 servings (2 slices each); 360 calories per serving.

☐ *Food Processor Directions:* Place egg, garlic, parsley, mustard, lemon juice, water, pepper sauce and salt in workbowl fitted with steel blade. Cover and process until smooth, about 5 seconds. With food processor running, slowly pour oil in thin stream down feed tube until thick sauce forms, about 15 seconds.

☆ ☆ ☆ ☆ ☆

Beef and Potato Broil

Good source of protein and niacin

    Herb Butter (below)
1   *pound ground beef*
½   *teaspoon salt*
⅛   *teaspoon pepper*
3   *medium potatoes*
2   *tablespoons vegetable oil*
½   *teaspoon salt*
½   *teaspoon paprika*

Prepare Herb Butter. Mix ground beef, ½ teaspoon salt and the pepper. Shape beef mixture into oval-shaped patty, ½ inch thick. Place patty on one end of rack in broiler pan. Cut potatoes lengthwise into ½-inch slices. Place potato slices in single layer on other end of rack. Mix oil, ½ teaspoon salt and the paprika; brush potatoes with half of the oil mixture.

Set oven control to broil and/or 550°. Broil patty and potatoes with tops about 3 inches from heat until brown, 5 to 7 minutes. Turn patty and potatoes; brush potatoes with remaining oil mixture. Broil until patty is done and potatoes are fork-tender, 5 to 7 minutes longer. Heat Herb Butter to boiling; serve with patty and potatoes.

Herb Butter

¼   *cup margarine or butter*
1   *tablespoon snipped parsley*
2   *teaspoons red wine vinegar*
2   *teaspoons water*
¼   *teaspoon dried basil leaves*
¼   *teaspoon dried tarragon leaves*
¼   *teaspoon dried savory leaves*

Heat margarine in 1-quart saucepan just until melted. Stir in remaining ingredients.

4 servings; 480 calories per serving.

☆ ☆ ☆ ☆ ☆

Oven Burger

Good source of protein

1½   *pounds ground beef*
1   *teaspoon salt*
1   *small green pepper, chopped (about ½ cup)*
1   *small onion, chopped (about ¼ cup)*
1   *tablespoon prepared horseradish*
1   *tablespoon prepared mustard*
⅓   *cup chili sauce or catsup*

Mix all ingredients except chili sauce. Press beef mixture in ungreased pie plate, 9 × 1¼ inches. Spread chili sauce over top. Cook uncovered in 350° oven until done, 45 to 50 minutes; drain off fat. Let stand 5 minutes before cutting into wedges.

6 servings; 260 calories per serving.

☆ ☆ ☆ ☆ ☆

Chili Burgers

Good source of protein

1½   *pounds ground beef*
1   *egg*
1   *can (4 ounces) chopped green chilies, drained*
½   *cup finely crushed corn chips*
1   *small onion, chopped (about ¼ cup)*
1   *medium clove garlic, crushed*
1   *tablespoon chili powder*
2   *medium tomatoes, each cut into 4 slices*
1   *cup shredded Monterey Jack cheese*
    (about 4 ounces)

Mix ground beef, egg, chilies, corn chips, onion, garlic and chili powder. Shape beef mixture into 8 patties, each about ½ inch thick. Place patties on rack in broiler pan.

Set oven control to broil and/or 550°. Broil patties with tops about 3 inches from heat until medium doneness, 5 to 7 minutes on each side. Place 1 tomato slice on each patty; sprinkle with 1 tablespoon cheese. Broil just until cheese is melted, about 2 minutes.

8 servings; 275 calories per serving.

☆ ☆ ☆ ☆ ☆

Vegetable Beef Burgers

Good source of protein, niacin and vitamin C

1½   pounds ground beef
1   cup bean sprouts, coarsely chopped
¼   cup chopped green pepper
1   small onion, chopped (about ¼ cup)
1   small carrot, shredded (about ¼ cup)
1   small stalk celery, chopped (about ¼ cup)
1   teaspoon salt
¼   teaspoon pepper
1½   cups alfalfa sprouts
2   medium tomatoes, each cut into 3 slices

Mix ground beef, bean sprouts, green pepper, onion, carrot, celery, salt and pepper. Shape beef mixture into 6 patties, each about ½ inch thick. Place patties on rack in broiler pan. Set oven control to broil and/or 550°. Broil patties with tops about 3 inches from heat until medium doneness, 3 to 5 minutes on each side. Top each patty with ¼ cup alfalfa sprouts and 1 tomato slice.

6 servings; 260 calories per serving.

☆ ☆ ☆ ☆ ☆

Burgers with Cheesy Vegetables

Good source of protein and niacin

2   medium potatoes, cut into ½-inch pieces
       (about 2 cups)
1   cup frozen green peas
1   can (2 ounces) mushroom stems and pieces,
       drained
2   pounds ground beef
1   small onion, chopped (about ¼ cup)
⅓   cup water
½   teaspoon salt
¼   teaspoon pepper
¾   cup shredded mozzarella cheese
       (about 3 ounces)
1   jar (2 ounces) diced pimiento, drained
½   teaspoon salt
⅛   teaspoon pepper

Heat 1 inch salted water (½ teaspoon salt to 1 cup water) to boiling. Add potatoes, peas and mushrooms. Cover and heat to boiling; reduce heat. Simmer until potatoes are tender, about 10 minutes; drain. Mix ground beef, onion, water, ½ teaspoon salt and ¼ teaspoon pepper. Shape beef mixture into 8 patties, each about ½ inch thick. Place patties on rack in broiler pan. Set oven control to broil and/or 550°. Broil patties with tops about 3 inches from heat until medium doneness, 4 to 6 minutes on each side. Mix potatoes, peas, mushrooms, cheese, pimiento, ½ teaspoon salt and ⅛ teaspoon pepper. Top each beef patty with vegetables.

8 servings; 320 calories per serving.

☆ ☆ ☆ ☆ ☆

Savory Beef Patties

Good source of protein

1   pound ground beef
1   small onion, chopped (about ¼ cup)
½   teaspoon salt
⅛   teaspoon pepper
3   tablespoons margarine or butter
2   tablespoons snipped chives or parsley
1   teaspoon dry mustard
¼   teaspoon garlic powder
1   teaspoon lemon juice
½   teaspoon Worcestershire sauce

Mix ground beef, onion, salt and pepper. Shape beef mixture into 4 patties, each about ½ inch thick. Cook in 10-inch skillet over medium heat, turning frequently, until desired doneness, about 10 minutes for medium. Remove patties; keep warm. Drain drippings from skillet. Heat margarine in same skillet until melted; stir in remaining ingredients. Serve over patties.

4 servings; 325 calories per serving.

☆ ☆ ☆ ☆ ☆

Hamburgers Ranchero

Good source of protein, niacin, vitamins A and C

	Ranchero Sauce (below)
1½	*pounds ground beef*
1	*medium onion, chopped (about ½ cup)*
1	*teaspoon salt*
1	*teaspoon dried oregano leaves*
¼	*teaspoon pepper*
6	*6- or 7-inch corn tortillas*
3	*cups shredded lettuce*

Prepare Ranchero Sauce. Mix ground beef, onion, salt, oregano and pepper. Shape beef mixture into 6 patties, each about ½ inch thick. Place patties on rack in broiler pan. Set oven control to broil and/or 550°. Broil patties with tops about 3 inches from heat until medium doneness, 4 to 6 minutes on each side. Soften tortillas as directed on package. Sprinkle ½ cup lettuce on each tortilla; place patty on lettuce. Spoon Ranchero Sauce over each patty.

Ranchero Sauce

1	*can (28 ounces) whole tomatoes, well drained*
1	*small onion, cut up*
1	*large clove garlic*
1	*canned jalapeño or green chili pepper, seeds and membrane removed*
1	*teaspoon lemon juice*
¼	*teaspoon ground coriander*

Place all ingredients in blender container. Cover and blend on medium speed until finely chopped, about 5 seconds.

6 servings; 330 calories per serving.

☐ *Food Processor Directions for Ranchero Sauce:* Place all ingredients in workbowl fitted with steel blade. Cover and process until finely chopped, about 10 seconds.

═══════════ ☆ ☆ ☆ ☆ ☆ ═══════════

Curried Meat Loaf

Good source of protein

1½	*pounds ground beef*
¾	*cup rolled oats*
½	*cup plain yogurt*
1	*medium onion, chopped (about ½ cup)*
1	*egg*
2	*teaspoons curry powder*
1	*teaspoon salt*
1	*teaspoon dry mustard*
¼	*teaspoon red pepper sauce*
	Vegetable Sauce (below)

Mix all ingredients except Vegetable Sauce. Spread beef mixture evenly in ungreased loaf pan, 9 × 5 × 3 inches. Cook uncovered in 350° oven until done, about 1½ hours. Prepare Vegetable Sauce; serve with meat loaf.

Vegetable Sauce

1	*medium tomato, chopped*
1	*small cucumber, seeded and chopped*
¼	*cup sliced green onions (with tops)*
1	*clove garlic, finely chopped*
¼	*cup plain yogurt*
½	*teaspoon curry powder*

Mix all ingredients.

6 servings; 330 calories per serving.

☐ *Microwave Directions:* Mix all ingredients except Vegetable Sauce. Spread beef mixture evenly in microwavable loaf dish, 9 × 5 × 3 inches. Cover with waxed paper and microwave on medium-high (70%) 12 minutes; rotate dish ½ turn. Microwave until center is no longer pink, 13 to 16 minutes longer. Cover and let stand 5 minutes. Prepare Vegetable Sauce; serve with meat loaf.

═══════════ ☆ ☆ ☆ ☆ ☆ ═══════════

Teriyaki Meat Loaf

Good source of protein and niacin

1½ pounds ground beef
 1 can (8 ounces) water chestnuts, chopped
 1 egg
½ cup orange juice
¼ cup soy sauce
 1 tablespoon packed brown sugar
½ teaspoon ground ginger
 1 large clove garlic, crushed
 1 can (8 ounces) crushed pineapple in juice,
     undrained

Mix all ingredients except pineapple. Spread beef mixture evenly in ungreased loaf pan, 9 × 5 × 3 inches. Cook uncovered in 350° oven 1 hour; drain. Spoon pineapple over meat loaf. Cook until meat loaf is done, about 30 minutes longer.

6 servings; 335 calories per serving.

☐ *Microwave Directions:* Mix all ingredients except pineapple. Spread beef mixture evenly in microwavable loaf dish, 9 × 5 × 3 inches. Drain pineapple; spoon pineapple over beef mixture. Cover with waxed paper and microwave on medium-high (70%) 12 minutes; rotate dish ½ turn. Microwave until center is no longer pink, 13 to 16 minutes longer. Cover and let stand 5 minutes.

☆ ☆ ☆ ☆ ☆

Barley-Beef Stew

Good source of protein, niacin, iron and vitamin A

1½ pounds ground beef
 1 large onion, chopped (about 1 cup)
 2 stalks celery, sliced (about 1 cup)
 1 can (28 ounces) whole tomatoes, undrained
2½ cups water
 1 cup uncooked barley
 1 tablespoon chili powder
 1 teaspoon salt
¼ teaspoon pepper

Cook and stir ground beef, onion and celery in 4-quart Dutch oven over medium heat until

beef is brown; drain. Stir in remaining ingredients. Break up tomatoes with fork. Heat to boiling; reduce heat. Cover and simmer until barley is done and stew is desired consistency, about 1 hour.

6 servings (about 1⅓ cups); 405 calories each.

☆ ☆ ☆ ☆ ☆

Beef and Bulgur Stew

Good source of protein

1½ pounds ground beef
 1 medium onion, chopped (about ½ cup)
 1 small eggplant (about 1 pound),
     cut into 1-inch pieces
 2 cups water
 1 cup uncooked cracked wheat (bulgur)
 1 tablespoon snipped mint leaves or 1 teaspoon
     dried mint leaves
1½ teaspoons salt
 1 teaspoon dried oregano leaves
 2 medium tomatoes, chopped (about 1½ cups)
¼ cup grated Parmesan cheese

Cook and stir ground beef and onion in 4-quart Dutch oven until beef is brown; drain. Stir in eggplant, water, cracked wheat, mint, salt and oregano. Heat to boiling; reduce heat. Cover and simmer, stirring occasionally, until wheat is tender, about 30 minutes (add small amount of water if necessary). Stir in tomatoes and cheese. Heat just until tomatoes are hot, about 5 minutes. Serve with additional Parmesan cheese if desired.

8 servings (about 1 cup); 290 calories each.

☆ ☆ ☆ ☆ ☆

Cheese-Topped Pie

Good source of protein

1	pound ground beef
1	small green pepper, chopped (about ½ cup)
1	small onion, chopped (about ¼ cup)
1	jar (2 ounces) diced pimiento, drained
½	cup all-purpose flour
½	cup milk
2	egg yolks
1	egg
1	teaspoon salt
⅛	teaspoon pepper
1	tablespoon margarine or butter
1	tablespoon all-purpose flour
½	teaspoon dry mustard
¼	teaspoon salt
	Dash of cayenne pepper
½	cup milk
1	cup shredded Cheddar cheese (about 4 ounces)
2	egg whites

Cook and stir ground beef, green pepper and onion until beef is brown; drain. Stir in pimiento. Spread beef mixture in ungreased pie plate, 9 × 1¼ inches. Beat ½ cup flour, ½ cup milk, the egg yolks, egg, 1 teaspoon salt and the pepper with hand beater until smooth. Pour over beef mixture in pie plate.

Heat oven to 375°. Heat margarine in 1-quart saucepan until melted. Blend in 1 tablespoon flour, the mustard, ¼ teaspoon salt and the cayenne pepper. Cook over low heat, stirring constantly, until smooth and bubbly; remove from heat. Stir in ½ cup milk. Heat to boiling, stirring constantly. Boil and stir 1 minute. Add cheese; cook and stir over low heat just until cheese is melted. Beat egg whites in 1½-quart bowl until stiff but not dry. Fold cheese mixture into egg whites; spread over beef mixture. Cook uncovered in oven until golden brown and knife inserted halfway between center and edge comes out clean, 20 to 25 minutes. Serve immediately.

8 servings; 275 calories per serving.

☆ ☆ ☆ ☆ ☆

Manicotti

minutes; drain. Stir in tomatoes (with liquid), mushrooms, parsley, salt, fennel seed and basil. Break up tomatoes with fork. Heat to boiling; reduce heat. Cover and simmer beef mixture 10 minutes.

Spoon about ⅓ of the beef mixture in ungreased rectangular baking dish, 13×9×2 inches. Rinse spinach under running cold water to separate; drain. Place spinach on towels and squeeze until dry. Mix spinach, cottage cheese, ⅓ cup Parmesan cheese, the nutmeg and pepper. Fill uncooked manicotti shells with spinach mixture; place shells on beef mixture in dish. Pour remaining beef mixture evenly over shells, covering shells completely; sprinkle with 2 tablespoons Parmesan cheese. Cover and cook in 350° oven until shells are tender, about 1½ hours.

7 servings; 405 calories per serving.

☆ ☆ ☆ ☆ ☆

Layered Beef Squares

Good source of protein and niacin

1½	pounds ground beef
1	medium onion, chopped (about ½ cup)
1	egg
½	cup milk
⅓	cup dry bread crumbs
1	teaspoon salt
1	teaspoon dried basil leaves
¼	teaspoon garlic powder
½	cup shredded Swiss cheese (about 2 ounces)
2	small zucchini, thinly sliced (about 1⅓ cups)
1	jar (2 ounces) diced pimiento, drained

Mix ground beef, onion, egg, milk, bread crumbs, salt, basil and garlic powder. Spread half of the beef mixture in ungreased square pan, 8×8×2 inches. Sprinkle cheese, zucchini and pimiento over beef mixture to within ½ inch of sides of pan; spread remaining beef mixture carefully over top. Cook uncovered in 350° oven until done, 45 to 50 minutes; drain off fat. Let stand 10 minutes before cutting into serving pieces.

6 servings; 335 calories per serving.

☆ ☆ ☆ ☆ ☆

Manicotti

Good source of protein, thiamin, niacin, riboflavin, iron and vitamin A

1	pound ground beef
1	large onion, chopped (about 1 cup)
2	large cloves garlic, crushed
1	can (28 ounces) whole tomatoes
1	can (8 ounces) mushroom stems and pieces, drained
¼	cup snipped parsley
1	teaspoon salt
1	teaspoon fennel seed
1	teaspoon dried basil leaves
2	packages (10 ounces each) frozen chopped spinach
2	cups creamed cottage cheese (small curd)
⅓	cup grated Parmesan cheese
¼	teaspoon ground nutmeg
¼	teaspoon pepper
14	uncooked manicotti shells
2	tablespoons grated Parmesan cheese

Cook and stir ground beef, onion and garlic in 10-inch skillet until beef is brown, about 10

Beef and Corn Pie

Good source of protein

1   pound ground beef
1   medium onion, chopped (about 1/2 cup)
1   can (8 3/4 ounces) whole kernel corn, drained
1   can (8 ounces) tomato sauce
1   small green pepper, chopped (about 1/2 cup)
1   teaspoon dried basil leaves
1/2   teaspoon salt
1/2   teaspoon dried oregano leaves
1/4   teaspoon red pepper sauce
    Cornmeal Crust (below)
1/2   cup shredded Cheddar cheese (about 2 ounces)

Cook and stir ground beef and onion in 10-inch skillet until beef is brown, about 10 minutes; drain. Stir in corn, tomato sauce, green pepper, basil, salt, oregano and pepper sauce. Prepare Cornmeal Crust. Press firmly and evenly against bottom and side of ungreased pie plate, 9 × 1 1/4 inches. Spoon beef mixture into pie plate. Cook uncovered in 400° oven 25 minutes. Sprinkle cheese over beef mixture. Cook until cheese is melted, about 5 minutes longer. Let stand 10 minutes before cutting.

Cornmeal Crust

1   cup all-purpose flour
1/4   cup yellow cornmeal
1/4   teaspoon salt
1/3   cup margarine or butter, softened
3   to 4 tablespoons water

Mix flour, cornmeal and salt. Stir in margarine and enough water to make a soft dough.

6 servings; 430 calories per serving.

☆ ☆ ☆ ☆ ☆

Macaroni and Beef

Good source of protein

1   pound ground beef
1   medium onion, chopped (about 1/2 cup)
1   can (8 ounces) tomato sauce
1/2   teaspoon dried oregano leaves
1/4   teaspoon salt
1/4   teaspoon ground cinnamon
1/8   teaspoon ground nutmeg
1   large clove garlic, crushed
4   cups cooked elbow macaroni
2   tablespoons margarine or butter
2   tablespoons all-purpose flour
1/4   teaspoon salt
    Dash of ground nutmeg
1 1/2   cups milk
1/4   cup grated Romano cheese

Cook and stir ground beef and onion in 10-inch skillet over medium heat until beef is brown, about 10 minutes; drain. Stir in tomato sauce, oregano, salt, cinnamon, 1/8 teaspoon nutmeg and the garlic. Alternate layers of macaroni and beef mixture in ungreased 2-quart casserole.

Heat margarine in 1-quart saucepan over low heat until melted. Blend in flour, 1/4 teaspoon salt and dash of nutmeg. Cook over low heat, stirring constantly, until smooth and bubbly; remove from heat. Stir in milk. Heat to boiling, stirring constantly. Boil and stir 1 minute. Spoon sauce over macaroni and beef mixture; sprinkle with cheese. Cook uncovered in 350° oven until bubbly and cheese is light brown, about 35 minutes.

6 servings (about 1 cup); 375 calories each.

☆ ☆ ☆ ☆ ☆

Sweet-Sour Cabbage Rolls

Good source of protein, niacin and iron

8	*large cabbage leaves*
1	*pound ground beef*
⅓	*cup uncooked cracked wheat (bulgur)*
⅓	*cup milk*
1	*egg*
1	*teaspoon salt*
1	*teaspoon dry mustard*
¼	*teaspoon pepper*
¼	*teaspoon ground cinnamon*
½	*cup packed brown sugar*
½	*cup water*
¼	*cup vinegar*
1	*teaspoon caraway seed*
4	*medium potatoes, cut into fourths*
1	*tablespoon cornstarch*
2	*tablespoons cold water*

Cover cabbage leaves with boiling water. Let stand until leaves are limp, about 10 minutes; drain. Mix ground beef, cracked wheat, milk, egg, salt, mustard, pepper and cinnamon. Shape beef mixture into eight 3½-inch rolls. Place 1 roll across stem end of each cabbage leaf. Roll leaf around roll, folding in sides. Place rolls, seam sides down in Dutch oven.

Mix brown sugar, water, vinegar and caraway seed; pour over rolls. Heat to boiling; reduce heat. Cover and simmer 30 minutes. Add potatoes. Cover and simmer until potatoes are tender, about 30 minutes. Remove rolls and potatoes; keep warm. Mix cornstarch and 2 tablespoons cold water; gradually stir into broth. Heat to boiling, stirring constantly. Boil and stir 1 minute. Serve with rolls.

4 servings (2 rolls each); 550 calories per serving.

☐ *Microwave Directions:* Prepare cabbage rolls as directed. Arrange in circle in 3-quart round microwavable casserole. Mix brown sugar, water, vinegar and caraway seed; pour over cabbage rolls. Add potatoes around edge of casserole. Cover tightly and microwave on high (100%) 10 minutes; rotate casserole ½ turn. Microwave until cabbage rolls are done and potatoes are tender, 10 to 15 minutes longer. Remove cabbage rolls and potatoes; keep warm. Mix cornstarch and 2 tablespoons cold water; gradually stir into broth. Microwave uncovered, stirring every minute until thickened, 3 to 4 minutes. Serve with rolls.

☆ ☆ ☆ ☆ ☆

Cheese-Topped Pork

Good source of protein, thiamin and niacin

3 - *pound pork boneless top loin roast*
1   *teaspoon salt*
1   *teaspoon dry mustard*
1/2 *teaspoon garlic powder*
1/2 *teaspoon ground sage*
1/8 *teaspoon pepper*
1/2 *cup shredded Gruyère or Swiss cheese*
      (about 2 ounces)
      Mustard Gravy (below)

Place pork, fat side up, on rack in shallow roasting pan. Mix salt, mustard, garlic powder, sage and pepper; rub over pork. Insert meat thermometer so tip is in thickest part of pork and does not rest in fat. Roast uncovered in 325° oven until thermometer registers 170°, about 2 hours. Remove pork; sprinkle cheese over top and keep warm. (Cheese will melt and form a lacy pattern over top of pork.) Reserve pork drippings. Prepare Mustard Gravy; serve with pork.

Mustard Gravy

      Reserved pork drippings
1/4 *cup all-purpose flour*
2   *tablespoons Dijon-style mustard*
1/2 *teaspoon salt*
1/8 *teaspoon pepper*
2   *cups water*

Heat reserved pork drippings to boiling in 2-quart saucepan. Blend in flour, mustard, salt and pepper. Cook over low heat, stirring constantly, until smooth and bubbly; remove from heat. Stir in water. Heat to boiling, stirring constantly. Boil and stir 1 minute.

12 servings; 280 calories per serving.

☆ ☆ ☆ ☆ ☆

Pork Roast with Raisin Sauce

Good source of protein, thiamin and niacin

4 - *pound pork boneless loin roast*
1   *teaspoon salt*
1/2 *teaspoon ground cinnamon*
1/4 *teaspoon garlic powder*
1/4 *teaspoon pepper*
1/4 *teaspoon ground cumin*
      Raisin Sauce (below)

Place pork, fat side up, on rack in shallow roasting pan. Mix salt, cinnamon, garlic powder, pepper and cumin; sprinkle over pork. Insert meat thermometer so tip is in center of thickest part of pork and does not rest in fat. Roast uncovered in 325° oven until thermometer registers 170°, about 2½ hours. Prepare Raisin Sauce; serve with pork.

Raisin Sauce

1½   *cups apple juice*
1½   *cups raisins*
 1/4 *cup maple-flavored syrup*
 1/2 *teaspoon ground cinnamon*
1   *teaspoon cornstarch*
2   *tablespoons cold water*

Heat apple juice, raisins, syrup and cinnamon to boiling, stirring occasionally; reduce heat. Simmer until raisins are plump and tender, about 10 minutes. Mix cornstarch and cold water; stir into raisin mixture. Heat to boiling, stirring constantly. Boil and stir 1 minute.

16 servings; 300 calories per serving.

☆ ☆ ☆ ☆ ☆

Sweet-Sour Pork 'n Onions

Good source of protein, thiamin and niacin

4	pork loin or rib chops, about ¾ inch thick
½	teaspoon salt
⅛	teaspoon pepper
2	medium onions, cut into ¼-inch slices
½	cup dry white wine
2	tablespoons red wine vinegar
2	teaspoons sugar
⅛	teaspoon ground cloves
1	teaspoon cornstarch
2	tablespoons cold water

Cook pork in 10-inch skillet over medium heat until brown on both sides; sprinkle with salt and pepper. Arrange onions on pork. Mix wine, vinegar, sugar and cloves; pour over onions and pork. Heat to boiling; reduce heat. Cover and simmer until pork is tender, 25 to 30 minutes.

Remove pork and onions; keep warm. Mix cornstarch and cold water; gradually stir into liquid in skillet. Heat to boiling, stirring constantly. Boil and stir 1 minute. Serve sauce over pork and onions.

4 servings; 385 calories per serving.

☆ ☆ ☆ ☆ ☆

Spicy-Sesame Spareribs

Good source of protein and thiamin

4	pounds fresh pork spareribs, cut into serving pieces
¼	cup soy sauce
¼	cup dry white wine
2	tablespoons toasted sesame seed
1	tablespoon sesame or vegetable oil
2	teaspoons sugar
⅛	teaspoon red pepper flakes
2	large cloves garlic, crushed
1	teaspoon cornstarch
2	tablespoons cold water

Place pork, meaty sides up, on rack in shallow roasting pan. Roast uncovered in 325° oven

1½ hours. Mix soy sauce, wine, sesame seed, oil, sugar, red pepper and garlic in 1-quart saucepan; heat to boiling. Mix cornstarch and cold water; gradually stir into soy mixture. Boil and stir 1 minute. Brush pork with soy sauce mixture. Roast, turning and brushing frequently with sauce, until pork is done, about 45 minutes.

6 servings; 575 calories per serving.

☆ ☆ ☆ ☆ ☆

Sweet 'n Pungent Spareribs

Good source of protein, thiamin, niacin and iron

4½	pounds fresh pork spareribs, cut into serving pieces
1	can (8 ounces) crushed pineapple in juice, undrained
¼	cup vinegar
¼	cup molasses
¼	cup chili sauce
1	medium clove garlic, crushed
¼	teaspoon ground ginger
⅛	teaspoon red pepper sauce
2	tablespoons soy sauce

Place pork, meaty sides up, on rack in shallow roasting pan. Roast uncovered in 325° oven 1½ hours. Mix remaining ingredients. Brush pork with pineapple mixture. Roast, turning and brushing frequently with pineapple mixture until pork is done, about 45 minutes. (About half of the pineapple mixture will be used to brush ribs.) Heat remaining pineapple mixture to boiling, stirring occasionally. Serve with pork.

6 servings; 665 calories per serving.

☆ ☆ ☆ ☆ ☆

Pork with Apple and Parsnips

Good source of protein and thiamin

4   pork loin or rib chops, about ½ inch thick
3   medium parsnips, cut crosswise into ½-inch slices
1   medium onion, sliced
½   cup chicken broth (page 56)
1   teaspoon dry mustard
½   teaspoon salt
¼   teaspoon ground allspice
⅛   teaspoon pepper
1   medium apple, cut into ¼-inch wedges
2   tablespoons snipped parsley

Cook pork in 10-inch skillet over medium heat until brown on both sides. Place parsnips and onion on pork. Mix chicken broth, mustard, salt, allspice and pepper; pour over vegetables. Heat to boiling; reduce heat. Cover and simmer until pork is done, 35 to 40 minutes. Arrange apple on vegetables. Cover and cook just until apple is tender, about 3 minutes. Sprinkle with parsley.

4 servings; 360 calories per serving.

☆ ☆ ☆ ☆ ☆

Pork Chops with Grapes

Good source of protein, thiamin and niacin

4   pork loin or rib chops, about ¾ inch thick
½   teaspoon salt
¼   teaspoon dried tarragon leaves
⅛   teaspoon pepper
1   cup chicken broth (page 56)
1   tablespoon lemon juice
1   clove garlic, crushed
2   teaspoons cornstarch
2   tablespoons cold water
1   cup seedless green grapes
1   can (4 ounces) mushroom stems and pieces, drained

Cook pork in 10-inch skillet until brown on both sides; sprinkle with salt, tarragon and pepper. Mix chicken broth, lemon juice and garlic; pour over pork. Heat to boiling; reduce heat. Cover and simmer until pork is done, 35 to 40 minutes. Remove pork; keep warm. Mix cornstarch and water; gradually stir into broth. Heat to boiling, stirring constantly. Boil and stir 1 minute. Stir in grapes and mushrooms; heat just until hot. Serve over pork.

4 servings; 395 calories per serving.

☆ ☆ ☆ ☆ ☆

Pork with Stuffed Yams

Good source of protein, thiamin, niacin and vitamin A

2 medium yams or sweet potatoes
   Vegetable oil
4 pork loin or rib chops, about ¾ inch thick
½ teaspoon salt
¼ teaspoon paprika
⅛ teaspoon garlic powder
⅛ teaspoon pepper
½ cup orange juice
2 tablespoons margarine or butter, softened
2 tablespoons orange juice
½ cup chopped apple
2 tablespoons finely chopped onion
2 tablespoons finely chopped celery

Rub skins of yams with oil; prick with fork. Cook in 350° oven until tender, 50 to 60 minutes. Place pork in ungreased rectangular pan, 13 × 9 × 2 inches. Mix salt, paprika, garlic powder and pepper; sprinkle half of the salt mixture over pork. Turn pork; sprinkle with remaining salt mixture. Pour ½ cup orange juice into pan. Cover and cook in 350° oven 45 minutes.

Cut each yam lengthwise into halves. Scoop out inside, leaving ¼-inch shell. Mash yams until no lumps remain. Beat in margarine and 2 tablespoons orange juice until light and fluffy. Stir in apple, onion and celery. Fill shells with yam mixture.

Push pork to one end of pan; place yams in other end of pan. Cook uncovered until pork is done and yams are hot, 30 to 35 minutes.

4 servings; 530 calories per serving.

☆ ☆ ☆ ☆ ☆

Autumn Pork Chops

Good source of protein, thiamin and vitamin A

6 pork loin or rib chops, about ½ inch thick
¼ teaspoon salt
⅛ teaspoon pepper
2 medium onions, sliced and separated into rings
2 medium acorn squash, cut into 1-inch rings and seeded
3 medium apples, cored and cut into 1-inch rings
¼ cup margarine or butter, melted
2 tablespoons honey
2 tablespoons water
1 teaspoon pumpkin pie spice

Cook pork over medium heat until brown on both sides. Place pork in ungreased rectangular baking dish, 13 × 9 × 2 inches; sprinkle with salt and pepper. Arrange onions, squash and apples on pork. Mix remaining ingredients; pour over apples. Cover and cook in 350° oven until pork is done and squash is tender, 45 to 55 minutes. Serve pan drippings with pork.

6 servings; 460 calories per serving.

☆ ☆ ☆ ☆ ☆

Pork-Sauerkraut Skillet

Good source of protein, thiamin and niacin

4 pork blade steaks, about ½ inch thick
¼ teaspoon salt
⅛ teaspoon pepper
1 medium onion, thinly sliced
1 can (16 ounces) sauerkraut, drained
1 cup dry white wine
1 teaspoon paprika
2 cloves garlic, crushed

Cook pork in 10-inch skillet over medium heat until brown on both sides; drain. Sprinkle with salt and pepper; reduce heat. Place onion and sauerkraut over pork. Mix wine, paprika and garlic; pour over sauerkraut. Cover and simmer until pork is tender, about 35 minutes.

4 servings; 480 calories per serving.

☆ ☆ ☆ ☆ ☆

Pork in Lettuce Leaves

Good source of protein, thiamin, riboflavin, niacin and iron

1¼ pounds pork boneless loin or leg
 1 teaspoon cornstarch
 1 teaspoon soy sauce
 ½ teaspoon salt
 ¼ teaspoon pepper
 2 tablespoons vegetable oil
 2 large cloves garlic, finely chopped
 4 medium stalks celery, diagonally sliced
   (about 2 cups)
 4 green onions (with tops), sliced
 1 can (4 ounces) mushroom stems and pieces,
   drained
 ¼ cup hot water
 1 teaspoon instant chicken bouillon
 1 teaspoon cornstarch
 1 teaspoon soy sauce
 2 tablespoons cold water
 8 large lettuce leaves

Trim fat from pork. Cut pork with grain into 2-inch strips. Cut strips across grain into ⅛-inch slices. Stack slices and cut into thin strips. Toss pork, 1 teaspoon cornstarch, 1 teaspoon soy sauce, the salt and pepper; cover and refrigerate 30 minutes.

Heat oil in 12-inch skillet or wok over high heat until hot. Add pork and garlic. Cook and stir until pork is no longer pink, about 8 minutes. Add celery, onions and mushrooms. Cook and stir 1 minute. Mix ¼ cup hot water and the chicken bouillon; stir into pork mixture. Mix cornstarch, 1 teaspoon soy sauce and the cold water; gradually stir into pork mixture. Heat to boiling, stirring constantly. Boil and stir 1 minute; remove from heat. Divide pork mixture among lettuce leaves, placing it at stem end of each lettuce leaf. Roll leaf around pork mixture, folding in sides.

4 servings (2 leaves each); 370 calories per serving.

Pork in Lettuce Leaves

Pork-Vegetable Stew

Good source of protein, thiamin and niacin

 4   slices bacon, cut into ½-inch pieces
 1½   pounds pork boneless shoulder, cut into 1-inch
        pieces
 1   large onion, chopped
 2   medium cloves garlic, crushed
 1   teaspoon salt
 1   teaspoon dried rosemary leaves
 ¼   teaspoon pepper
 ⅛   teaspoon ground cloves
 1   can (10 ounces) condensed chicken broth
 ½   cup water
 2   medium rutabagas, cut into 1-inch pieces
        (about 3 cups)
 1   package (10 ounces) frozen baby Brussels
        sprouts
 1   tablespoon cornstarch
 2   tablespoons cold water

Fry bacon in 4-quart Dutch oven over medium heat until crisp. Remove with slotted spoon and drain; reserve. Pour off all but 2 tablespoons bacon fat. Cook pork in bacon fat, stirring occasionally, until brown. Stir in onion, garlic, salt, rosemary, pepper, cloves, chicken broth and water. Heat to boiling; reduce heat. Cover and simmer 30 minutes.

Add rutabagas. Heat to boiling; reduce heat. Cover and simmer 20 minutes. Rinse Brussels sprouts under running cold water to separate; drain. Stir Brussels sprouts and bacon into pork mixture. Cover and simmer until Brussels sprouts are done, about 10 minutes. Mix cornstarch and 2 tablespoons cold water; gradually stir into pork mixture. Heat to boiling, stirring constantly. Boil and stir 1 minute.

6 servings (about 1 cup); 440 calories each.

☆ ☆ ☆ ☆ ☆

Coconut-Curried Pork

Good source of protein, thiamin, riboflavin, niacin and iron

 1   cup flaked coconut
 1½   cups boiling water
 3   pounds pork boneless shoulder
 1   medium onion, chopped (about ½ cup)
 1   large clove garlic, finely chopped
 1   tablespoon chili powder
 2   teaspoons curry powder
 1   teaspoon salt
 1   teaspoon ground ginger
 ⅛   teaspoon cayenne pepper
 2   tablespoons vegetable oil
 1   medium green pepper, cut into ¾-inch pieces
 2   tablespoons cornstarch
 3   tablespoons cold water
 2   medium tomatoes, cut into wedges
 4½   cups hot cooked rice

Line bowl with double thickness cheesecloth. Place coconut in cheesecloth; pour 1½ cups boiling water over coconut. Let stand 30 minutes. Gather ends of cheesecloth together and squeeze liquid into bowl. Reserve coconut and liquid separately.

Trim excess fat from pork; cut pork into 1-inch pieces. Cook and stir onion, garlic, chili powder, curry powder, salt, ginger and cayenne pepper in oil in 10-inch skillet until onion is tender, about 5 minutes. Add pork and reserved coconut liquid. Heat to boiling; reduce heat. Cover and simmer, stirring occasionally, until pork is tender, about 1 hour.

Toast reserved coconut in 350° oven, stirring occasionally, until dry and golden brown, 10 to 15 minutes. Stir green pepper into pork mixture. Cover and simmer until green pepper is crisp-tender, about 5 minutes. Mix cornstarch and 3 tablespoons cold water; gradually stir into pork mixture. Heat to boiling, stirring constantly. Boil and stir 1 minute. Add tomato wedges; heat just until tomatoes are hot. Serve over rice; sprinkle with coconut.

6 servings; 690 calories per serving.

☆ ☆ ☆ ☆ ☆

Coconut-Curried Pork

Stir-Fried Pork and Pasta

Good source of protein, thiamin and niacin

1¼	pounds pork boneless loin or leg
1	teaspoon cornstarch
1	teaspoon soy sauce
¼	teaspoon salt
⅛	teaspoon pepper
2	tablespoons vegetable oil
2	large cloves garlic, finely chopped
¼	to ½ teaspoon finely crushed dried red pepper
2	medium stalks celery, diagonally cut into ¼-inch slices (about 1 cup)
1	small green pepper, cut into 1-inch pieces
2	cups bean sprouts (about 4 ounces)
4	ounces mushrooms, sliced (about 1¼ cups)
2	cups cooked vermicelli (about 4 ounces uncooked)
3	green onions (with tops), sliced
1	tablespoon soy sauce

Trim fat from pork. Cut pork into strips, 2 × 1 × ⅛ inch. Toss pork, cornstarch, 1 teaspoon soy sauce, the salt and pepper. Cover and refrigerate 20 minutes.

Heat oil in 12-inch skillet or wok over high heat until hot. Add pork, garlic and red pepper; cook and stir until pork is no longer pink, about 5 minutes. Add celery and green pepper; cook and stir 2 minutes. Add bean sprouts and mushrooms; cook and stir 2 minutes. Add vermicelli, green onions and 1 tablespoon soy sauce; toss until thoroughly mixed, about 2 minutes.

6 servings (about 1 cup); 305 calories each.

☆ ☆ ☆ ☆ ☆

Stir-Fried Pork and Pasta

Sweet-and-Sour Ham

Good source of protein, thiamin and niacin

1   *can (15¼ ounces) pineapple chunks in juice*
1   *medium onion, sliced*
2   *tablespoons margarine or butter*
1   *pound fully cooked smoked ham, cut into strips,*
     4 × ¼ inch
1   *small green pepper, chopped (about ½ cup)*
¼   *teaspoon salt*
¼   *teaspoon pepper*
1   *tablespoon cornstarch*
2   *tablespoons cold water*
4   *cups hot cooked rice*

Drain pineapple; reserve juice. Add enough water to juice to measure 1 cup. Cook and stir onion in margarine in 10-inch skillet over medium heat until onion is tender, about 5 minutes. Stir in ham, green pepper, salt, pepper, pineapple chunks and reserved pineapple juice. Heat to boiling; reduce heat. Cover and simmer until green pepper is crisp-tender, about 5 minutes. Mix cornstarch and cold water; gradually stir into ham mixture. Heat to boiling, stirring constantly. Boil and stir 1 minute. Serve over rice.

5 servings; 545 calories per serving.

☆ ☆ ☆ ☆ ☆

Ham with Mustard Fruits

Good source of protein, thiamin and vitamin A

1   *fully cooked smoked ham slice, about 1 inch*
     thick (about 2 pounds)
1   *can (30 ounces) apricot halves in juice, drained*
1   *can (15¼ ounces) pineapple chunks in juice,*
     drained
¼   *cup margarine or butter, melted*
2   *tablespoons prepared mustard*
2   *tablespoons honey*
1   *teaspoon prepared horseradish*
1   *medium clove garlic, crushed*

Slash diagonally outer edge of fat on ham at 1-inch intervals to prevent curling. Place ham in ungreased rectangular baking dish, 12 ×

7½ × 2 inches. Arrange fruit on ham. Mix remaining ingredients; pour over fruit and ham. Cook uncovered in 350° oven until ham is hot, about 40 minutes.

8 servings; 450 calories per serving.

☐ *Microwave Directions:* Prepare ham as directed. Place ham in microwavable dish, 12 × 7½ × 2 inches. Cover with waxed paper and microwave on medium-high (70%) 8 minutes. Turn ham; arrange fruit on ham. Mix remaining ingredients; pour over fruit and ham. Cover and microwave 5 minutes; rotate dish ½ turn. Microwave until ham is hot, 5 to 7 minutes longer.

☆ ☆ ☆ ☆ ☆

Ham Waldorf Salad

Good source of protein

¾   *cup plain yogurt*
½   *teaspoon ground nutmeg*
½   *teaspoon Worcestershire sauce*
2½   *cups cut-up fully cooked smoked ham*
2   *medium apples, coarsely chopped*
     (about 2 cups)
2   *stalks celery, sliced (about 1 cup)*
1   *cup seedless red or green grapes*
½   *cup coarsely chopped walnuts*
¼   *cup sliced green onions (with tops)*
     Lettuce
1   *medium apple, cut into wedges*

Mix yogurt, nutmeg and Worcestershire sauce; toss with ham, apples, celery, grapes, walnuts and green onions. Cover and refrigerate at least 2 hours. Serve ham mixture on lettuce; garnish with apple wedges.

6 servings (about 1 cup); 310 calories each.

☆ ☆ ☆ ☆ ☆

Ham and Pasta Salad

Good source of protein and thiamin

Italian Dressing (below)
1   *package (10 ounces) frozen chopped broccoli, cooked and drained*
1   *package (10 ounces) pasta bows (farfalle), cooked and drained*
1   *pound fully cooked smoked ham, cut into julienne strips*
1   *small green pepper, chopped (about ½ cup)*
2   *tablespoons finely chopped onion*

Prepare Italian Dressing. Gently toss with remaining ingredients. Cover and refrigerate at least 6 hours.

Italian Dressing

¼   *cup grated Parmesan cheese*
¼   *cup olive or vegetable oil*
2   *tablespoons snipped parsley*
2   *tablespoons lemon juice*
2   *tablespoons vinegar*
1   *teaspoon dry mustard*
1   *teaspoon dried basil leaves*
¼   *teaspoon dried oregano leaves*
¼   *teaspoon dried marjoram leaves*
⅛   *teaspoon pepper*
1   *medium clove garlic, crushed*

Shake all ingredients in tightly covered jar.

6 servings (about 1½ cups); 505 calories each.

☆ ☆ ☆ ☆ ☆

Ham Roll

Good source of protein, thiamin and calcium

1   *package active dry yeast*
1   *cup warm water (105 to 115°)*
1½ *cups all-purpose flour*
1   *tablespoon sugar*
1   *teaspoon salt*
1   *to 1½ cups all-purpose flour*
2   *cups chopped fully cooked smoked ham*
1½ *cups shredded Swiss cheese (about 6 ounces)*
1   *small onion, chopped (about ¼ cup)*
¼   *cup grated Parmesan cheese*
1   *can (4 ounces) mushroom stems and pieces, drained*
1   *jar (2 ounces) diced pimiento, drained*
1   *egg*
1   *tablespoon water*
1   *tablespoon sesame seed*

Dissolve yeast in 1 cup warm water in large bowl. Add 1½ cups flour, the sugar and salt. Beat on low speed until moistened; beat on medium speed, scraping bowl occasionally, until smooth. Stir in enough remaining flour to make dough easy to handle. Turn dough onto lightly floured surface; knead 3 minutes. Shape into ball; cover.

Heat oven to 375°. Grease jelly roll pan, 15½ × 10½ × 1 inch. Mix ham, Swiss cheese, onion, Parmesan cheese, mushrooms and pimiento. Roll dough into rectangle, 14 × 12 inches. Spread ham mixture over rectangle, leaving 1-inch strip on one 14-inch side and ½-inch strip on the 12-inch sides. Roll up tightly, beginning at filled 14-inch side. Pinch unfilled strip of dough into roll to seal well; seal ends. Place roll, seam side down, in pan. Mix egg and 1 tablespoon water; brush over roll. Sprinkle with sesame seed. Bake until golden brown, about 40 minutes. Let stand 10 minutes before cutting.

8 servings; 325 calories per serving.

☆ ☆ ☆ ☆ ☆

Ham Roll

Shaping Ham Roll

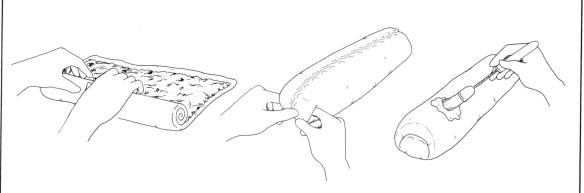

Spread ham mixture over rectangle, roll up tightly, beginning at filled 1-inch side.

Pinch unfilled strip of dough into roll to seal well; seal ends.

Brush egg mixture over roll.

Sausage and Vegetable Spaghetti

Good source of protein and vitamin A

1	spaghetti squash (about 3 pounds)
1	pound Italian sausage
1	medium onion, chopped (about 1/2 cup)
1	medium zucchini, coarsely chopped (about 1 cup)
1/4	cup snipped parsley
1	large clove garlic, crushed
1	tablespoon dried basil leaves
4	medium tomatoes, coarsely chopped (about 3 cups)
1/2	cup grated Parmesan cheese
1/2	teaspoon salt
1/4	teaspoon pepper

Prick squash with fork. Cook in 400° oven until tender, about 1 hour. Remove sausage from casing. Cook and stir sausage and onion in 10-inch skillet over medium heat until sausage is done, about 10 minutes. Stir in zucchini, parsley, garlic and basil. Cover and cook 3 minutes. Stir in tomatoes and Parmesan cheese. Cut squash into halves; remove seeds and fibrous strings. Remove squash strands with 2 forks; toss with salt and pepper. Serve sausage mixture over squash. Serve with additional Parmesan cheese if desired.

6 servings (about 1³/₄ cups); 230 calories each.

☆ ☆ ☆ ☆ ☆

Sausage and Vegetable Spaghetti

Sausage-Bean Soup

Good source of protein, thiamin, niacin and vitamin A

1 pound fully cooked smoked kielbasa, cut into
     $1/4$-inch slices
1 medium onion, chopped (about $1/2$ cup)
1 medium green pepper, chopped (about 1 cup)
$2/3$ cup uncooked regular rice
$1 1/2$ cups water
1 can (28 ounces) whole tomatoes, undrained
1 can ($10 1/2$ ounces) condensed beef broth
1 teaspoon dried oregano leaves
$1/4$ teaspoon pepper
1 can (20 ounces) red kidney beans, drained

Cook and stir kielbasa and onion in 4-quart Dutch oven over medium heat until onion is tender, about 10 minutes. Stir in remaining ingredients except beans. Break up tomatoes with fork. Heat to boiling; reduce heat. Cover and simmer 30 minutes. Stir in beans. Heat, stirring occasionally, just until beans are hot, about 5 minutes.

6 servings (about $1 1/3$ cups); 355 calories each.

☆ ☆ ☆ ☆ ☆

Individual Pork Pies

Good source of protein and thiamin

1 pound bulk pork sausage
1 cup cubed fully cooked smoked ham
1 medium green pepper, chopped (about 1 cup)
1 medium onion, chopped (about $1/2$ cup)
1 medium stalk celery, thinly sliced (about $1/2$ cup)
$1/2$ teaspoon ground sage
$1/8$ teaspoon pepper
1 can ($10 3/4$ ounces) condensed cream of
     chicken soup
4 cups thinly sliced apples (about 4 medium)
     Pastry (below)

Cook and stir sausage in 10-inch skillet until done, about 10 minutes; drain. Stir in ham, green pepper, onion, celery, sage, pepper and soup. Divide sausage mixture among 6 ungreased 10-ounce individual casseroles or custard cups. Place apples on sausage mixture in each casserole. Prepare Pastry. Gather into ball; divide into 6 equal parts. Roll each part 1 inch larger than casserole. Fold in half; place on casserole and unfold. Seal pastry to edge of casserole; cut several slits in top. Cook in 375° oven until crust is brown, about 30 minutes.

Pastry

$1/3$ cup plus 1 tablespoon shortening
1 cup all-purpose flour
$1/4$ cup grated Parmesan cheese
$1/2$ teaspoon salt
2 to 3 tablespoons cold water

Cut shortening into flour, cheese and salt until particles are size of small peas. Sprinkle in water, 1 tablespoon at a time, tossing with fork until all flour is moistened and pastry almost cleans side of bowl (1 to 2 teaspoons water can be added if necessary).

6 servings; 500 calories per serving.

☆ ☆ ☆ ☆ ☆

Bratwurst and Cabbage

Good source of protein, thiamin and niacin

12 fully cooked bratwurst (about 2 pounds)
1 tablespoon vegetable oil
6 cups coarsely shredded green cabbage
     (about 1 pound)
1 teaspoon salt
$1/2$ teaspoon caraway seed
     Dash of pepper
$1/3$ cup dry white wine
     Prepared mustard

Cook bratwurst in oil in 4-quart Dutch oven over medium heat until brown, about 10 minutes; remove and reserve. Stir cabbage, salt, caraway seed and pepper into drippings in Dutch oven. Cook and stir 1 minute; stir in wine. Place bratwurst on cabbage mixture. Heat to boiling; reduce heat. Cover and simmer until cabbage and bratwurst are hot, about 10 minutes. Serve with mustard.

6 servings (2 bratwurst and $1/2$ cup cabbage); 500 calories each.

☆ ☆ ☆ ☆ ☆

Lamb with Parsley Rice

Good source of protein, thiamin and niacin

4   lamb sirloin or shoulder chops, about 3/4 inch
      thick
1/2 lemon
1   tablespoon vegetable oil
1   cup uncooked regular rice
2   cups water
1   can (4 ounces) mushroom stems and pieces,
      drained
1   large clove garlic, crushed
1   teaspoon salt
1   teaspoon dried rosemary leaves
1   teaspoon dry mustard
1/2 teaspoon salt
1   jar (1 ounce) pine nuts
1/4 cup snipped parsley

Remove fell (the paperlike covering) if it is on
lamb. Slash diagonally outer edge of fat on
lamb at 1-inch intervals to prevent curling (do
not cut into lean). Squeeze lemon on both sides
of lamb. Cook lamb in oil in 10-inch skillet
over medium heat until brown on both sides,
about 10 minutes. Remove lamb and reserve;
drain fat from skillet.

Mix rice, water, mushrooms, garlic and 1 teaspoon salt in same skillet; place lamb on top.
Mix rosemary, mustard and 1/2 teaspoon salt;
sprinkle evenly over lamb. Heat to boiling;
reduce heat. Cover and simmer 14 minutes
(do not lift cover or stir). Remove from heat;
let stand 10 minutes. Remove lamb; keep
warm. Stir pine nuts and parsley into rice mixture; serve with lamb.

4 servings (1 chop and 1 cup rice); 390 calories each.

☆ ☆ ☆ ☆ ☆

Lamb with Kasha

Good source of protein and niacin

1 1/2 pounds lamb boneless shoulder
1   tablespoon olive or vegetable oil
1   medium onion, chopped (about 1/2 cup)
1   large clove garlic, finely chopped
1   teaspoon salt
1/2 teaspoon dried thyme leaves
1/2 teaspoon dried oregano leaves
1 1/4 cups water
2   tablespoons lemon juice
1   package (10 ounces) frozen cut green beans
1/2 cup medium buckwheat kernels (kasha)

Trim excess fat from lamb. Cut lamb into 3/4-
inch pieces. Cook and stir lamb in oil in 4-
quart Dutch oven over medium heat until
brown, about 10 minutes. Add onion, garlic,
salt, thyme, oregano, water and lemon juice.
Heat to boiling; reduce heat. Cover and simmer until lamb is tender, about 1 hour.

Rinse frozen green beans under running cold
water to separate; drain. Stir beans and buckwheat kernels into lamb mixture. Heat to
boiling; reduce heat. Cover and simmer until
beans are tender and liquid is absorbed, 10 to
12 minutes.

6 servings (about 3/4 cup); 235 calories each.

☐ *Pressure Cooker Directions:* Prepare lamb as
directed. Cook and stir lamb in oil in 4-quart
pressure cooker over medium heat until
brown, about 10 minutes. Add onion, garlic,
salt, thyme, oregano, water and lemon juice.
Following manufacturer's directions, cover
and cook at 15 pounds pressure 12 minutes.
Cool 5 minutes; reduce pressure. Remove all
but 1 cup liquid. Stir beans and buckwheat
kernels into lamb mixture. Heat to boiling;
reduce heat. Simmer uncovered, stirring occasionally, until beans are tender and liquid is
absorbed, about 6 minutes.

☆ ☆ ☆ ☆ ☆

Mustard Lamb Chops

Good source of protein, niacin and vitamin A

6	lamb sirloin or shoulder chops, about ¾ inch thick
2	tablespoons Dijon-style mustard
2	teaspoons vegetable oil
1	teaspoon dried thyme leaves
½	teaspoon salt
2	medium carrots, cut into strips, 2 × ½ inch
½	small head cauliflower, separated into flowerets
2	medium zucchini, cut into strips, 2 × ½ inch
2	tablespoons margarine or butter, melted
½	teaspoon salt
¼	teaspoon pepper

Remove fell (the paperlike covering) if it is on lamb. Slash diagonally outer edge of fat on lamb at 1-inch intervals to prevent curling (do not cut into lean). Place lamb on rack in broiler pan. Mix mustard, oil, thyme and ½ teaspoon salt; brush half of the mustard mixture evenly over lamb.

Place steamer basket in ½ inch water in saucepan or skillet (water should not touch bottom of basket). Place carrots, cauliflower and zucchini in basket. Cover tightly and heat to boiling; reduce heat. Steam until vegetables are tender, 12 to 15 minutes. Set oven control to broil and/or 550°. Broil lamb with top about 3 inches from heat until brown, about 6 minutes; turn. Brush lamb with remaining mustard mixture. Broil until medium doneness, 5 to 8 minutes longer. Mix margarine, ½ teaspoon salt and the pepper. Spoon over vegetables; serve with lamb.

6 servings; 500 calories per serving.

☆ ☆ ☆ ☆ ☆

Mustard Lamb Chops

Braised Veal Shanks

Good source of protein and niacin

8	veal shanks (about 4 pounds)
1/4	cup all-purpose flour
2	tablespoons vegetable oil
1	cup dry white wine
1/2	cup beef broth
1/2	teaspoon salt
1/2	teaspoon dried oregano leaves
1/8	teaspoon pepper
1	clove garlic, crushed
2	tablespoons snipped parsley
1	teaspoon finely shredded lemon peel
1	clove garlic, finely chopped
1	teaspoon cornstarch
2	tablespoons cold water

Coat veal with flour. Heat oil in 4-quart Dutch oven; cook veal over medium heat until brown, about 10 minutes. Mix wine, beef broth, salt, oregano, pepper and crushed garlic; pour over veal. Heat to boiling; reduce heat. Cover and simmer until veal is tender, 1½ to 2 hours. Remove veal from broth; keep warm. Mix parsley, lemon peel and chopped garlic; sprinkle over veal. Mix cornstarch and cold water; gradually stir into broth. Heat to boiling, stirring constantly. Boil and stir 1 minute. Serve sauce with veal.

8 servings (1 shank); 310 calories each.

☐ *Pressure Cooker Directions:* Coat veal with flour. Heat oil in 6-quart pressure cooker; cook veal over medium heat until brown, about 10 minutes. Mix wine, beef broth, salt, oregano, pepper and crushed garlic; pour over veal. Following manufacturer's directions, cover and cook at 15 pounds pressure, about 40 minutes. Cool 5 minutes; reduce pressure. Remove veal from broth; keep warm. Mix parsley, lemon peel and chopped garlic; sprinkle over veal. Remove all but 1⅓ cups broth. Mix cornstarch and cold water; gradually stir into broth. Heat to boiling, stirring constantly. Boil and stir 1 minute. Serve sauce with veal.

☆ ☆ ☆ ☆ ☆

Veal with Tuna Sauce

Good source of protein and niacin

2	- pound veal boneless shoulder roast
2	tablespoons olive or vegetable oil
1	medium onion, chopped (about ½ cup)
2	large cloves garlic, crushed
1/2	cup chicken broth (page 56)
1/2	cup dry white wine
1/2	teaspoon salt
1/2	teaspoon dried basil leaves
1/4	teaspoon pepper
1	can (6½ ounces) tuna in water, drained
1/4	cup olive or vegetable oil
1	tablespoon lemon juice
1/4	teaspoon salt
2	tablespoons capers
2	tablespoons snipped parsley

Cook veal in 2 tablespoons oil in 4-quart Dutch oven over medium heat, turning occasionally, until brown. Add onion, garlic, chicken broth, wine, ½ teaspoon salt, the basil and pepper. Heat to boiling; reduce heat. Cover and simmer until veal is tender, about 2 hours. Remove veal from broth; cover and refrigerate until cold, at least 12 hours. Reserve ½ cup broth; cover and refrigerate.

Place tuna, reserved broth, ¼ cup oil, the lemon juice and ¼ teaspoon salt in blender container. Cover and blend on medium speed, stopping blender occasionally to scrape down sides, until mixture is smooth and creamy, about 2 minutes. Cut veal into thin slices. Spoon tuna mixture over veal; sprinkle with capers and parsley. Garnish with lemon slices if desired.

10 servings; 250 calories per serving.

☐ *Food Processor Directions:* Place tuna, reserved broth, ¼ cup oil, the lemon juice and ¼ teaspoon salt in workbowl fitted with steel blade. Cover and process until smooth, about 15 seconds.

☆ ☆ ☆ ☆ ☆

Nutrition Information Per Serving or Unit

Recipe and Page Number	Protein	Carbo-hydrates	Fat	Sodium	Potas-sium	Protein	Calcium	Iron
		Grams		Milligrams		Percent U.S. Recommended Daily Allowance		
BEEF								
Beef and Beer Stew, 117	21	12	7	390	350	46	4	16
Beef and Eggplant Salad, 117	15	5	24	350	400	32	2	14
Beef-Baguette Slices, 118	27	23	18	350	370	56	4	22
Beef Roll-Ups, 111	27	9	10	505	565	60	4	22
Beef with Tomatoes and Rice, 108	25	2	32	395	490	50	2	26
Broiled Herbed Steak, 110	24	1	8	460	315	54	2	18
Chili con Carne, 116	32	49	10	865	820	64	10	40
Dilled Steak, 110	27	23	8	240	720	62	6	22
Easy Burgundy Stew, 116	23	19	4	430	845	50	4	22
French-Style Beef Roast, 106	26	9	18	380	640	58	6	22
Fruited Beef Roast, 107	33	38	22	215	785	72	4	28
Garlic Beef Roast, 109	25	3	31	285	415	56	0	20
Italian-Style Liver, 114	18	6	8	305	320	40	2	34
Lemon-Honey Beef Ribs, 113	19	11	43	210	380	42	0	14
Mustard-Marinated Steak, 113	15	1	28	65	260	34	0	12
Oriental Pot Roast, 107	33	15	22	490	685	74	8	30
Roast with Peppers, 106	32	6	32	275	600	72	2	26
Sausage-Stuffed Steak, 112	26	9	15	695	445	58	2	18
Spicy Stir-Fried Beef, 115	29	15	14	505	850	66	4	24
Stir-Fried Beef, 114	22	12	13	840	585	50	4	20
Tangy Short Ribs, 113	19	11	37	720	490	42	2	16
Vegetable-Chili Steak, 109	30	25	7	565	830	60	8	28
GROUND BEEF								
Barley-Beef Stew, 122	26	35	18	620	895	52	4	26
Beef and Bulgur Stew, 122	20	21	14	490	515	40	6	20
Beef and Corn Pie, 125	21	31	25	815	505	40	12	20
Beef and Potato Broil, 119	23	17	36	730	730	50	2	20

Nutrition Information Per Serving or Unit

Recipe and Page Number	Protein	Carbo-hydrates	Fat	Sodium	Potas-sium	Protein	Calcium	Iron
		Grams		Milligrams		Percent U.S. Recommended Daily Allowance		
Burgers with Cheesy Vegetables, 120	25	10	20	375	555	54	8	20
Cheese-Topped Pie, 123	19	9	18	510	315	42	16	14
Chili Burgers, 119	21	5	19	140	400	46	12	14
Curried Meat Loaf, 121	25	12	20	435	605	56	8	22
Hamburgers Ranchero, 121	24	18	18	605	765	52	8	24
Layered Beef Squares, 124	26	8	22	495	515	58	16	20
Macaroni and Beef, 125	21	30	19	505	550	42	14	20
Manicotti, 124	30	38	15	865	880	60	22	30
Oven Burger, 119	21	5	17	615	480	48	2	16
Savory Beef Patties, 120	21	1	26	425	420	46	2	16
Sweet-Sour Cabbage Rolls, 126	28	65	20	630	1065	62	12	32
Teriyaki Meat Loaf, 122	24	19	18	745	690	52	2	20
Vegetable Beef Burgers, 120	22	4	17	415	565	50	2	18
PORK Autumn Pork Chops, 130	19	29	30	235	730	44	4	18
Bratwurst and Cabbage, 139	23	8	42	1350	510	50	12	14
Cheese-Topped Pork, 127	28	2	18	380	360	62	6	20
Coconut-Curried Pork, 132	29	51	41	1025	705	54	4	32
Ham and Pasta Salad, 136	24	40	28	70	270	48	10	24
Ham Roll, 136	22	35	11	710	235	44	26	16
Ham Waldorf Salad, 135	16	17	20	45	300	36	6	12
Ham with Mustard Fruits, 135	22	28	28	980	305	48	2	18
Individual Pork Pies, 139	20	39	30	1160	500	44	8	14
Pork Chops with Grapes, 129	24	10	29	525	480	52	2	20
Pork in Lettuce Leaves, 131	34	7	23	755	745	76	6	28

Nutrition Information Per Serving or Unit

Recipe and Page Number	Protein	Carbo-hydrates	Fat	Sodium	Potas-sium	Protein	Calcium	Iron
		Grams		Milligrams		Percent U.S. Recommended Daily Allowance		
Pork Roast with Raisin Sauce, 127	27	18	13	200	490	60	2	22
Pork-Sauerkraut Skillet, 130	27	9	33	975	555	60	6	24
Pork-Vegetable Stew, 132	27	15	30	780	775	60	8	22
Pork with Apple and Parsnips, 129	20	18	23	425	660	44	6	18
Pork with Stuffed Yams, 130	24	27	36	405	445	52	2	20
Sausage and Vegetable Spaghetti, 138	13	18	12	640	755	28	16	12
Sausage-Bean Soup, 139	18	24	21	1320	825	36	8	24
Spicy-Sesame Spareribs, 128	27	4	50	765	535	60	2	20
Stir-Fried Pork and Pasta, 134	26	17	15	400	600	50	4	22
Sweet-and-Sour Ham, 135	23	57	25	785	245	46	4	24
Sweet 'n Pungent Spareribs, 128	29	20	52	570	765	64	6	26
Sweet-Sour Pork 'n Onions, 128	22	9	27	335	455	48	2	18
LAMB AND VEAL Braised Veal Shanks, 142	31	5	16	280	620	70	2	22
Lamb with Kasha, 140	23	11	11	530	355	48	6	16
Lamb with Parsley Rice, 140	22	4	32	880	300	42	4	18
Mustard Lamb Chops, 141	28	7	40	575	635	62	6	16
Veal with Tuna Sauce, 142	22	2	17	405	405	48	2	14

Vegetables
★★★

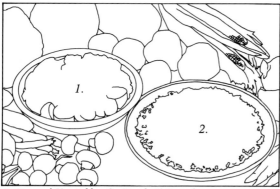

1. Steamed Vegetables, 2. Spaghetti Squash

Artichokes with Curried Hollandaise Sauce

4   medium artichokes
4   teaspoons lemon juice
4   cups water
1   teaspoon salt
    Curried Hollandaise Sauce (below)

Remove small leaves at base of each artichoke; trim stem even with base of artichoke. Slice 1 inch off top; discard top. Snip off thorny tips of the remaining leaves with scissors. Gently pull apart leaves and remove the choke (fuzzy growth covering artichoke heart) with small spoon. Sprinkle each artichoke with 1 teaspoon lemon juice. Heat artichokes, water and salt to boiling in Dutch oven; reduce heat. Cover and simmer until leaves pull out easily and bottom is tender when pierced with a knife, 25 to 30 minutes. Remove artichokes with tongs; place upside down to drain. Serve hot with Curried Hollandaise Sauce.

Curried Hollandaise Sauce

2   egg yolks, slightly beaten
3   tablespoons lemon juice
1/2 cup margarine or butter
1/8 teaspoon curry powder

Stir egg yolks and lemon juice vigorously with wooden spoon in 1-quart saucepan. Add 1/4 cup of the margarine. Heat over very low heat, stirring constantly, until margarine is melted. Add remaining margarine, stirring vigorously until margarine is melted and sauce thickens.

(Be sure margarine melts slowly; this gives eggs time to cook and thicken the sauce without curdling.) Stir in curry powder.

4 servings (1 artichoke and about 3 tablespoons sauce); 300 calories per serving.

☐ *Microwave Directions for Curried Hollandaise Sauce:* Place margarine in 2-cup microwavable measure. Microwave uncovered on high (100%) until melted, 1 to 1½ minutes. Add lemon juice and 1 tablespoon water. Beat in egg yolks with fork. Microwave uncovered on medium (50%), stirring every 15 seconds, until thickened, 1 to 1½ minutes (sauce will curdle if overcooked). Stir in curry powder.

☆ ☆ ☆ ☆ ☆

Asparagus with Bacon

Good source of vitamin A and thiamin

1½ pounds asparagus, cut diagonally into
       1-inch pieces*
2   tablespoons snipped parsley
2   teaspoons lemon juice
1/4 teaspoon salt
2   slices bacon, crisply fried and crumbled

Place steamer basket in ½ inch water in saucepan or skillet (water should not touch bottom of basket). Place lower stalk pieces in basket. Cover tightly and heat to boiling; reduce heat. Steam 4 minutes. Add tips. Cover tightly and steam until crisp-tender, 4 to 5 minutes longer. Toss asparagus with parsley, lemon juice and salt. Sprinkle with bacon.

4 servings (about 3/4 cup); 75 calories each.

*2 packages (10 ounces each) frozen cut asparagus can be substituted for the fresh asparagus. Cook as directed on package; drain.

☐ *Microwave Directions:* Place asparagus, 1/4 cup water and 1/4 teaspoon salt in 1½-quart microwavable casserole. Cover tightly and microwave on high (100%) 3 minutes; stir. Cover and microwave until crisp-tender, 2 to 3 minutes longer. Let stand 1 minute; drain. Continue as directed.

☆ ☆ ☆ ☆ ☆

Green Beans Piquant

1½ pounds green beans, cut into 1-inch pieces*
12 medium radishes, cut into fourths
 3 sprigs parsley
 1 teaspoon salt
½ teaspoon mustard seed
 2 tablespoons margarine or butter
 1 tablespoon lime juice

Heat beans and 1 inch salted water (½ teaspoon salt to 1 cup water) to boiling; reduce heat. Simmer uncovered 5 minutes. Cover and simmer until tender, 15 to 20 minutes longer; drain. Place radishes and parsley in blender container. Cover and blend on high speed, stopping blender frequently to scrape sides, until finely chopped, about 20 seconds. Cook and stir radish mixture, salt and mustard seed in margarine over medium heat until hot, about 5 minutes. Toss with green beans and lime juice.

8 servings (about ⅔ cup); 50 calories each.

*2 packages (10 ounces each) frozen cut green beans can be substituted for the fresh green beans. Cook as directed on package; drain.

☆ ☆ ☆ ☆ ☆

Sesame Green Beans

1½ pounds green beans, cut into 1½-inch pieces*
 2 teaspoons sesame seed
 1 medium clove garlic, finely chopped
 2 tablespoons margarine or butter
 2 tablespoons soy sauce

Heat beans and 1 inch salted water (½ teaspoon salt to 1 cup water) to boiling; reduce heat. Simmer uncovered 5 minutes. Cover and simmer until crisp-tender, 10 to 15 minutes longer; drain. Cook and stir sesame seed and garlic in 1-quart saucepan over medium heat until sesame seed are light golden brown, 3 to 5 minutes. Add margarine and soy sauce. Heat until margarine is melted, stirring occasionally. Toss with green beans.

8 servings (about ⅔ cup); 60 calories each.

*2 packages (10 ounces each) frozen cut green beans can be substituted for the fresh green beans. Cook as directed on package; drain.

☆ ☆ ☆ ☆ ☆

Mixed Vegetables

Mixed Vegetables

1 tablespoon instant chicken bouillon
½ cup water
1 tablespoon cornstarch
1 tablespoon cold water
1 tablespoon soy sauce
8 ounces bean sprouts
2 tablespoons vegetable oil
1 medium onion, thinly sliced
2 large cloves garlic, finely chopped
1 teaspoon finely chopped gingerroot
4 medium stalks celery, cut into ¼-inch slices
     (about 2 cups)
1 package (10 ounces) frozen green peas
8 ounces mushrooms, cut into ¼-inch slices
     (about 3 cups)

Mix bouillon in ½ cup water. Dissolve cornstarch in 1 tablespoon water and the soy sauce.

Rinse bean sprouts under running cold water; drain. Heat wok or 12-inch skillet over medium-high heat until 1 or 2 drops water bubble and skitter when sprinkled in wok. Add oil; rotate wok to coat side. Add onion, garlic and gingerroot; stir-fry until garlic is light brown. Add celery and peas; stir-fry 3 minutes. Add mushrooms and bean sprouts; stir-fry 1 minute. Stir in chicken bouillon; heat to boiling. Stir in cornstarch mixture; cook and stir until thickened, about 10 seconds.

8 servings (about ¾ cup); 90 calories each.

☆ ☆ ☆ ☆ ☆

Honeyed Beets

6 cups water
1 tablespoon vinegar
1 teaspoon salt
5 medium beets (about 1¼ pounds)*
1 medium onion, chopped (about ½ cup)
2 tablespoons margarine or butter
2 tablespoons honey
1 tablespoon lemon juice
½ teaspoon salt
⅛ teaspoon ground cinnamon
1 tablespoon snipped parsley

Heat water, vinegar and 1 teaspoon salt to boiling. Add beets. Cover and heat to boiling; reduce heat. Simmer until tender, 35 to 45 minutes; drain. Run cold water over beets; slip off skins and remove root ends. Cut beets into shoestring pieces. Cook and stir onion in margarine in 10-inch skillet over medium heat until onion is tender, about 5 minutes. Stir in beets, honey, lemon juice, ½ teaspoon salt and the cinnamon. Heat, stirring occasionally, until beets are hot, about 5 minutes. Sprinkle with parsley.

7 servings (about ½ cup); 65 calories each.

*2 cans (16 ounces each) shoestring beets, drained, can be substituted for the fresh beets; stir in with onion. Continue as directed.

☆ ☆ ☆ ☆ ☆

Broccoli With Herbed Mushrooms

Good source of vitamins A and C

1   pound broccoli*
4   ounces mushrooms, sliced (about 1½ cups)
½   teaspoon instant beef bouillon
¼   teaspoon dried thyme leaves
2   teaspoons margarine or butter

Cut broccoli stalks lengthwise into thin spears. Place steamer basket in ½ inch water in saucepan or skillet (water should not touch bottom of basket). Place broccoli in basket. Cover tightly and heat to boiling; reduce heat. Steam until tender, about 15 minutes. Cook and stir mushrooms, bouillon and thyme in margarine until mushrooms are hot, about 3 minutes. Toss with broccoli.

4 servings (about 3 spears); 70 calories each.

*1 package (10 ounces) frozen broccoli spears can be substituted for the fresh broccoli. Cook as directed on package; drain.

☐ *Microwave Directions:* Cut broccoli stalks lengthwise into thin spears. Place ¼ cup water and ½ teaspoon salt in 2-quart microwavable casserole. Arrange broccoli spears with flowery ends in center of casserole. Cover tightly and microwave on high (100%) 3 minutes; rotate casserole ½ turn. Microwave until tender, 2 to 4 minutes longer; drain. Mix remaining ingredients in 1-quart microwavable casserole. Cover tightly and microwave until mushrooms are hot, 1 to 2 minutes. Toss mushroom mixture with broccoli.

☆ ☆ ☆ ☆ ☆

Broccoli with Garlic Mayonnaise

Good source of vitamins A and C

½   cup mayonnaise or salad dressing
2   medium cloves garlic, crushed
1½ pounds broccoli*
    Paprika

Mix mayonnaise and garlic; cover and refrigerate at least 4 hours.

Cut broccoli stalks lengthwise into thin spears. Place steamer basket in ½ inch water in saucepan or skillet (water should not touch bottom of basket). Place broccoli in basket. Cover tightly and heat to boiling; reduce heat. Steam until tender, about 15 minutes. Cover and refrigerate until chilled, at least 2 hours.

Sprinkle mayonnaise mixture with paprika; serve with broccoli.

6 servings (about 3 spears and 1½ tablespoons mayonnaise); 180 calories each.

*2 packages (10 ounces each) frozen broccoli spears can be substituted for the fresh broccoli. Prepare as directed on packge; drain.

☐ *Microwave Directions:* Cut broccoli stalks lengthwise into thin spears. Place ¼ cup water and ½ teaspoon salt in microwavable dish, 12 × 7½ × 2 inches, or pie plate, 10 × 1½ inches. Arrange broccoli spears lengthwise in dish with flowery ends in center of dish. Or arrange in circle in pie plate with flowery ends in center of plate. Cover tightly and microwave on high (100%) 4 minutes; rotate dish ½ turn. Microwave until tender, 3 to 5 minutes longer; drain.

☆ ☆ ☆ ☆ ☆

Brussels Sprouts with Carrots

Good source of vitamins A and C

1   pound Brussels sprouts (about 5 cups)*
1/4 cup milk
3   tablespoons margarine or butter
1/4 teaspoon salt
1/4 teaspoon dry mustard
2   medium carrots, shredded (about 1 cup)

Place steamer basket in 1/2 inch water in saucepan or skillet (water should not touch bottom of basket). Place Brussels sprouts in basket. Cover tightly and heat to boiling; reduce heat. Steam until tender, 12 to 15 minutes. Heat milk, margarine, salt and mustard to boiling, stirring constantly; reduce heat. Stir in carrots. Cover and simmer 2 minutes. Spoon over Brussels sprouts.

4 servings (about 5 sprouts); 145 calories each.

*2 packages (10 ounces each) frozen Brussels sprouts can be substituted for the fresh Brussels sprouts. Cook sprouts as directed on package; drain.

☐ *Microwave Directions:* Place Brussels sprouts and 1/4 cup water in 1 1/2-quart microwavable casserole. Cover tightly and microwave on high (100%) 5 minutes; stir. Cover and microwave until tender, 4 to 6 minutes longer; drain. Place remaining ingredients in 1-quart microwavable casserole. Cover tightly and microwave 1 minute; stir. Cover and microwave until hot, about 1 minute longer. Spoon over Brussels sprouts.

☆ ☆ ☆ ☆ ☆

Cabbage Wedges

1   small head green cabbage (about 1 pound), cut into 6 wedges
1   tablespoon sugar
3   tablespoons white vinegar
1   tablespoon margarine or butter
1   teaspoon finely chopped onion
1/4 teaspoon salt
1/4 teaspoon celery seed
1/4 teaspoon ground ginger

Heat 1 inch salted water (1/2 teaspoon salt to 1 cup water) to boiling in 10-inch skillet. Add cabbage. Cover and heat to boiling; reduce heat. Simmer until crisp-tender, 15 to 20 minutes. Remove to serving platter with slotted spoon. Heat remaining ingredients to boiling in small saucepan, stirring occasionally. Pour sauce over cabbage wedges.

6 servings (1 wedge); 50 calories each.

☐ *Microwave Directions:* Place 1/2 cup water and 1/2 teaspoon salt in 2-quart round microwavable casserole. Arrange cabbage wedges spoke fashion with cores at edge of casserole. Cover tightly and microwave on high (100%) 5 minutes; rotate casserole 1/2 turn. Microwave until crisp-tender, 4 to 6 minutes longer. Let stand 5 minutes. Mix 2 tablespoons vinegar and the remaining ingredients in 1-cup microwavable measure. Microwave uncovered to boiling, 30 to 60 seconds.

☆ ☆ ☆ ☆ ☆

Cabbage Wedges, and Brussels Sprouts with Carrots

Cabbage-Rice Casserole

6   cups coarsely shredded green cabbage
        (about 1 large head)
    Mushroom Sauce (below)
2   cups cooked brown or regular rice
½   cup shredded Swiss cheese (about 2 ounces)

Heat ½ inch salted water (½ teaspoon salt to 1 cup water) to boiling. Add cabbage. Cover and heat to boiling; reduce heat. Simmer until crisp-tender, about 5 minutes; drain. Prepare Mushroom Sauce. Place rice in ungreased 1½-quart casserole. Top with cabbage. Pour Mushroom Sauce over cabbage; sprinkle with cheese. Cook uncovered in 350° oven until hot and bubbly, about 30 minutes.

Mushroom Sauce

8   ounces mushrooms, sliced (about 3 cups)
2   tablespoons margarine or butter
2   tablespoons flour
1   tablespoon prepared horseradish
1   teaspoon salt
½   teaspoon dry mustard
⅛   teaspoon pepper
1½ cups milk

Cook and stir mushrooms in margarine until tender. Remove with slotted spoon; reserve. Blend flour, horseradish, salt, mustard and pepper into margarine. Cook over low heat, stirring constantly, until smooth and bubbly; remove from heat. Stir in milk. Heat to boiling, stirring constantly. Boil and stir 1 minute. Stir in reserved mushrooms.

8 servings (about ½ cup); 190 calories each.

☆ ☆ ☆ ☆ ☆

Savory Carrot Casserole

Good source of vitamin A

3   cups shredded carrots (about 6 medium)
1   small onion, chopped (about ¼ cup)
½   teaspoon salt
½   teaspoon dried savory leaves
¼   teaspoon dry mustard
½   cup hot water
¼   cup coarsely chopped walnuts
1   tablespoon margarine or butter

Mix carrots, onion, salt, savory and mustard in ungreased 1½-quart casserole. Pour water over carrot mixture. Cover and cook in 350° oven until carrots are tender, about 45 minutes. Cook and stir walnuts in margarine over medium heat until walnuts are toasted, about 2 minutes. Spoon over carrots.

4 servings (about ½ cup); 110 calories each.

☐ *Microwave Directions:* Mix carrots, onion, salt, savory, mustard and 1 tablespoon water in ungreased 1½-quart microwavable casserole. Cover tightly and microwave on high (100%) 3 minutes; stir. Cover and microwave until carrots are tender, 2 to 4 minutes longer. Place walnuts and margarine in small microwavable bowl. Microwave uncovered, stirring every 30 seconds until toasted, 3 to 4 minutes. Spoon over carrots.

☆ ☆ ☆ ☆ ☆

Carrots with Coconut

Good source of vitamin A

¹/₄   cup flaked coconut
2   pounds carrots, cut crosswise into ¹/₄-inch slices
        (about 5 cups)
2   tablespoons margarine or butter
1   teaspoon salt
¹/₂   teaspoon ground nutmeg

Sprinkle coconut evenly in ungreased jelly roll pan, 15¹/₂ × 10¹/₂ × 1 inch. Toast in 350° oven until golden brown, 10 to 15 minutes, stirring occasionally (watch carefully).

Place steamer basket in ¹/₂ inch water in saucepan or skillet (water should not touch bottom of pan). Place carrots in basket. Cover tightly and heat to boiling; reduce heat. Steam until carrots are tender, 12 to 15 minutes. Toss carrots with margarine, salt and nutmeg. Sprinkle with coconut.

6 servings (about ³/₄ cup); 115 calories each.

☆ ☆ ☆ ☆ ☆

Carrots with Fennel

Good source of vitamin A

1   medium onion, thinly sliced
1   large clove garlic, finely chopped
2   tablespoons margarine or butter
¹/₂   cup water
1   tablespoon instant chicken bouillon
¹/₂   teaspoon salt
¹/₄   teaspoon dried dill weed
¹/₈   teaspoon pepper
1   pound carrots, cut crosswise into thirds,
        then lengthwise into ³/₈-inch strips
2   medium fennel bulbs, cut into ¹/₄-inch slices

Cook and stir onion and garlic in margarine in 10-inch skillet over medium heat until onion is tender, about 5 minutes. Stir in water, chicken bouillon, salt, dill weed and pepper. Add carrots and fennel. Heat to boiling; reduce heat. Cover and simmer until carrots are tender, about 12 minutes. Sprinkle with snipped parsley if desired.

6 servings (about 1 cup); 75 calories each.

☆ ☆ ☆ ☆ ☆

Tri-Colored Cauliflower

1   medium head cauliflower (about 2 pounds)
3   medium tomatoes, chopped (about 3 cups)
1   medium onion, chopped (about ½ cup)
1   can (4 ounces) chopped green chilies, drained
2   tablespoons vegetable oil
1   teaspoon salt
¼   teaspoon ground cinnamon
2   tablespoons chopped ripe olives
½   cup shredded Monterey Jack or Cheddar
      cheese (about 2 ounces)

Heat 1 inch salted water (½ teaspoon salt to 1 cup water) to boiling. Add cauliflower. Cover and heat to boiling; reduce heat. Simmer until tender, 20 to 25 minutes; drain. Cook and stir tomatoes, onion and chilies in oil in 10-inch skillet until onion is tender, about 5 minutes. Stir in salt and cinnamon. Simmer uncovered 5 minutes. Stir in olives; heat until hot. Place cauliflower on serving plate. Cut into 8 wedges; separate wedges slightly. Spoon tomato sauce over and around cauliflower wedges. Sprinkle with cheese.

8 servings (1 cauliflower wedge and about ⅓ cup tomato sauce); 115 calories each.

☐ *Microwave Directions:* Cut cone-shaped center from core of cauliflower. Place cauliflower and ¼ cup water in microwavable pie plate, 9 × 1¼ inches. Cover tightly and microwave on high (100%) 4 minutes; rotate pie plate ¼ turn. Microwave until tender, 3 to 4 minutes longer; drain. Mix remaining ingredients except cheese in microwavable 1½-quart casserole. Cover tightly and microwave, stirring every 2 minutes, until onion is tender, 4 to 5 minutes. Continue as directed.

☆ ☆ ☆ ☆ ☆

Tri-Colored Cauliflower

Corn Amandine

2   packages (10 ounces each) frozen whole
      kernel corn
½   cup slivered almonds
1   medium clove garlic, finely chopped
2   tablespoons margarine or butter
¼   cup dry white wine
1   teaspoon instant chicken bouillon
½   teaspoon salt
⅛   teaspoon pepper
1   tablespoon snipped parsley

Rinse corn under running cold water to separate; drain. Cook and stir almonds and garlic in margarine in 10-inch skillet over medium heat until almonds are golden, about 8 minutes. Add corn, wine, instant bouillon, salt and pepper. Heat to boiling, stirring occasionally; reduce heat. Cover and simmer until corn is tender, about 5 minutes. Sprinkle with snipped parsley.

6 servings (about ½ cup); 195 calories each.

☐ *Microwave Directions:* Place almonds, garlic and 1 teaspoon margarine in 1½-quart microwavable casserole. Microwave uncovered on high (100%), stirring every 30 seconds, until almonds are golden, 4 to 5 minutes. Stir in corn, 2 tablespoons wine, the bouillon, salt and pepper. Cover tightly and microwave 5 minutes; stir. Cover and microwave until done, 3 to 5 minutes longer. Sprinkle with parsley.

☆ ☆ ☆ ☆ ☆

SPICES AND HERBS
FOR TODAY'S COOKING

More spices and herbs are being consumed in the United States than ever before, reflecting today's cooking trends. Adding spices and herbs is an easy and economical way to add variety to foods.

Spices and herbs are naturally low in sodium, and can often replace some of the salt used when preparing foods. They also add flavor without adding calories. Try them in place of higher calorie toppings, such as butter, sour cream and rich sauces often used on vegetables. Keep in mind that seasonings should enhance the flavor of food, not overpower it.

Corn with Basil

5   ears corn*
1   medium onion, chopped (about 1/2 cup)
1/2   cup thinly sliced celery
1   clove garlic, finely chopped
2   tablespoons margarine or butter
1   jar (2 ounces) diced pimiento, drained
1/2   teaspoon salt
1   teaspoon snipped basil or 1/4 teaspoon dried
       basil leaves

Cut enough kernels from corn to measure 3 cups. Cook and stir corn, onion, celery and garlic in margarine in 3-quart saucepan over medium heat until onion is tender, about 10 minutes. Stir in remaining ingredients; reduce heat. Cover and cook until corn is tender, 3 to 5 minutes longer.

8 servings (about 1/2 cup); 95 calories each.

*2 packages (10 ounces each) frozen whole kernel corn can be substituted for the fresh corn. Rinse under running cold water to separate; drain.

☆ ☆ ☆ ☆ ☆

Eggplant Bake

1/2   cup dry bread crumbs
1/2   teaspoon dried marjoram leaves
1/2   teaspoon dried oregano leaves
1/2   teaspoon garlic salt
1   medium eggplant (about 1 1/2 pounds),
       cut crosswise into 1/2-inch slices
1/2   cup margarine or butter, melted
1   can (8 ounces) mushroom stems and
       pieces, drained
1   cup shredded Monterey Jack cheese
2   tablespoons grated Parmesan cheese

Mix crumbs, marjoram, oregano and garlic salt. Dip eggplant in margarine, then in crumb mixture. Place in single layer in greased jelly roll pan, 15 1/2 × 10 1/2 × 1 inch. Mix mushrooms and Monterey Jack cheese; spoon onto eggplant slices. Sprinkle with Parmesan cheese. Cook in 400° oven until eggplant is tender, 25 to 30 minutes.

6 servings (2 slices); 280 calories each.

☆ ☆ ☆ ☆ ☆

Corn with Basil

Stuffed Eggplant

1   small eggplant (about 1 pound)
1/4   cup chopped green pepper
2   tablespoons finely chopped onion
1   clove garlic, finely chopped
1/4   cup margarine or butter
1/2   cup crushed herb seasoned stuffing
1   jar (2 ounces) diced pimiento, drained
    Grated Parmesan cheese

Cut eggplant lengthwise into halves. Remove eggplant, leaving 1/2-inch shells. Cut eggplant into cubes. Cook and stir green pepper, onion and garlic in margarine in 10-inch skillet over medium heat until onion is tender, about 5 minutes. Stir in cubed eggplant. Cook and stir over medium heat until eggplant darkens, about 5 minutes longer. Stir in stuffing and pimiento. Fill eggplant halves with green pepper mixture; sprinkle with cheese. Cook uncovered in 350° oven until eggplant shell is tender, 30 to 35 minutes. To serve, cut each half crosswise into halves.

4 servings (about 1/3 cup); 160 calories each.

□ *Microwave Directions:* Cut eggplant as directed. Mix green pepper, onion, garlic and margarine in 1½-quart microwavable casserole. Cover tightly and microwave on high (100%) until onion is tender, 1 to 2 minutes. Stir in cubed eggplant. Cover and microwave until eggplant is crisp-tender, 1 to 2 minutes longer. Stir in stuffing and pimiento. Fill eggplant halves with green pepper mixture; sprinkle with cheese. Place on microwavable serving plate. Microwave uncovered until eggplant shell is tender and filling is hot, 4 to 6 minutes. Let stand 5 minutes.

☆ ☆ ☆ ☆ ☆

Steamed Vegetables

    Yogurt Sauce (below)
1/2   small cauliflower, separated into flowerets
2   medium zucchini, cut crosswise into
    1-inch slices
1   medium red or green pepper, cut into
    1/4-inch strips
1   lemon half

Prepare Yogurt Sauce. Place steamer basket in 1/2 inch water in saucepan or skillet (water should not touch bottom of basket). Place cauliflower, zucchini and red pepper in basket. Cover tightly and heat to boiling; reduce heat. Steam until vegetables are crisp-tender, about 6 minutes. Arrange vegetables on plate; squeeze lemon over vegetables. Serve with Yogurt Sauce.

Yogurt Sauce

3/4   cup plain yogurt
1   teaspoon honey
1/4   teaspoon salt
1/4   teaspoon dried basil leaves
1/4   teaspoon dried tarragon leaves
1   clove garlic, crushed
    Pinch of dried dill weed

Mix all ingredients. Cover and refrigerate at least 2 hours but no longer than 24 hours.

6 servings (about 1 cup vegetables and 2 tablespoons sauce); 70 calories each.

□ *Microwave Directions:* Place cauliflower, zucchini, red pepper, 1/4 cup water and 1/4 teaspoon salt in 2-quart microwavable casserole. Cover tightly and microwave on high (100%) 4 minutes; stir. Cover and microwave until crisp-tender, 3 to 5 minutes longer; drain. Continue as directed.

☆ ☆ ☆ ☆ ☆

Baked Whole Onions

Lettuce with Mushrooms

8	ounces mushrooms, sliced (about 3 cups)
1	small leek, thinly sliced
1	small clove garlic, finely chopped
2	tablespoons vegetable oil
1	tablespoon white wine vinegar
1/2	teaspoon salt
1/2	teaspoon dry mustard
1/8	teaspoon pepper
1	medium firm head lettuce (about 1 pound), coarsely shredded (about 6 cups)

Cook and stir mushrooms, leek and garlic in oil in 10-inch skillet over medium heat until mushrooms are tender. Stir in vinegar, salt, mustard and pepper. Add lettuce. Cover and simmer just until lettuce is wilted, about 5 minutes. Toss; serve immediately.

8 servings (about 1/2 cup); 50 calories each.

☆ ☆ ☆ ☆ ☆

Baked Whole Onions

6	medium onions (with skins)
2	small cloves garlic, finely chopped
1/4	cup margarine or butter
1/4	cup dry white wine
1/4	cup grated Parmesan cheese
2	tablespoons snipped parsley

Place onions directly on middle oven rack. Cook in 350° oven until onions are tender, 30 to 40 minutes. Remove skins; place onions upright in serving dish. Cut each onion into fourths about halfway through; separate slightly. Cook garlic in margarine over medium heat until garlic is golden brown. Remove from heat; stir in wine. Stir in cheese and parsley; pour immediately over onions.

6 servings; 135 calories each.

☆ ☆ ☆ ☆ ☆

Glazed Parsnips

2   pounds parsnips, cut crosswise into
        1/4-inch slices
2   tablespoons margarine or butter
1   tablespoon packed brown sugar
1/4 cup snipped parsley

Heat 1 inch salted water (1/2 teaspoon salt to 1 cup water) to boiling. Add parsnips. Cover and heat to boiling; reduce heat. Simmer until parsnips are tender, about 10 minutes; drain. Heat margarine over medium heat until melted; stir in brown sugar. Mix parsnips and brown sugar mixture until parsnips are coated; stir in parsley.

6 servings (about 1/2 cup); 150 calories each.

☐ *Microwave Directions:* Place parsnips, 1/4 cup water and 1/8 teaspoon salt in 1 1/2-quart microwavable casserole. Cover tightly and microwave on high (100%) 3 minutes; stir. Cover and microwave until tender, 3 to 5 minutes longer. Let stand 1 minute; drain. Place margarine in small microwavable bowl. Microwave uncovered until margarine is melted, about 15 seconds; stir in brown sugar. Continue as directed above.

☆ ☆ ☆ ☆ ☆

Peas with Parmesan

2   packages (10 ounces each) frozen green peas
1   tablespoon grated Parmesan cheese
1/8 teaspoon grated lemon peel
1   tablespoon lemon juice
1/2 teaspoon salt
1/8 teaspoon dried tarragon leaves

Cook peas as directed on package; drain. Toss with remaining ingredients. Serve with additional Parmesan cheese if desired.

6 servings (about 1/2 cup); 70 calories each.

☆ ☆ ☆ ☆ ☆

Peas in Curry Sauce

2   packages (10 ounces each) frozen green peas
2   slices bacon
1   medium onion, chopped (about 1/2 cup)
1   large clove garlic, finely chopped
1/4 cup finely chopped salted peanuts
1   teaspoon finely chopped gingerroot
2   teaspoons flour
1   teaspoon curry powder
1/4 teaspoon dry mustard
1/2 cup milk

Rinse peas under running cold water to separate; drain and reserve. Fry bacon in 10-inch skillet until crisp. Remove from skillet and drain; crumble and reserve. Cook and stir onion, garlic, peanuts and gingerroot in bacon fat over medium heat until onion is tender, about 5 minutes. Blend in flour, curry powder and mustard. Cook over low heat, stirring constantly, until mixture is bubbly; remove from heat. Stir in milk; add peas. Heat to boiling, stirring constantly; reduce heat. Cover and simmer, stirring occasionally, until peas are tender, about 5 minutes. Sprinkle with reserved bacon.

6 servings (about 1/2 cup); 140 calories each.

☆ ☆ ☆ ☆ ☆

USING WHEAT GERM

Wheat germ has a delicate, nutty flavor and can be used in a wide variety of recipes. Try it as a coating for Crunchy Zucchini Sticks (page 167) or sprinkled inside the pan for Vegetable Terrine (page 169). The part of the wheat kernel which would grow or germinate if planted is called the wheat germ. It is the most nutritious part of the wheat kernel or berry and provides protein, vitamins B_1 and B_2, iron and vitamin E. The wheat germ is removed from the kernel during milling and is lightly toasted before it is vacuum-packed. Because wheat germ is high in oil, it should be stored tightly covered in the refrigerator to help prevent rancidity.

Skillet Peppers

Sweet Potato Slices

Good source of vitamin A

> Coating Mix (below)
> 4   medium sweet potatoes (about 1½ pounds), each cut lengthwise into ¼-inch slices
> ¼   cup milk

Prepare Coating Mix. Dip potatoes in milk, then shake in Coating Mix. Place in single layer on rack in shallow roasting pan. Cook in 425° oven until tender, 30 to 35 minutes. Serve with cranberry sauce if desired.

Coating Mix

> 2   tablespoons yellow cornmeal
> 2   tablespoons whole wheat flour
> 1   teaspoon salt
> 1   teaspoon ground sage
> ½   teaspoon onion powder
> ½   teaspoon sugar
> ½   teaspoon paprika

Shake all ingredients in plastic bag.

4 servings (about 4 slices); 260 calories each.

☆ ☆ ☆ ☆ ☆

Baked Potato Wedges

> 2   tablespoons margarine or butter
> 2   large potatoes (about 1 pound)
> 1   egg
> ¾   teaspoon salt
>   Dash of pepper
> 2   tablespoons flour
> ½   teaspoon paprika
> ¼   cup finely shredded Gruyère cheese

Heat margarine in pie plate, 9 × 1¼ inches, in 400° oven until melted. Shred potatoes into bowl of cold water; drain. Mix potatoes, egg, salt and pepper; gradually mix in flour. Pack potato mixture firmly in pie plate; sprinkle with paprika and cheese. Cook uncovered until golden brown, about 40 minutes. Cut into 6 wedges.

6 servings (1 wedge); 120 calories each.

☆ ☆ ☆ ☆ ☆

Skillet Peppers

Good source of vitamin C

> 3   medium green or red peppers, cut into ¼-inch strips
> 1   medium onion, thinly sliced
> ¼   cup golden raisins
> 2   tablespoons olive oil or vegetable oil
> 2   tablespoons salted sunflower nuts
> 2   teaspoons lemon juice
> ½   teaspoon salt

Cook and stir green peppers, onion and raisins in oil in 10-inch skillet over medium heat until green peppers are tender, about 15 minutes. Stir in remaining ingredients.

4 servings (about ½ cup); 155 calories each.

□ *Microwave Directions:* Mix green peppers, onion, raisins and oil in 2-quart microwavable casserole. Cover tightly and microwave on high (100%) 3 minutes; stir. Cover and microwave until peppers are almost tender, 3 to 5 minutes longer. Continue as directed.

☆ ☆ ☆ ☆ ☆

Potato Planks

3   *medium potatoes, each cut lengthwise*
    into eighths
    Vegetable oil
1   *teaspoon salt*
½   *teaspoon sugar*
½   *teaspoon paprika*
¼   *teaspoon dry mustard*
⅛   *teaspoon garlic powder*

Set oven control to broil and/or 550°. Place potatoes, cut sides down, in ungreased jelly roll pan, 15½ × 10½ × 1 inch; brush with oil. Mix remaining ingredients; sprinkle potatoes with half of the mixture. Broil potatoes with tops about 3 inches from heat until potatoes begin to bubble slightly, about 10 minutes. Turn; brush with oil and sprinkle with remaining salt mixture. Broil until golden brown and tender, about 5 minutes longer. Serve with dairy sour cream if desired.

6 servings (4 wedges); 60 calories each.

☆ ☆ ☆ ☆ ☆

Potato Ring with Sprouts

2   *pounds potatoes (about 6 medium)*
1   *tablespoon prepared mustard*
½   *teaspoon salt*
⅛   *teaspoon pepper*
½   *cup shredded Cheddar cheese (about 2 ounces)*
    Margarine or butter, softened
2   *tablespoons wheat germ*
2   *packages (8 ounces each) frozen baby*
    Brussels sprouts
¼   *cup margarine or butter*
2   *teaspoons lemon juice*
½   *teaspoon salt*
1   *jar (2 ounces) diced pimiento, drained*

Heat 1 inch salted water (½ teaspoon salt to 1 cup water) to boiling. Add potatoes. Cover and heat to boiling; reduce heat. Simmer until tender, 20 to 25 minutes; drain. Mash potatoes until no lumps remain. Beat in mustard, ½ teaspoon salt and the pepper. Stir in cheese. Brush 4-cup ring mold with margarine; sprinkle with wheat germ. Press potato mixture in mold. Cook uncovered in 400° oven until golden brown, about 25 minutes.

Cook Brussels sprouts as directed on package; drain. Toss sprouts with ¼ cup margarine, the lemon juice, ½ teaspoon salt and the pimiento. Unmold potato ring onto serving plate. Fill center of ring with Brussels sprouts; place remaining sprouts around outside of ring.

8 servings (about ½ cup potatoes and ¼ cup Brussels sprouts); 180 calories each.

☆ ☆ ☆ ☆ ☆

Stuffed Potatoes

6   *large potatoes*
1   *carton (6 ounces) plain yogurt or ½ cup*
    dairy sour cream
¼   *cup milk*
¼   *cup chopped green onions (with tops)*
2   *tablespoons margarine or butter*
1   *teaspoon salt*
¼   *teaspoon dried dill weed*
⅛   *teaspoon pepper*
    Paprika

Prick potatoes with fork. Cook in 350° oven until tender, 1 to 1¼ hours. Cut thin lengthwise slice from each potato. Scoop out inside, leaving thin shell. Mash potatoes until no lumps remain. Beat in remaining ingredients except paprika until light and fluffy. Fill shells with potato mixture; sprinkle with paprika. Place on ungreased cookie sheet. Cook uncovered in 450° oven until hot, about 10 minutes.

6 potatoes; 110 calories each.

☐ *Microwave Directions:* Prick potatoes with fork. Arrange in circle in microwave. Microwave uncovered on high (100%) until tender, 15 to 18 minutes. Let stand 5 minutes. Continue as directed. Arrange filled potatoes in circle on 12-inch microwavable plate. Cover with waxed paper and microwave until hot, 3 to 5 minutes.

☆ ☆ ☆ ☆ ☆

Spaghetti Squash

Good source of vitamin A

1   spaghetti squash (about 1½ pounds)
1   medium onion, chopped (about ½ cup)
1   small green pepper, chopped (about ½ cup)
1   large clove garlic, finely chopped
2   tablespoons olive or vegetable oil
4   medium tomatoes, chopped (about 4 cups)
½   teaspoon salt
¼   teaspoon dried oregano leaves
¼   teaspoon dried basil leaves
¼   teaspoon fennel seed
⅛   teaspoon pepper
2   tablespoons margarine or butter
¼   cup grated Parmesan cheese

Prick squash with fork. Cook in 400° oven until tender, about 40 minutes. Cook and stir onion, green pepper and garlic in oil in 3-quart saucepan over medium heat until onion is tender, about 5 minutes. Stir in tomatoes, salt, oregano, basil, fennel and pepper. Simmer uncovered, stirring occasionally, 5 minutes. Cut squash into halves; remove seeds and fibrous strings. Remove squash strands with two forks; toss with margarine and cheese. Spoon tomato mixture over squash.

6 servings (about ⅔ cup); 150 calories each.

☐ *Microwave Directions:* Pierce squash in several places to allow steam to escape. Place squash on paper towel in microwave. Microwave on high (100%) 5 minutes; turn squash over. Microwave until tender, 4 to 6 minutes longer. Place onion, green pepper, garlic and oil in 1½-quart microwavable casserole. Cover tightly and microwave until onion is tender, 2 to 3 minutes. Stir in tomatoes, salt, oregano, basil, fennel and pepper. Cover and microwave until hot, 2 to 4 minutes longer. Continue as directed.

——————— ☆ ☆ ☆ ☆ ☆ ———————

Squash Casserole

3   pounds butternut squash, cut into cubes
     (about 8 cups)
1   package (8 ounces) Neufchâtel cheese, softened
¼   cup chopped green onions (with tops)
¾   teaspoon salt
¼   teaspoon pepper
¼   teaspoon ground nutmeg
¼   cup coarsely chopped pecans

Heat 1 inch salted water (½ teaspoon salt to 1 cup water) to boiling. Add squash. Cover and heat to boiling; reduce heat. Simmer until tender, 15 to 20 minutes; drain. Mash squash; stir in cheese, onions, salt, pepper and nutmeg until cheese is melted. Pour into ungreased 1½-quart casserole. Sprinkle with pecans. Cook in 350° oven until hot, about 30 minutes.

8 servings (about ½ cup); 130 calories each.

——————— ☆ ☆ ☆ ☆ ☆ ———————

Spinach with Nutmeg

Good source of vitamins A and C

2   tablespoons olive or vegetable oil
1½   pounds spinach (about 10 cups)
½   teaspoon salt
¼   teaspoon ground nutmeg
2   tablespoons salted sunflower nuts

Place oil in Dutch oven; add spinach. Cover and cook over medium heat 5 minutes. Cook and stir until spinach is wilted, about 5 minutes longer. Stir in salt and nutmeg. Sprinkle with sunflower nuts.

5 servings (about ½ cup); 110 calories each.

——————— ☆ ☆ ☆ ☆ ☆ ———————

Spinach Strudel

Good source of vitamin A

2 pounds spinach (about 13 cups)*
6 slices bacon
1 medium onion, chopped (about ½ cup)
1 large clove garlic, finely chopped
1 can (8 ounces) water chestnuts, drained
      and chopped
1 tablespoon lemon juice
1 teaspoon salt
½ teaspoon prepared horseradish
6 frozen phyllo sheets, thawed
¼ cup margarine or butter, melted
1 teaspoon sesame seed

Wash spinach; drain. Cover and cook half of the spinach with just the water that clings to leaves in Dutch oven over medium heat until wilted, about 3 minutes. Repeat with remaining spinach. Fry bacon in 10-inch skillet until crisp. Remove from skillet and drain; crumble and reserve. Pour off all but 1 tablespoon bacon fat. Cook and stir onion and garlic in bacon fat until onion is tender, about 5 minutes. Stir reserved bacon, water chestnuts, lemon juice, salt and horseradish into onion mixture. Mix with spinach.

Unfold phyllo sheets; carefully separate 1 phyllo sheet and place on ungreased cookie sheet. Cover remaining sheets with damp towel to prevent them from drying out. Brush phyllo sheet with margarine. Layer remaining sheets, brushing each sheet with margarine. Spread spinach mixture within 2 inches of each edge; fold 2-inch edges on long sides over filling. Roll up, beginning at a narrow end. Move to center of cookie sheet, placing seam side down. Brush with margarine; sprinkle with sesame seed. Bake in 375° oven until light brown, about 45 minutes. Cut into about 1-inch slices.

8 servings (1 slice); 200 calories each.

*2 packages (10 ounces each) frozen spinach can be substituted for the fresh spinach. Thaw and drain thoroughly.

☆ ☆ ☆ ☆ ☆

Spinach Strudel

Rolling Spinach Strudel

Fold 2-inch edge on long sides over filling. Roll up, beginning at a narrow edge.

Tomatoes and Artichokes

Good source of vitamin C

½ cup coarsely chopped walnuts
2 tablespoons grated Parmesan cheese
½ teaspoon salt
⅛ teaspoon pepper
2 tablespoons olive oil
1 can (14 ounces) artichoke hearts, drained and
   cut into halves
1 pint cherry tomatoes
¼ cup snipped parsley

Cook and stir walnuts, cheese, salt and pepper in oil in 10-inch skillet over medium heat until nuts are coated and golden brown, about 5 minutes. Add artichokes and tomatoes. Cook, stirring constantly, just until vegetables are hot, about 3 minutes. Stir in parsley.

6 servings (about ⅔ cup); 175 calories each.

☆ ☆ ☆ ☆ ☆

Corn-Filled Tomatoes

Good source of vitamin A

8 medium tomatoes
1 package (12 ounces) frozen corn
      soufflé, thawed
4 slices bacon, crisply fried and crumbled
¼ cup dry bread crumbs
2 tablespoons chopped green onions (with tops)

Remove stem ends from tomatoes. Scoop out pulp, leaving ½-inch walls. Place tomatoes in pie plate, 9 × 1¼ inches. Mix remaining ingredients. Fill tomatoes with corn mixture. Cook uncovered in 350° oven until filling is hot, 20 to 25 minutes.

8 servings (1 tomato); 145 calories each.

☆ ☆ ☆ ☆ ☆

Tomatoes and Artichokes, Turnips with Cheese, and Corn-Filled Tomatoes

Turnips with Cheese

Good source of vitamin A

1   pound turnips (about 3 medium), cut into
        2 × ½ × ½-inch strips
2   medium stalks celery, thinly sliced (about 1 cup)
1   medium onion, sliced
    Dash of pepper
½   cup shredded Cheddar cheese (about 2 ounces)

Heat 1 inch salted water (½ teaspoon salt to 1 cup water) to boiling. Add turnips, celery, onion and pepper. Cover and heat to boiling; reduce heat. Simmer until turnips are tender, about 20 minutes; drain. Toss vegetables with cheese just until mixed.

6 servings (about ½ cup); 65 calories each.

☆ ☆ ☆ ☆ ☆

Crunchy Zucchini Sticks

3   medium zucchini
½   cup wheat germ
½   cup finely chopped almonds
¼   cup grated Parmesan cheese
½   teaspoon salt
¼   cup margarine or butter, melted

Cut each zucchini lengthwise into fourths, then crosswise into halves to form sticks. Cut each stick lengthwise into halves. (Each zucchini makes 16 sticks.) Mix wheat germ, almonds, cheese and salt in plastic bag. Roll about 8 zucchini sticks at a time in margarine until evenly coated. Lift with fork, allowing excess margarine to drip off. Shake sticks in wheat germ mixture until evenly coated. Place in single layer on ungreased cookie sheet. Repeat with remaining sticks. Cook in 350° oven until crisp-tender, about 15 minutes.

6 servings (8 sticks); 205 calories each.

☆ ☆ ☆ ☆ ☆

Vegetable Terrine, and Cornish Hens with Glazed Oranges (page 76)

Preparing Pan

Line bottom and end sides of pan with foil; sprinkle with wheat germ. Layer vegetables in pan.

Broiling Green Pepper

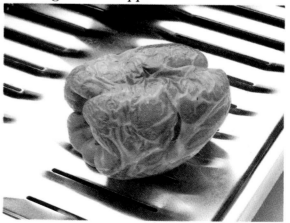

Broil green pepper about 5 inches from heat until skin blisters and brown spots appear.

Vegetable Terrine

Good source of vitamin A and riboflavin

½	medium head green cabbage (about 1 pound), coarsely shredded
2	teaspoons salt
½	teaspoon pepper
1	pound spinach
6	medium carrots, coarsely shredded (about 4 cups)
1	large onion, cut into ¼-inch slices
	Herbed Sauce (below)
2	tablespoons lemon juice
	Margarine or butter, softened
¼	cup wheat germ
1	medium green pepper

Heat ½ inch salted water (½ teaspoon salt to 1 cup water) to boiling. Add cabbage. Cover and heat to boiling; reduce heat. Simmer until crisp-tender, about 5 minutes. (Do not drain water.) Transfer cabbage to salad spinner or strainer with slotted spoon. Rinse under running cold water; spin dry or press against strainer with back of spoon to remove excess moisture. Place cabbage in 1½-quart bowl; sprinkle with ½ teaspoon of the salt and ⅛ teaspoon of the pepper.

Add spinach to reserved water. Cover and heat to boiling; reduce heat. Simmer until wilted, about 3 minutes. Transfer to salad spinner or strainer with slotted spoon. Rinse under running cold water; spin dry or press against strainer with back of spoon. Place in 1½-quart bowl; sprinkle with ½ teaspoon of the salt and ⅛ teaspoon of the pepper.

Place carrots in 1½-quart bowl; sprinkle with ½ teaspoon of the salt and ⅛ teaspoon of the pepper. Place onion in 1½-quart bowl; sprinkle with remaining salt and pepper.

Prepare Herbed Sauce; divide in half. Stir lemon juice into one half; cover and refrigerate. Stir ¼ of the remaining sauce (about ⅓ cup) into each of the 4 vegetables.

Generously grease bottom and sides of loaf pan, 9 × 5 × 3 inches, with margarine. Line bottom and end sides with aluminum foil; grease foil and sprinkle with wheat germ. Layer onion, carrots, spinach and cabbage in pan. Cook uncovered in 400° oven until golden brown, about 50 minutes. Let stand 10 minutes; unmold onto serving plate. Carefully remove foil.

Set oven control to broil and/or 550°. Place green pepper on rack in broiler pan. Broil pepper with top 4 to 5 inches from heat until skin blisters and browns, turning frequently, about 5 minutes on each side. Wrap in towel; let stand 5 minutes. Heat refrigerated Herbed Sauce just to boiling; keep warm. Remove skin, stem, seeds and membrane from pepper. Place pepper in blender container. Cover and blend on medium speed until smooth, about 10 seconds; stir into Herbed Sauce. Cut terrine into about 1-inch slices; serve with Herbed Sauce.

Herbed Sauce

⅓	cup margarine or butter
⅓	cup all-purpose flour
1	tablespoon snipped chives
1	teaspoon salt
1	teaspoon dry mustard
1	teaspoon dried tarragon leaves
1	teaspoon dried savory leaves
⅛	teaspoon pepper
3	cups milk
3	eggs

Heat margarine in 2-quart saucepan over low heat until melted. Blend in flour, chives, salt, mustard, tarragon, savory and pepper. Cook over low heat, stirring constantly, until smooth and bubbly; remove from heat. Stir in milk. Heat to boiling, stirring constantly. Boil and stir 1 minute. Stir at least half of the hot mixture gradually into eggs. Blend into hot mixture in saucepan.

8 servings (1 slice); 280 calories each.

☐ *Food Processor Directions:* Place green pepper in workbowl fitted with steel blade. Cover and process until smooth, about 5 seconds.

☆ ☆ ☆ ☆ ☆

Nutrition Information Per Serving or Unit

Recipe and Page Number	Protein	Carbo-hydrates	Fat	Sodium	Potas-sium	Protein	Calcium	Iron
		Grams		Milligrams		Percent U.S. Recommended Daily Allowance		
Artichokes with Curried Hollandaise Sauce, 148	5	13	26	320	400	8	8	10
Asparagus with Bacon, 148	6	9	2	175	435	10	6	8
Baked Potato Wedges, 162	4	13	6	345	240	6	4	4
Baked Whole Onions, 160	3	11	9	170	205	6	8	4
Broccoli with Garlic Mayonnaise, 151	4	7	15	120	450	6	12	8
Broccoli with Herbed Mushrooms, 151	5	8	2	110	545	8	12	8
Brussels Sprouts with Carrots, 152	5	11	9	280	455	6	6	6
Cabbage-Rice Casserole, 154	8	21	8	575	340	12	22	6
Cabbage Wedges, 152	1	7	2	130	180	0	4	2
Carrots with Coconut, 155	2	16	5	480	525	2	6	6
Carrots with Fennel*, 155	1	9	4	590	290	2	4	4
Corn Amandine, 157	5	21	10	340	275	8	4	8
Corn with Basil, 158	2	15	3	180	175	4	0	4
Corn-Filled Tomatoes, 166	5	18	6	320	410	8	2	6
Crunchy Zucchini Sticks, 167	7	11	15	340	420	10	12	10
Eggplant Bake, 158	8	13	22	560	205	12	20	8
Glazed Parsnips, 161	2	25	5	60	600	4	8	6
Green Beans Piquant, 149	1	5	3	310	145	2	4	4
Honeyed Beets, 150	1	9	3	215	105	0	*0	2
Lettuce with Mushrooms, 160	1	3	4	145	200	2	0	2
Mixed Vegetables, 150	4	10	4	455	335	6	2	8
Peas in Curry Sauce, 161	8	16	5	170	240	12	6	12
Peas with Parmesan, 161	5	11	1	305	135	8	2	10
Potato Planks, 163	1	9	2	365	180	2	0	2
Potato Ring with Sprouts, 163	6	19	9	430	460	10	8	8
Savory Carrot Casserole, 154	2	10	7	350	330	2	4	4

Nutrition Information Per Serving or Unit

Recipe and Page Number	Protein	Carbo-hydrates	Fat	Sodium	Potas-sium	Protein	Calcium	Iron
		Grams			Milligrams	Percent U.S. Recommended Daily Allowance		
Sesame Green Beans, 149	2	6	3	295	165	4	4	4
Skillet Peppers, 162	3	16	9	295	405	4	2	10
Spaghetti Squash, 164	4	12	10	300	515	6	10	8
Spinach with Nutmeg, 164	5	7	7	315	675	8	14	24
Spinach Strudel, 165	8	22	9	485	715	12	12	24
Squash Casserole, 164	5	7	9	320	315	8	8	6
Steamed Vegetables, 159	4	11	1	115	480	6	8	8
Stuffed Eggplant, 159	3	10	12	235	215	4	4	6
Stuffed Potatoes, 163	3	13	5	430	290	4	6	2
Sweet Potato Slices, 162	5	55	2	630	505	8	12	10
Tomatoes and Artichokes, 166	4	15	11	215	195	6	6	16
Tri-Colored Cauliflower, 157	5	10	6	345	430	8	10	8
Turnips with Cheese, 167	4	5	3	100	210	8	22	6
Vegetable Terrine, 169	11	23	16	1075	850	18	24	22

*Complete nutrition information not available.

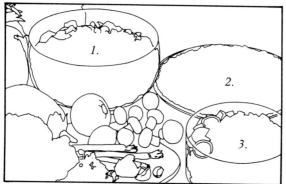

1. Elegant Tossed Salad, 2. Pineapple-Tomato Salad,
3. Ratatouille Salad

Citrus-Radish Salad

Good source of vitamin C

6   medium radishes, thinly sliced
2   grapefruit, pared, sectioned and cut into halves
2   medium oranges, pared and sectioned
1   small onion, thinly sliced and separated
        into rings
     Lemon Dressing (below)
     Lettuce leaves

Mix radishes, grapefruit, oranges and onion. Prepare Lemon Dressing; pour over fruit mixture. Cover and refrigerate, stirring occasionally, at least 1 hour. Remove fruit with slotted spoon. Serve on lettuce leaves.

Lemon Dressing

1/4   cup water
2   tablespoons sugar
1   tablespoon lemon juice
1/8   teaspoon salt
1/8   teaspoon paprika

Shake all ingredients in tightly covered jar.

6 servings (about 1/2 cup); 60 calories each.

☆ ☆ ☆ ☆ ☆

Apple-Pear Salad

2   medium apples, sliced
2   medium pears, sliced
1   medium stalk celery, diagonally sliced
        (about 1/2 cup)
2   tablespoons lemon juice
1   tablespoon honey
1/4 teaspoon salt
1/4 teaspoon pumpkin pie spice
     Lettuce leaves

Mix apples, pears and celery. Shake lemon juice, honey, salt and pumpkin pie spice in tightly covered container. Pour over apple mixture; toss until evenly coated. Cover and refrigerate at least 1 hour. Arrange apple mixture on lettuce leaves.

8 servings (about 2/3 cup); 55 calories each.

☆ ☆ ☆ ☆ ☆

Fresh Fruit Salad

Good source of vitamin C

     Lime Dressing (below)
3   medium peaches, sliced
2   medium bananas, sliced
1   cup raspberries or blueberries

Prepare Lime Dressing. Mix remaining ingredients. Toss with dressing until evenly coated. Serve on salad greens if desired.

Lime Dressing

3   tablespoons lime juice
3   tablespoons honey
2   tablespoons vegetable oil
1/2 teaspoon poppy seed

Shake all ingredients in tightly covered container. Refrigerate at least 1 hour. Shake before using.

6 servings (about 2/3 cup); 150 calories each.

☆ ☆ ☆ ☆ ☆

Avocado-Papaya Salad

Good source of vitamins A and C

    Lime-Sesame Dressing (below)
1   *large avocado*
1   *lime, cut into halves*
1   *large papaya*
    Lettuce leaves
5   *lime wedges*

Prepare Lime-Sesame Dressing. Cut avocado lengthwise into halves; remove pit and skin. Cut each half lengthwise into 4 slices. Squeeze juice from one lime half over avocado. Pare papaya; cut lengthwise into halves. Remove seeds; cut each half lengthwise into 4 slices. Squeeze juice from remaining lime half over papaya. Arrange avocado and papaya on lettuce leaves; drizzle with Lime-Sesame Dressing. Garnish with lime wedges.

Lime-Sesame Dressing

⅓   *cup vegetable oil*
2   *tablespoons lime juice*
1   *tablespoon honey*
1   *clove garlic, crushed*
½   *teaspoon salt*
2   *tablespoons sesame seed*

Shake oil, lime juice, honey, garlic and salt in tightly covered container. Refrigerate at least 1 hour. Cook and stir sesame seed over medium heat until golden brown; cool. Add sesame seed to dressing; shake.

5 servings (about 3 slices); 290 calories each.

☆ ☆ ☆ ☆ ☆

Avocado-Papaya Salad

Winter Fruit Salad

Almond Dressing (below)
1 *bunch Bibb lettuce, separated*
2 *oranges, pared and sectioned*
2 *medium pears, cut into ¾-inch pieces*
1 *avocado, cut into ¾-inch pieces*
1 *small onion, thinly sliced and separated into rings*
1 *medium apple, cut into thin wedges*

Prepare Almond Dressing. Arrange Bibb lettuce leaves on plate or in shallow bowl. Toss oranges, pears, avocado and onion with Almond Dressing until evenly coated. Spoon fruit mixture in center of lettuce. Arrange apple wedges around fruit mixture. Garnish with whole toasted almonds if desired.

Almond Dressing

2 *tablespoons finely chopped toasted almonds*
2 *tablespoons orange juice*
2 *tablespoons vegetable oil*
1 *teaspoon lemon juice*
⅛ *teaspoon salt*
⅛ *teaspoon paprika*

Shake all ingredients in tightly covered container. Refrigerate at least 1 hour.

8 servings (about ⅔ cup); 150 calories each.

☆ ☆ ☆ ☆ ☆

Pineapple-Tomato Salad

Good source of vitamin C

Curry Dressing (below)
1 *small pineapple*
2 *medium tomatoes, cut into ¼-inch slices*
2 *cups alfalfa sprouts*

Prepare Curry Dressing. Pare pineapple; cut lengthwise into halves. Remove core; cut pineapple crosswise into ⅜-inch slices. Pour Curry Dressing evenly over pineapple and tomato slices. Cover and refrigerate at least 2 hours. Remove pineapple and tomatoes with slotted spoon; arrange on alfalfa sprouts.

Curry Dressing

1 *teaspoon curry powder*
½ *teaspoon paprika*
1 *tablespoon vegetable oil*
⅓ *cup vegetable oil*
¼ *cup lemon juice*
2 *tablespoons chopped green onions (with tops)*
1 *teaspoon honey*
½ *teaspoon salt*
¼ *teaspoon ground mace*

Cook and stir curry powder and paprika in 1 tablespoon oil until deep brown. Shake curry powder mixture and the remaining ingredients in tightly covered container.

6 servings; 105 calories each.

☆ ☆ ☆ ☆ ☆

KIWI FRUIT AND PAPAYA — NEWLY POPULAR

Two once exotic fruits, now grown in the United States, are kiwi fruit and papaya. Both are low in calories and high in vitamin C. Because they contain an enzyme that breaks down protein, neither fruit can be used in gelatin mixtures since the enzyme prevents them from thickening. They can be prepared ahead since neither fruit discolors on standing.

The fuzzy brown skin of the kiwi fruit encases lime green flesh with tiny, edible black seeds. The flavor of kiwi fruit resembles a combination of strawberry and melon. If it is firm, let ripen at room temperature for a day or two, then refrigerate. To serve, cut in half and eat with spoon or pare and slice the fruit.

Papaya has a firm, smooth skin that turns a rich golden color as the fruit ripens. Its texture is like that of melon with the sweet flavor of peach. Ripen papaya at room temperature, then refrigerate. To serve, cut papaya in half, remove the black seeds with a spoon and eat the fruit directly from the shell like a melon with a lime wedge; or pare and slice, dice or cut the fruit into pieces.

Cantaloupe Salads

Good source of vitamins A and C

2   small cantaloupe
1   cup sliced strawberries
1   cup seedless green grapes
    Lettuce leaves
½   cup dairy sour cream
¼   cup mayonnaise or salad dressing
2   tablespoons packed brown sugar
¼   cup chopped nuts

Pare each cantaloupe. Cut off about 1 inch from ends of each cantaloupe. Cut up end pieces; mix with strawberries and grapes. Remove seeds from cantaloupe. Cut each cantaloupe into 3 even rings. Place rings on lettuce leaves on each of 6 plates; cut each ring into 1-inch pieces, retaining shape of ring. Spoon mixed fruit onto each ring. Mix sour cream, mayonnaise and brown sugar until sugar is dissolved and mixture is smooth. Stir in nuts. Spoon sour cream mixture on each salad.

6 servings (1 cantaloupe ring and ½ cup fruit); 245 calories each.

☆ ☆ ☆ ☆ ☆

Plum-Celery Salad

2   medium stalks celery, diagonally sliced
        (about 1 cup)
¼   cup vegetable oil
2   tablespoons vinegar
½   teaspoon salt
¼   teaspoon dry mustard
6   plums, thinly sliced (about 2 cups)
2   cups watercress
¼   cup toasted slivered almonds
⅓   cup mayonnaise or salad dressing

Heat 1 inch salted water (½ teaspoon salt to 1 cup water) to boiling. Add celery. Cover and heat to boiling; reduce heat. Simmer until crisp-tender, about 3 minutes. Rinse immediately under running cold water; drain. Shake oil, vinegar, salt and mustard in tightly covered container; pour over celery. Cover and refrigerate at least 2 hours, stirring occasionally; drain. Mix celery, plums, watercress and almonds. Toss celery mixture with mayonnaise until evenly coated.

6 servings (about ¾ cup); 160 calories each.

☆ ☆ ☆ ☆ ☆

Pears in Lime Dressing

Cabbage with Fruit

Good source of vitamin C

2   cups finely shredded green cabbage
       (about 1 small head)
1   can (8 ounces) crushed pineapple in juice,
       drained
2   medium apples, chopped (about 2 cups)
1   cup seedless red or green grapes
1   cup plain yogurt
1/3 cup mayonnaise or salad dressing
1   tablespoon packed brown sugar
1/4 teaspoon salt

Mix cabbage, pineapple, apples and grapes.
Mix remaining ingredients; toss with cabbage
mixture until evenly coated.

6 servings (about 3/4 cup); 200 calories each.

☆ ☆ ☆ ☆ ☆

Pears in Lime Dressing

1/4 cup lime juice
1   tablespoon snipped mint leaves
3   tablespoons vegetable oil
2   tablespoons honey
1   teaspoon finely shredded lime peel
3   large pears
     Bibb lettuce leaves

Mix lime juice and mint. Let stand at room
temperature at least 1 hour. Remove mint and
discard. Shake lime juice, oil, honey and lime
peel in tightly covered container. Cut each
pear lengthwise into halves; remove core and
seeds. Place each pear half, cut side down, on
cutting surface. Cut crosswise diagonally into
thin slices. With spatula, place each pear half
on lettuce leaves; separate and overlap slices
slightly, retaining pear shape. Drizzle lime
juice mixture over pears. Garnish with mint
leaves if desired.

6 servings (1/2 pear); 145 calories each.

☆ ☆ ☆ ☆ ☆

Chili Slaw

Good source of vitamin C

1/2 cup mayonnaise or salad dressing
1/4 cup dairy sour cream
3   tablespoons snipped parsley
2   tablespoons chopped onion
2   tablespoons lemon juice
1/2 teaspoon salt
     Dash of pepper
3   cups finely shredded green cabbage
       (about 1 small head)
1   can (4 ounces) chopped green chilies, drained
3   slices bacon, crisply fried and crumbled

Mix mayonnaise, sour cream, parsley, onion,
lemon juice, salt and pepper. Toss with cabbage and chilies until evenly coated. Sprinkle
with bacon.

5 servings (about 1/2 cup); 235 calories each.

☆ ☆ ☆ ☆ ☆

Confetti Slaw

Good source of vitamin C

    Cumin Dressing (below)
3   *cups chopped red cabbage (about 1 small head)*
1   *medium tomato, chopped (about 1 cup)*
1/3 *cup sliced pimiento-stuffed olives*
1/4 *cup chopped onion*
1/4 *cup crumbled feta cheese*
1   *tablespoon snipped coriander (cilantro)*

Prepare Cumin Dressing. Mix remaining ingredients. Pour Cumin Dressing over mixture; toss until evenly coated.

Cumin Dressing

1/4 *cup vegetable oil*
2   *tablespoons tarragon or wine vinegar*
3/4 *teaspoon salt*
1/2 *teaspoon ground cumin*
    Dash of pepper
1   *small clove garlic, crushed*

Shake all ingredients in tightly covered jar.

7 servings (about 1/2 cup); 125 calories each.

☆ ☆ ☆ ☆ ☆

Vegetable-Raisin Toss

Good source of vitamin A

2   *medium carrots, finely shredded (about 1 cup)*
1   *cup finely shredded green cabbage*
3   *tablespoons raisins*
1   *tablespoon finely chopped green pepper*
1   *tablespoon finely chopped onion*
1/2 *teaspoon prepared horseradish*
1/8 *teaspoon salt*
2   *tablespoons mayonnaise or salad dressing*

Mix all ingredients except mayonnaise. Toss with mayonnaise until evenly coated. Spoon into lettuce cups if desired.

4 servings (about 1/3 cup); 95 calories each.

☆ ☆ ☆ ☆ ☆

Cauliflower-Grape Salad

1   *small head cauliflower (about 1 1/2 pounds),
    separated into flowerets*
1/2 *teaspoon salt*
1   *cup seedless green grapes or Tokay grapes,
    halved and seeded*
2   *medium stalks celery, diagonally sliced
    (about 1 cup)*
2   *tablespoons sliced green onions (with tops)*
1   *tablespoon snipped parsley*
1   *tablespoon sugar*
2   *tablespoons vegetable oil*
1   *tablespoon vinegar*
1/2 *teaspoon salt*
    Dash of pepper
    Dash of red pepper sauce
    Sugared Almonds (below)

Place steamer basket in 1/2 inch water in saucepan or skillet (water should not touch bottom of basket). Place cauliflower in basket. Cover tightly and heat to boiling; reduce heat. Steam until crisp-tender, about 6 minutes. Immediately rinse under running cold water; drain. Place cauliflower in 2-quart bowl. Sprinkle with 1/2 teaspoon salt; stir. Add grapes and celery. Shake green onions, parsley, sugar, oil, vinegar, 1/2 teaspoon salt, the pepper and pepper sauce in tightly covered container. Pour over cauliflower, grapes and celery; toss until evenly coated. Cover and refrigerate, stirring occasionally, at least 4 hours. Prepare Sugared Almonds. Just before serving, toss almonds with cauliflower mixture.

Sugared Almonds

Cook 1/4 cup sliced almonds and 1 tablespoon plus 1 teaspoon sugar over low heat, stirring constantly, until sugar is caramelized and almonds are coated; cool and break apart. Store at room temperature.

6 servings (about 3/4 cup); 155 calories each.

☆ ☆ ☆ ☆ ☆

Oriental Salad

2   cups bean sprouts
     Sesame Dressing (below)
1   tablespoon vegetable oil
1   egg, beaten
1   cup sliced mushrooms
1   package (6 ounces) frozen pea pods, thawed
1/2 cup sliced water chestnuts
1   medium stalk celery, diagonally sliced
        (about 1/2 cup)
1/4 cup sliced green onions (with tops)

Cover bean sprouts with cold water. Let stand 10 minutes; drain. Prepare Sesame Dressing. Heat oil in 10-inch skillet over medium heat until hot; add egg. Cook egg, turning once, until firm, about 10 seconds (do not stir). Cut egg into thin strips. Mix bean sprouts, mushrooms, pea pods, water chestnuts, celery and onions. Toss dressing with vegetable mixture until evenly coated. Sprinkle with egg strips.

Sesame Dressing

1   tablespoon sesame seed
1/4 cup chili sauce
2   tablespoons vegetable oil
1   tablespoon wine vinegar
2   teaspoons soy sauce
1   clove garlic, crushed

Cook and stir sesame seed over medium heat until golden brown. Shake sesame seed and remaining ingredients in tightly covered jar.

8 servings (about 3/4 cup); 125 calories each.

━━━━━━ ☆ ☆ ☆ ☆ ☆ ━━━━━━

Artichoke-Asparagus Salad

1   package (6 ounces) frozen artichoke hearts
     Lemon-Mustard Dressing (below)
1   can (15 ounces) white asparagus spears,
        drained and cut crosswise into halves
1   cup sliced mushrooms
     Boston lettuce
18   small pitted ripe olives

Cook artichoke hearts as directed on package; drain. Immediately rinse under running cold water; drain. Prepare Lemon-Mustard Dressing; pour over artichokes, asparagus and mushrooms. Cover and refrigerate at least 2 hours.

Remove vegetables with slotted spoon; reserve Lemon-Mustard Dressing. Arrange vegetables on lettuce on each of 6 plates. Garnish with ripe olives. Serve with remaining Lemon-Mustard Dressing.

Lemon-Mustard Dressing

1/2 cup olive or vegetable oil
1/4 cup lemon juice
2   tablespoons snipped chives
1   tablespoon Dijon-style mustard
1/2 teaspoon salt
1/2 teaspoon grated lemon peel

Shake all ingredients in tightly covered jar.

6 servings (about 3/4 cup); 225 calories each.

━━━━━━ ☆ ☆ ☆ ☆ ☆ ━━━━━━

Artichoke-Asparagus Salad

Hot Avocado Salad

3   slices bacon
1   medium onion, sliced
1/4   cup vinegar
2   teaspoons sugar
1/2   teaspoon salt
4   to 6 drops red pepper sauce
2   medium tomatoes, chopped (about 2 cups)
2   medium avocados, chopped (about 2 cups)
1   tablespoon snipped coriander (cilantro),
        if desired

Fry bacon in 10-inch skillet over medium heat until crisp. Remove from skillet and drain; crumble and reserve. Cook and stir onion in bacon fat until tender, about 5 minutes. Stir in vinegar, sugar, salt and pepper sauce; heat to boiling. Pour over tomatoes, avocados and coriander; toss until evenly coated. Sprinkle with reserved bacon.

6 servings (about 1/2 cup); 195 calories each.

═══════ ☆ ☆ ☆ ☆ ☆ ═══════

Hot Avocado Salad

Zucchini-Apricot Salad

1/3   cup cut-up dried apricots
1/2   cup water
3   tablespoons vegetable oil
2   tablespoons lemon juice
1/2   teaspoon salt
1/8   teaspoon dry mustard
1/8   teaspoon paprika
    Dash of red pepper sauce
2   medium zucchini, thinly sliced (about 3 cups)
    Lettuce leaves
    Roasted salted pumpkin seeds

Heat apricots and water to boiling; remove from heat. Cover and let stand 15 minutes; drain. Shake oil, lemon juice, salt, mustard, paprika and pepper sauce in tightly covered container. Pour over apricots and zucchini; toss until evenly coated. Cover and refrigerate at least 2 hours. Serve on lettuce leaves; sprinkle with pumpkin seeds.

4 servings (about 1/2 cup); 110 calories each.

ZUCCHINI-RAISIN SALAD: Substitute 1/3 cup raisins for the apricots.

═══════ ☆ ☆ ☆ ☆ ☆ ═══════

Vegetable-Pasta Salad

2   cups cooked small macaroni shells
2   medium tomatoes, chopped (about 1 1/2 cups)
1   small leek, thinly sliced (about 1/2 cup)
1/2   cup sliced ripe olives
2   tablespoons capers
1/2   cup mayonnaise or salad dressing
1   tablespoon lemon juice
1/2   teaspoon dried basil leaves
1/2   teaspoon salt
1   large clove garlic, crushed
    Dash of red pepper sauce
2   cups shredded lettuce

Mix macaroni, tomatoes, leek, olives and capers. Stir together mayonnaise, lemon juice, basil, salt, garlic and pepper sauce; toss with macaroni mixture until evenly coated. Cover and refrigerate at least 2 hours. Just before serving, toss macaroni mixture with lettuce.

8 servings (about 3/4 cup); 170 calories each.

═══════ ☆ ☆ ☆ ☆ ☆ ═══════

Marinated Roasted Peppers

Good source of vitamin C

6	large red or green peppers
1/4	cup olive or vegetable oil
2	tablespoons snipped parsley
2	tablespoons lemon juice
2	tablespoons lime juice
1/2	teaspoon salt
1/4	teaspoon dried oregano leaves
1/4	teaspoon dried basil leaves
1/8	teaspoon pepper
1/8	teaspoon dried sage leaves
2	large cloves garlic, finely chopped

Set oven control to broil and/or 550°. Place red peppers on rack in broiler pan. Broil peppers with tops 4 to 5 inches from heat until skin blisters and browns, about 5 minutes on each side. Wrap in towels; let stand 5 minutes. Remove skin, stems, seeds and membrane from peppers; cut peppers into 1/4-inch slices. Shake remaining ingredients in tightly covered container; pour over peppers. Cover and refrigerate at least 4 hours, stirring occasionally.

8 servings (about 1/2 cup); 100 calories each.

☆ ☆ ☆ ☆ ☆

Marinated Asparagus

1 1/2	pounds asparagus*
1	teaspoon finely shredded orange peel
1/4	cup orange juice
1/4	cup vegetable oil
2	teaspoons lemon juice
1/4	teaspoon salt
	Dash of cayenne pepper

Place steamer basket in 1/2 inch water in saucepan or skillet (water should not touch bottom of basket). Place asparagus spears in basket. Cover tightly and heat to boiling; reduce heat. Steam until crisp-tender, 8 to 10 minutes. Immediately rinse under running cold water; drain. Shake remaining ingredients in tightly covered container; pour over asparagus. Cover and refrigerate at least 4 hours, turning asparagus occasionally; drain. Garnish with orange slices if desired.

4 servings (about 5 spears); 60 calories each.

*1 package (10 ounces) frozen asparagus spears can be substituted for the fresh asparagus. Cook as directed on package just until crisp-tender; drain. Immediately rinse under running cold water; drain. Continue as directed.

☆ ☆ ☆ ☆ ☆

Ratatouille Salad

1	small eggplant (about 1 pound), cut into 1/2-inch pieces
	Basil Dressing (below)
2	medium tomatoes, chopped (about 1 1/2 cups)
1	medium zucchini, thinly sliced
1	small onion, sliced and separated into rings
1	small green pepper, chopped (about 1/2 cup)
1/3	cup snipped parsley

Heat small amount salted water (1/2 teaspoon salt to 1 cup water) to boiling. Add eggplant. Cover and heat to boiling, reduce heat. Simmer just until tender, 5 to 8 minutes; drain and cool. Prepare Basil Dressing. Mix eggplant, tomatoes, zucchini, onion, green pepper and parsley. Pour Basil Dressing over vegetables; toss until evenly coated. Cover and refrigerate at least 4 hours. Serve on lettuce leaves if desired.

Basil Dressing

1/3	cup olive or vegetable oil
2	tablespoons lemon juice
1	teaspoon salt
1/2	teaspoon dried basil leaves
1/2	teaspoon dry mustard
1/8	teaspoon pepper

Shake all ingredients in tightly covered jar.

8 servings (about 1/2 cup); 110 calories each.

☆ ☆ ☆ ☆ ☆

Mushroom and Fennel Salad

Mushroom and Fennel Salad

¼ cup olive or vegetable oil
2 tablespoons white wine vinegar
½ teaspoon salt
⅛ teaspoon dried dill weed
2 large cloves garlic, crushed
2 cups thinly sliced fennel bulb
3 cups sliced mushrooms (about 8 ounces)
¼ cup sliced green onions (with tops)
   Bibb lettuce leaves

Shake oil, vinegar, salt, dill weed and garlic in tightly covered container. Pour over fennel, mushrooms and green onions; toss until evenly coated. Cover and refrigerate at least 2 hours. Serve on lettuce leaves. Sprinkle with freshly ground pepper if desired.

6 servings (about ½ cup); 95 calories each.

☆ ☆ ☆ ☆ ☆

Italian Potato Salad

Good source of vitamin C

2 pounds potatoes (about 6 medium)
1 jar (6 ounces) marinated artichoke hearts
1 small green pepper, chopped (about ½ cup)
1 small onion, chopped (about ¼ cup)
1 jar (2 ounces) diced pimiento, drained
¼ cup sliced ripe olives
3 tablespoons olive or vegetable oil
2 tablespoons vinegar
1 tablespoon snipped basil or ½ teaspoon dried basil leaves
1½ teaspoons salt
¼ teaspoon pepper

Heat 1 inch salted water (½ teaspoon salt to 1 cup water) to boiling. Add potatoes. Cover and heat to boiling; reduce heat. Simmer until tender, 30 to 35 minutes; drain and cool. Cut potatoes lengthwise into halves; cut crosswise into ¼-inch slices. Drain artichokes, reserving liquid. Cut artichokes into halves. Mix potatoes, artichokes, green pepper, onion, pimiento and olives. Shake reserved artichoke liquid, the oil, vinegar, basil, salt and pepper in tightly covered container; pour over vegetables. Toss until vegetables are evenly coated. Cover and refrigerate at least 2 hours. Garnish with anchovies and basil leaves if desired.

8 servings (about ¾ cup); 180 calories each.

☆ ☆ ☆ ☆ ☆

DISCOVER FENNEL

Fennel has the aroma and flavor of anise or licorice and is a favorite seasoning in Italian cooking. The whitish colored bulb and celerylike stalks can be used raw in salads or can be cooked and served as a vegetable or part of a main dish. The yellowish brown seeds give Italian sausage its characteristic taste and are an ingredient in many main dish, vegetable, salad and bread recipes. You can discover and experiment with fennel in these recipes: Carrots with Fennel (page 155), Mushroom and Fennel Salad (page 184) and Swordfish with Cucumber (page 14).

Bulgur-Tomato Salad

Good source of vitamin C

1	cup bulgur (cracked wheat)
2	medium tomatoes, chopped (about 1½ cups)
1	medium onion, chopped (about ½ cup)
½	cup finely snipped parsley
¼	cup finely chopped green pepper
2	tablespoons finely snipped mint leaves
¼	cup olive or vegetable oil
¼	cup lemon juice
1	teaspoon salt
⅛	teaspoon pepper
	Lettuce leaves

Cover bulgur with cold water. Let stand until bulgur is tender, about 1 hour; drain. Mix bulgur, tomatoes, onion, parsley, green pepper and mint. Sprinkle with oil, lemon juice, salt and pepper; stir until evenly coated. Cover and refrigerate at least 2 hours. Arrange lettuce leaves around bulgur mixture. Garnish with mint leaves if desired.

8 servings (about ½ cup); 155 calories each.

☆ ☆ ☆ ☆ ☆

Elegant Tossed Salad

Good source of vitamin A

	Mustard Dressing (below)
4	slices French bread, each ½ inch thick
2	large cloves garlic, cut lengthwise into halves
2	tablespoons olive or vegetable oil
4	ounces watercress (about 4 cups)
1½	cups sliced mushrooms (about 4 ounces)
1	medium leek, thinly sliced
½	head Boston lettuce, torn into bite-size pieces
½	small bunch romaine, torn into bite-size pieces

Prepare Mustard Dressing. Tear bread into ½-inch pieces. Cook and stir garlic in oil in 8-inch skillet over medium heat until garlic is deep golden brown; remove garlic and discard. Add bread to oil. Cook and stir until bread is golden brown and crusty; cool. Shake Mustard Dressing; toss with watercress, mushrooms, leek, lettuce and romaine. Sprinkle with bread.

Mustard Dressing

2	tablespoons olive or vegetable oil
1	tablespoon red wine vinegar
2	teaspoons grated Parmesan cheese
2	teaspoons Dijon-style mustard
¼	teaspoon salt

Shake all ingredients in tightly covered container. Refrigerate at least 1 hour.

8 servings (about 1¼ cups); 70 calories each.

☆ ☆ ☆ ☆ ☆

Blue Cheese Tossed Salad

Good source of vitamins A and C

	Blue Cheese Dressing (below)
4	cups bite-size salad greens
1½	cups sliced mushrooms (about 4 ounces)
½	cup sliced radishes

Prepare Blue Cheese Dressing. Toss salad greens, mushrooms and radishes; serve with Blue Cheese Dressing.

Blue Cheese Dressing

3	ounces Neufchâtel or cream cheese, softened
¼	cup crumbled blue cheese
¼	cup apple juice
2	tablespoons vegetable oil

Beat Neufchâtel cheese, blue cheese and apple juice on low speed until smooth, about 3 minutes. Gradually add oil on low speed; continue beating until blended.

6 servings (about 1 cup); 120 calories each.

☆ ☆ ☆ ☆ ☆

Mexican Tossed Salad

Good source of vitamin A

 Sour Cream Dressing (below)
1 small head lettuce, shredded (about 4 cups)
1 small jicama, chopped (about 2 cups)
1 small avocado, chopped (about 1 cup)
1 cup cherry tomato halves
1 small onion, chopped (about ¼ cup)
1 can (4 ounces) chopped green chilies, drained

Prepare Sour Cream Dressing. Mix remaining ingredients; toss with Sour Cream Dressing until evenly coated. Sprinkle with coarsely crushed tortilla chips if desired.

Sour Cream Dressing

⅓ cup dairy sour cream
⅓ cup mayonnaise or salad dressing
2 teaspoons lemon juice
½ teaspoon chili powder
¼ teaspoon ground cumin
1 large clove garlic, crushed

Stir together all ingredients until smooth.

5 servings (about 1½ cups); 235 calories each.

☆ ☆ ☆ ☆ ☆

Chinese Tossed Salad

Good source of vitamins A and C

 Vegetable oil
2 ounces cellophane noodles (bean threads)
 Ginger Dressing (below)
½ medium head lettuce, shredded (about 4½ cups)
2 medium carrots, shredded (about 1 cup)
1 small green pepper, chopped (about ½ cup)
⅓ cup sliced green onions (with tops)

Heat oil (1 inch) in Dutch oven or wok to 425°. Fry ¼ of the noodles at a time until puffed but not browned, turning once, about 5 seconds. Drain on paper towels. Prepare Ginger Dressing. Mix lettuce, carrots, green pepper, onions and about ¾ of the noodles. Pour Ginger Dressing over mixture; toss until vegetables are evenly coated. Break up remaining noodles slightly; sprinkle over salad.

Ginger Dressing

¼ cup vegetable oil
3 tablespoons white wine vinegar
2 teaspoons sugar
2 teaspoons soy sauce
¼ teaspoon pepper
¼ teaspoon ground ginger
1 clove garlic, crushed

Shake all ingredients in tightly covered jar.

6 servings (about 1⅓ cups); 130 calories each.

☆ ☆ ☆ ☆ ☆

Wilted Vegetable Salad

3 slices bacon
1 small onion, chopped (about ¼ cup)
1 small green pepper, chopped (about ½ cup)
1 clove garlic, crushed
¼ cup vinegar
1 teaspoon sugar
½ teaspoon salt
⅛ teaspoon pepper
1 can (about 8 ounces) whole kernel corn, drained
1 bunch leaf lettuce, torn into bite-size pieces
1 small yellow summer squash or zucchini, thinly sliced

Fry bacon in 10-inch skillet until crisp. Remove from skillet and drain; crumble and reserve. Stir onion, green pepper, garlic, vinegar, sugar, salt and pepper into bacon fat; heat to boiling. Pour over corn, lettuce and squash; toss until evenly coated. Sprinkle with reserved bacon.

8 servings (about 1¼ cups); 105 calories each.

☆ ☆ ☆ ☆ ☆

Molded Tangerine Salad

Molded Tangerine Salad

Good source of vitamin C

1   envelope unflavored gelatin
1   cup cold water
1   can (6 ounces) frozen tangerine juice
      concentrate, thawed
1   package (8 ounces) Neufchâtel or cream
      cheese, softened
1   can (8 ounces) crushed pineapple in juice,
      well drained
     Watercress
1   kiwi, sliced

Sprinkle gelatin on cold water in 1-quart saucepan to soften; heat over low heat, stirring constantly, until gelatin is dissolved. Remove from heat; stir in juice concentrate. Beat cheese in 2½-quart bowl on medium speed until fluffy. Gradually beat in gelatin mixture on low speed until smooth. Refrigerate until slightly thickened, about 1 hour. Stir in pineapple. Pour into 4-cup mold. Refrigerate until firm, about 2 hours. Unmold on serving plate. Garnish with watercress and kiwi.

6 servings (about ½ cup); 145 calories each.

MOLDED ORANGE SALAD: Substitute 1 can (6 ounces) frozen orange juice concentrate for the tangerine juice concentrate.

—————— ☆ ☆ ☆ ☆ ☆ ——————

Avocado Mold

Good source of vitamin C

1   envelope unflavored gelatin
1   cup cold water
1¼ cups mashed avocado (about 2 medium)
 ¼   cup mayonnaise or salad dressing
 ¼   cup plain yogurt
 ½   teaspoon grated lime or lemon peel
2   tablespoons lime or lemon juice
 ½   teaspoon salt
      Salad greens
2   medium tomatoes, each cut into 6 slices
1   tablespoon snipped chives

Sprinkle gelatin on cold water in 2-quart saucepan to soften; heat over low heat, stirring constantly, until gelatin is dissolved. Stir into avocado, mayonnaise, yogurt, lime peel, juice and salt. Beat with hand beater until smooth. Pour into 3-cup mold. Refrigerate until firm, at least 4 hours. Unmold on salad greens. Arrange tomato slices around mold; sprinkle tomatoes with chives.

6 servings (about ½ cup mold and 2 tomato slices); 90 calories each.

—————— ☆ ☆ ☆ ☆ ☆ ——————

Layered Vegetable Salad

Good source of vitamins A and C

Flavored Gelatin (below)
4 *medium carrots, cut crosswise into ¼-inch slices (about 2 cups)*
2 *cups small cauliflowerets*
1 *package (10 ounces) frozen green peas*

Prepare Flavored Gelatin. Place steamer basket in ½ inch water in saucepan or skillet (water should not touch bottom of basket). Place carrots in basket. Cover tightly and heat to boiling; reduce heat. Steam until crisp-tender, about 8 minutes. Immediately rinse under running cold water; drain. Place cauliflowerets in steamer basket. Cover tightly and heat to boiling; reduce heat. Steam until crisp-tender, about 6 minutes. Immediately rinse under running cold water; drain. Rinse peas under running cold water; drain.

Layer peas, cauliflowerets and carrots in 4-cup mold. Pour Flavored Gelatin over vegetables. Refrigerate until firm, at least 4 hours. Unmold on salad greens and serve with mayonnaise or salad dressing if desired.

Flavored Gelatin

1 *can (10¾ ounces) condensed chicken broth*
1 *cup water*
1 *small onion, cut into fourths*
½ *lemon, cut into wedges*
2 *cloves garlic, crushed*
½ *teaspoon salt*
   Dash of cayenne pepper
2 *envelopes unflavored gelatin*
½ *cup cold water*

Heat chicken broth, 1 cup water, the onion, lemon, garlic, salt and cayenne pepper to boiling; reduce heat. Cover and simmer 10 minutes; remove from heat. Let stand 10 minutes; strain. Sprinkle gelatin on ½ cup cold water to soften. Heat broth mixture just to boiling; stir in gelatin mixture just until gelatin is dissolved. Cool to room temperature.

8 servings (about ½ cup); 70 calories each.

══════════ ☆ ☆ ☆ ☆ ☆ ══════════

Layered Vegetable Salad

Gazpacho Salad

Good source of vitamin C

1 *can (16 ounces) whole tomatoes*
1 *medium green pepper, chopped (about 1 cup)*
1 *medium cucumber, seeded and chopped (about 1 cup)*
1 *medium onion, chopped (about ½ cup)*
2 *large cloves garlic, chopped*
2 *tablespoons lemon juice*
1 *teaspoon ground cumin*
½ *teaspoon salt*
2 *or 3 drops red pepper sauce*
2 *envelopes unflavored gelatin*
¼ *cup chilled cocktail vegetable juice*
1 *cup hot cocktail vegetable juice*
   Salad greens

Place tomatoes (with liquid), ¼ cup of the green pepper, ¼ cup of the cucumber, ¼ cup of the onion, the garlic, lemon juice, cumin, salt and pepper sauce in blender container. Cover and blend on medium speed until smooth, 10 to 15 seconds. Pour into 2-quart bowl. Sprinkle gelatin on ¼ cup vegetable juice to soften; stir in 1 cup vegetable juice until gelatin is dissolved. Stir gelatin mixture into vegetable mixture. Refrigerate until slightly thickened but not set. Stir in remaining green pepper, cucumber and onion. Pour into 4-cup mold. Refrigerate until firm, about 4 hours. Unmold on salad greens. Serve with dairy sour cream if desired.

8 servings (about ½ cup); 40 calories each.

☐ *Food Processor Directions:* Place tomatoes (with liquid), ¼ cup of the green pepper, ¼ cup of the cucumber, ¼ cup of the onion, the garlic, lemon juice, cumin, salt and pepper sauce in workbowl fitted with steel blade. Cover and process until smooth, about 10 seconds. Continue as directed.

══════════ ☆ ☆ ☆ ☆ ☆ ══════════

Nutrition Information Per Serving or Unit

Recipe and Page Number	Protein	Carbo-hydrates	Fat	Sodium	Potas-sium	Protein	Calcium	Iron
		Grams		Milligrams		Percent U.S. Recommended Daily Allowance		
Apple-Pear Salad, 174	1	13	0	75	145	0	0	2
Artichoke-Asparagus Salad, 180	3	6	21	430	285	4	4	8
Avocado Mold, 187	3	6	6	240	345	4	2	4
Avocado-Papaya Salad, 175	3	16	24	225	520	4	4	6
Blue Cheese Tossed Salad, 185	4	4	10	165	315	6	8	8
Bulgur-Tomato Salad,* 185	3	20	7	275	190	4	2	8
Cabbage with Fruit, 178	2	23	11	185	250	4	8	2
Cantaloupe Salads, 177	3	27	14	90	665	6	8	10
Cauliflower-Grape Salad, 179	4	17	8	405	505	8	6	10
Chili Slaw, 178	3	6	22	405	165	4	4	4
Chinese Tossed Salad, 186	1	7	11	130	205	2	2	4
Citrus-Radish Salad, 174	1	14	0	50	185	0	2	2
Confetti Slaw, 179	2	5	11	520	140	2	6	4
Elegant Tossed Salad, 185	2	7	4	50	220	2	2	4
Fresh Fruit Salad, 174	1	26	5	5	310	2	0	2
Gazpacho Salad, 189	3	7	0	295	335	4	2	6
Hot Avocado Salad, 182	3	8	17	225	395	4	2	4
Italian Potato Salad, 184	3	22	9	445	370	4	2	8
Layered Vegetable Salad, 189	6	10	1	395	340	10	4	8
Marinated Asparagus, 183	4	5	3	45	280	6	2	8
Marinated Roasted Peppers, 183	2	7	7	155	285	2	2	6
Mexican Tossed Salad,* 186	3	11	20	125	510	4	6	6
Molded Tangerine Salad, 187	5	11	9	155	165	8	4	2
Mushroom and Fennel Salad,* 184	1	3	9	190	250	2	2	6
Oriental Salad, 180	4	12	7	210	335	6	2	8
Pears in Lime Dressing,* 178	1	20	7	5	195	0	2	4

Nutrition Information Per Serving or Unit

Recipe and Page Number	Protein	Carbo- hydrates	Fat	Sodium	Potas- sium	Protein	Calcium	Iron
		Grams		Milligrams		Percent U.S. Recommended Daily Allowance		
Pineapple-Tomato Salad, 176	1	14	5	65	230	2	2	4
Plum-Celery Salad, 177	2	9	13	460	220	2	4	4
Ratatouille Salad, 183	2	6	9	275	265	2	2	6
Vegetable-Pasta Salad*, 182	2	12	13	280	150	4	2	4
Vegetable-Raisin Toss, 179	1	10	6	130	200	2	2	2
Wilted Vegetable Salad, 186	2	9	7	235	170	4	2	4
Winter Fruit Salad, 176	2	16	10	40	410	2	2	6
Zucchini-Apricot Salad, 182	2	8	8	185	235	2	2	6

*Complete nutrition information not available.

Breads,
Grains
& Pasta

★ ★ ★

1. Cornmeal Noodles, 2. Whole Wheat Croissants,
3. Honey-Nut Muffins, 4. Cottage Herb Bread,
5. Green Fettuccine, 6. Granola, 7. Egg Noodles

Oven Crunchy French Toast

¼	cup margarine or butter
3	tablespoons wheat germ
½	cup orange juice
2	tablespoons honey
4	eggs
12	slices French bread, each 1 inch thick
2	tablespoons wheat germ

Heat margarine in jelly roll pan, 15½ × 10½ × 1 inch, in 450° oven until melted; sprinkle 3 tablespoons wheat germ evenly over margarine. Beat orange juice, honey and eggs with hand beater until foamy. Dip bread into egg mixture; place in pan. Drizzle any remaining egg mixture over bread. Sprinkle 2 tablespoons wheat germ evenly over bread. Bake until bottoms are golden brown, about 10 minutes. Turn bread; bake until bottoms are golden brown, 6 to 8 minutes longer.

6 servings (2 slices); 380 calories each.

☆ ☆ ☆ ☆ ☆

Buttermilk Pancakes

1	egg
1	cup whole wheat or all-purpose flour
1	cup buttermilk
1	tablespoon sugar
2	tablespoons vegetable oil
1	teaspoon baking powder
½	teaspoon salt
½	teaspoon baking soda

Beat egg in large bowl with hand beater until fluffy; beat in remaining ingredients just until smooth. Grease heated griddle if necessary. (To test griddle, sprinkle with few drops water. If bubbles skitter around, griddle temperature is correct.) Pour about ¼ cup batter onto hot griddle for each pancake. Cook until pancakes are puffed and dry around edges. Turn and cook until golden brown.

About nine 4-inch pancakes; 110 calories each.

BLUEBERRY PANCAKES: Substitute milk for the buttermilk. Stir ½ cup fresh or frozen blueberries (thawed and well drained) into batter.

CRANBERRY-ORANGE PANCAKES: Substitute milk for the buttermilk. Sprinkle 1 tablespoon sugar over ½ cup finely chopped cranberries; stir cranberries and 1 tablespoon grated orange peel into batter.

OATMEAL-BROWN SUGAR PANCAKES: Substitute milk for the buttermilk and ¼ cup packed brown sugar for the 1 tablespoon sugar. Stir ½ cup quick-cooking oats into batter.

YOGURT PANCAKES: Substitute ⅔ cup milk and ½ cup plain yogurt for the buttermilk.

☆ ☆ ☆ ☆ ☆

USING UNBLEACHED FLOUR FOR BREADS

All the breads recipes in this chapter were tested with bleached all-purpose enriched flour. If you prefer to use unbleached flour, the baking results may not always be the same as the tested recipe. Unbleached all-purpose enriched flour can be used satisfactorily for yeast breads, but white breads will be more of an off-white color. However, quick breads made with unbleached flour may vary from baking to baking. The reason? Unbleached flour skips a bleaching and maturing process that makes bleached flour consistent cup after cup.

Pear Oven Pancake

¼ cup margarine or butter
¼ cup packed brown sugar
¼ teaspoon ground nutmeg
2 pears, cut into ⅛-inch slices
4 eggs, separated
⅓ cup milk
⅓ cup all-purpose flour
1 teaspoon baking powder
Lemon Sauce (below)

Heat oven to 400°. Heat margarine in round pan, 9 × 1½ inches, in oven until melted. Sprinkle brown sugar and nutmeg evenly over margarine. Arrange pear slices in pan, overlapping slices slightly.

Beat egg whites in 1½-quart bowl on high speed until stiff but not dry. Beat egg yolks, milk, flour and baking powder in 1-quart bowl on low speed just until smooth, about 30 seconds. Fold egg yolk mixture into beaten whites. Pour batter over pears. Bake until pancake is golden brown and firm, about 20 minutes. Prepare Lemon Sauce. Loosen edge of pancake with metal spatula; invert onto heatproof serving plate. Let pan remain a few minutes. Serve pancake with Lemon Sauce.

Lemon Sauce

⅓ cup sugar
2 teaspoons cornstarch
⅔ cup water
1 tablespoon margarine or butter
1 tablespoon grated lemon peel
1 tablespoon lemon juice

Mix sugar and cornstarch in 1-quart saucepan. Gradually stir in water. Cook over medium heat, stirring constantly, until mixture thickens and boils. Boil and stir 1 minute. Remove from heat; stir in remaining ingredients.

1 pancake (4 servings); 450 calories per serving.

☆ ☆ ☆ ☆ ☆

Waffles

2 eggs
1¾ cups milk
1 cup all-purpose flour
1 cup whole wheat flour
½ cup margarine or butter, melted, or vegetable oil
1 tablespoon sugar
4 teaspoons baking powder
½ teaspoon salt

Heat waffle iron. Beat eggs in large bowl with hand beater until fluffy; beat in remaining ingredients just until smooth. Pour batter from cup or pitcher onto center of hot waffle iron. Bake until steaming stops, about 5 minutes. Remove waffles carefully.

About four 10-inch waffles (½ per serving); 540 calories per waffle.

CRISP WAFFLES: Omit whole wheat flour. Increase all-purpose flour to 2 cups.

☆ ☆ ☆ ☆ ☆

Whole Wheat Popovers

1 cup milk
¾ cup all-purpose flour
¼ cup whole wheat flour
¼ teaspoon salt
2 eggs

Heat oven to 450°. Generously grease six 6-ounce custard cups. Mix all ingredients with hand beater just until smooth (do not overbeat). Fill cups about ½ full. Bake 20 minutes. Reduce oven temperature to 350°. Bake 20 minutes longer. Immediately remove from cups; serve hot.

6 popovers; 130 calories each.

TRADITIONAL POPOVERS: Omit whole wheat flour; increase all-purpose flour to 1 cup.

☆ ☆ ☆ ☆ ☆

Honey-Nut Muffins

1 egg
¾ cup milk
½ cup chopped nuts
⅓ cup vegetable oil
¼ cup honey
2 cups whole wheat or all-purpose flour
3 teaspoons baking powder
½ teaspoon salt

Heat oven to 400°. Grease bottoms only of about 12 medium muffin cups, 2½ × 1¼ inches. Beat egg; stir in milk, nuts, oil and honey. Stir in remaining ingredients all at once just until flour is moistened (batter will be lumpy). Fill muffin cups about ¾ cup full; sprinkle with sugar if desired. Bake until golden brown, about 20 minutes. Immediately remove from pan.

About 12 muffins; 190 calories each.

BLUEBERRY MUFFINS: Stir in 1 cup fresh or ¾ cup frozen blueberries (thawed and well drained) with the milk. Sprinkle tops with mixture of ¼ cup packed brown sugar and ½ teaspoon ground cinnamon before baking if desired.

BRAN MUFFINS: Increase milk to 1½ cups. Pour milk over 1½ cups whole bran cereal; let stand 2 minutes. Stir in with the oil.

FRUIT MUFFINS: Stir in 1 medium apple, pared and chopped, ½ cup raisins and 1 tablespoon finely shredded orange peel with the milk and ½ teaspoon pumpkin pie spice with the flour.

PUMPERNICKEL MUFFINS: Substitute molasses for the honey, and rye flour for the whole wheat flour; omit nuts. Stir in 2 tablespoons caraway seed with the flour if desired.

SEED MUFFINS: Omit nuts. Stir in ½ cup sunflower nuts and 1 tablespoon poppy seed with the milk.

☆ ☆ ☆ ☆ ☆

Apricot-Date Bread

1½ cups boiling water
1 cup cut-up dried apricots
½ cup cut-up dates
1½ cups all-purpose flour
1 cup whole wheat flour
1 cup chopped nuts
¾ cup packed brown sugar
3 tablespoons vegetable oil
3½ teaspoons baking powder
2 teaspoons finely shredded lemon peel
½ teaspoon ground nutmeg
1 egg

Mix boiling water, apricots and dates; cool. Heat oven to 350°. Grease bottom only of loaf pan, 9 × 5 × 3 inches. Mix all ingredients; beat 30 seconds. Pour into pan. Bake until wooden pick inserted in center comes out clean, 55 to 65 minutes; cool slightly. Loosen sides of loaf from pan; remove from pan. Cool completely before slicing. Wrap and refrigerate no longer than 1 week.

1 loaf (24 slices); 145 calories per slice.

BANANA-NUT BREAD: Omit water, apricots and dates. Mix in 1¼ cups mashed ripe bananas (2 to 3 medium), ½ cup milk and ½ teaspoon salt. Bake 65 to 75 minutes.

CARROT-PINEAPPLE BREAD: Omit water, apricots, dates and lemon peel. Drain 1 can (8 ounces) crushed pineapple in juice; reserve juice. Add enough water to juice to measure ¾ cup. Mix in pineapple, pineapple juice, 1 cup shredded carrots and 2 teaspoons finely shredded orange peel. Bake 65 to 75 minutes.

ZUCCHINI BREAD: Omit water, apricots and dates. Mix in 1 cup milk and 1 cup shredded zucchini. Bake 65 to 75 minutes.

☆ ☆ ☆ ☆ ☆

Gruyère Puff Ring

1   cup milk
¼   cup margarine or butter
1   cup all-purpose flour
4   eggs
¾   cup shredded Gruyère or Swiss cheese
¼   cup grated Parmesan cheese

Heat oven to 400°. Heat milk and margarine to rolling boil in 2-quart saucepan. Stir in flour. Stir vigorously over low heat until mixture forms a ball, about 1 minute; remove from heat. Beat in eggs, all at once; continue beating until smooth and thickened. Beat in ½ cup of the Gruyère cheese and the Parmesan cheese. Drop ¾ of the dough by tablespoonfuls into 8 mounds in a circle onto greased cookie sheet. (Each mound of dough should just touch the next one.) Drop a teaspoonful of remaining dough onto center of each mound. Sprinkle with remaining ¼ cup Gruyère cheese. Bake on center oven rack until ring is puffed and golden, 40 to 45 minutes.

1 ring (8 servings); 210 calories per serving.

☆ ☆ ☆ ☆ ☆

Carrot-Whole Wheat Coffee Cake

Good source of vitamin A

1   cup all-purpose flour
1   cup whole wheat flour
1   cup plain yogurt
⅔   cup sugar
⅓   cup margarine or butter, softened
1   teaspoon baking powder
1   teaspoon baking soda
¼   teaspoon ground ginger
2   eggs
1   cup shredded carrots (about 1½ medium)
½   cup chopped nuts
3   tablespoons sugar
1   tablespoon finely shredded orange peel

Heat oven to 350°. Beat all-purpose flour, whole wheat flour, yogurt, ⅔ cup sugar, the margarine, baking powder, baking soda, ginger and eggs in large bowl on low speed, scraping bowl frequently, 30 seconds. Beat on medium speed, scraping bowl occasionally, 2 minutes. Stir in carrots and nuts. Spread batter in greased square pan, 9×9×2 inches. Mix 3 tablespoons sugar and the orange peel; sprinkle over batter. Bake until wooden pick inserted in center comes out clean, 35 to 40 minutes.

1 coffee cake (9 servings); 300 calories per serving.

☆ ☆ ☆ ☆ ☆

Apple-Granola Coffee Cake

Granola Streusel (below)
1   cup all-purpose flour
1   cup whole wheat flour
1   cup milk
³/₄ cup sugar
¹/₄ cup margarine or butter, softened
3   teaspoons baking powder
1   teaspoon ground cinnamon
¹/₂ teaspoon salt
¹/₄ teaspoon ground nutmeg
¹/₄ teaspoon ground allspice
1   egg
2   cups chopped pared apples (about 2 medium)

Heat oven to 350°. Prepare Granola Streusel. Beat remaining ingredients except apples in large bowl on low speed, scraping bowl frequently, 30 seconds. Beat on medium speed, scraping bowl occasionally, 2 minutes. Stir in apples. Spread half of the batter in greased square pan, 9 × 9 × 2 inches; sprinkle with half of the Granola Streusel. Top with remaining batter; sprinkle with remaining Granola Streusel. Bake until wooden pick inserted in center comes out clean, 40 to 45 minutes.

Granola Streusel

1   cup granola
¹/₂ cup chopped nuts
¹/₄ cup all-purpose flour
¹/₄ cup packed brown sugar
3   tablespoons firm margarine or butter

Mix all ingredients until crumbly.

1 coffee cake (9 servings); 250 calories per serving.

☆ ☆ ☆ ☆ ☆

Apple-Granola Coffee Cake

Oatmeal-Raisin Bread

¾ cup oats
1 package active dry yeast
1 cup warm water (105 to 115°)
2 cups all-purpose flour
¼ cup molasses
3 tablespoons shortening
2 teaspoons salt
1 egg
1 cup raisins
¾ cup all-purpose flour
2 tablespoons packed brown sugar
1 egg white, slightly beaten

Spread oats in single layer in ungreased rectangular pan, 13 × 9 × 2 inches. Toast in 350° oven, stirring occasionally, until golden brown, about 10 minutes; cool. Remove ¼ cup oats; crush and reserve.

Dissolve yeast in warm water in large bowl. Add 2 cups flour, the molasses, shortening, salt and egg. Beat on low speed until moistened; beat on medium speed, scraping bowl occasionally, 2 minutes. Stir in raisins, ¾ cup flour and ½ cup oats. Spread evenly in greased loaf pan, 9 × 5 × 3 inches. (Batter will be sticky.) Round top of loaf by patting with floured hands. Mix reserved oats and brown sugar. Brush loaf with egg white; sprinkle with oat mixture. Let rise in warm place until batter is about level with top of pan, about 1 hour.

Heat oven to 375°. Bake until loaf is brown and sounds hollow when tapped, 40 to 45 minutes. Immediately remove from pan; cool on wire rack.

1 loaf (20 slices); 130 calories per slice.

ANADAMA BREAD: Omit oats, raisins and brown sugar. Add ½ cup yellow cornmeal with the ¾ cup flour. Brush loaf with egg white; sprinkle with 2 tablespoons cornmeal.

☆ ☆ ☆ ☆ ☆

Honey Wheat Batter Bread

1 package active dry yeast
1¼ cups warm water (105 to 115°)
1 cup all-purpose flour
1 cup whole wheat flour
2 tablespoons wheat germ
2 tablespoons honey
2 tablespoons shortening
2 teaspoons salt
1 cup whole wheat flour

Dissolve yeast in warm water in large bowl. Add all-purpose flour, 1 cup whole wheat flour, the wheat germ, honey, shortening and salt. Beat on low speed until moistened; beat on medium speed, scraping bowl occasionally, 2 minutes. Stir in remaining whole wheat flour until smooth, 1 to 1½ minutes. Scrape batter from side of bowl. Cover; let rise in warm place until double, about 45 minutes.

Stir down batter by beating about 25 strokes. Spread evenly in greased loaf pan, 9 × 5 × 3 inches. (Batter will be sticky.) Smooth top of loaf by patting into shape with floured hands. Let rise until batter is about 1 inch below top of pan, about 30 minutes.

Heat oven to 375°. Bake until loaf is brown and sounds hollow when tapped, 45 to 50 minutes. Immediately remove from pan. Brush top of loaf with margarine or butter if desired; cool on wire rack.

1 loaf (20 slices); 90 calories per slice.

HONEY-NUT BATTER BREAD: Add ¾ cup chopped nuts and 2 teaspoons finely shredded orange peel with the second addition of whole wheat flour.

☆ ☆ ☆ ☆ ☆

Four-Grain Batter Bread

2   packages active dry yeast
½   cup warm water (105 to 115°)
3½   cups all-purpose flour
2   cups lukewarm milk (scalded then cooled)
2   tablespoons sugar
1   teaspoon salt
¼   teaspoon baking soda
½   cup whole wheat flour
½   cup wheat germ
½   cup quick-cooking oats
1   to 1¼ cups all-purpose flour
     Cornmeal

Dissolve yeast in warm water in large bowl. Add 3½ cups all-purpose flour, the milk, sugar, salt and baking soda. Beat on low speed until moistened; beat on medium speed, scraping bowl occasionally, 3 minutes. Stir in whole wheat flour, wheat germ, oats and enough remaining all-purpose flour to make a stiff batter.

Grease 2 loaf pans, 8½ × 4½ × 2½ inches; sprinkle with cornmeal. Divide batter evenly between loaf pans. Round tops of loaves by patting with floured hands; sprinkle with cornmeal. Cover; let rise in warm place until batter is about 1 inch below top of pan, about 30 minutes.

Heat oven to 400°. Bake until loaves are light brown, about 25 minutes. Immediately remove from pans; cool on wire rack.

2 loaves (18 slices each); 80 calories per slice.

WHOLE WHEAT BATTER BREAD: Increase whole wheat flour to 2 cups. Omit wheat germ and oats. Stir in 1 cup raisins with second addition of all-purpose flour.

☆ ☆ ☆ ☆ ☆

Cottage Herb Bread

1   cup large curd creamed cottage cheese
1   package active dry yeast
¾   cup warm water (105 to 115°)
1½   cups all-purpose flour
⅓   cup shortening
2   teaspoons parsley flakes
1   teaspoon salt
¾   teaspoon dried basil leaves
2   eggs
2½   to 3 cups all-purpose flour

Place cottage cheese in blender container. Cover and blend on high speed, stopping blender occasionally to scrape sides until smooth, about 1 minute. Dissolve yeast in warm water in large bowl. Add cottage cheese, 1½ cups flour, the shortening, parsley, salt, basil and eggs. Beat on low speed until moistened; beat on medium speed, scraping bowl occasionally, 3 minutes. Stir in enough remaining flour to make dough easy to handle.

Turn dough onto lightly floured surface; knead until smooth and elastic, about 5 minutes. Place in greased bowl; turn greased side up. Cover; let rise in warm place until double, about 1½ hours. (Dough is ready if indentation remains when touched.)

Punch down dough; divide into halves. Divide each half into 6 equal parts; shape each part into ball. Place 6 balls in zigzag pattern in each of 2 greased loaf pans, 9 × 5 × 3 inches. Let rise until double, about 1 hour.

Heat oven to 425°. Place pans on low oven rack so that tops of pans are in center of oven. Bake until loaves are golden brown and sound hollow when tapped, 25 to 30 minutes. Immediately remove from pans. Brush tops of loaves with margarine or butter if desired; cool on wire racks.

2 loaves (20 slices each); 80 calories per slice.

☆ ☆ ☆ ☆ ☆

Sesame Loaves

1	package active dry yeast
¼	cup warm water (105 to 115°)
1	cup all-purpose flour
1	cup lukewarm milk (scalded then cooled)
¼	cup sugar
¼	cup margarine or butter, softened
1½	teaspoons salt
2	eggs
3	to 3½ cups all-purpose flour
1	egg white
1	tablespoon water
	Sesame seed

Dissolve yeast in warm water in large bowl. Beat in 1 cup flour, the milk, sugar, margarine, salt and eggs. Stir in enough flour to make soft, sticky dough. Cover; let rise in warm place until double, about 1 hour. (Dough is ready if indentation remains.)

Stir down dough by beating about 25 strokes. Turn dough onto well-floured surface. Divide dough into 6 equal parts; shape each part into ball. Flatten each into rectangle, 6 × 2½ inches; taper ends. Place 3 rectangles on each of 2 lightly greased cookie sheets. Make ¼-inch deep slashes across loaves at 1-inch intervals. Beat egg white and 1 tablespoon water slightly; brush over loaves. Sprinkle with sesame seed. Let rise uncovered until double, about 40 minutes. Brush with egg white mixture.

Heat oven to 400°. Refrigerate one cookie sheet of loaves while other sheet of loaves bakes. Bake until loaves are golden brown, about 10 minutes. Repeat with second sheet. Cool on wire rack.

6 loaves; 160 calories per loaf.

ONION ROLLS: Omit sesame seed. Cook and stir ¾ cup chopped onion in 2 tablespoons margarine or butter until tender. Stir in 1 teaspoon poppy seed; cool. Divide dough into 10 equal parts; shape each part into ball. Flatten ball to ½-inch thickness. Make a hole 1 inch in diameter in center of each with floured fingers. Fill each hole with about 1 heaping teaspoon onion mixture; brush with egg white mixture. Let rise until double, about 40 minutes. Brush with egg white mixture. Bake until golden brown, about 10 minutes. 10 rolls.

CHEESE CRESCENTS: Omit sesame seed. Roll dough into 12-inch circle. Sprinkle with 3 tablespoons grated Parmesan cheese or American cheese food. Cut into 16 wedges. Roll up each wedge, beginning at rounded edge. Place rolls, with points underneath, on lightly greased cookie sheet; curve to form crescents. Let rise until double, about 40 minutes. Brush with egg white mixture. Bake until golden brown, about 11 minutes. 16 rolls.

☆ ☆ ☆ ☆ ☆

Sourdough French Bread

1 package active dry yeast
1¼ cups warm water (105 to 115°)
3 cups all-purpose flour
1 cup Sourdough Starter (below)
1 tablespoon sugar
1½ teaspoons salt
1 cup all-purpose flour
¼ teaspoon baking soda
½ to 1 cup all-purpose flour
Cornmeal
Cold water
1 egg white
2 tablespoons cold water

Dissolve yeast in warm water in large bowl. Beat in 3 cups flour, the Sourdough Starter, sugar and salt. Mix 1 cup flour and the baking soda; stir into sourdough mixture. Beat with wooden spoon until smooth and flour is completely absorbed. (Dough should be just firm enough to gather into ball.) If necessary, gradually add enough remaining flour, stirring until all flour is absorbed.

Turn dough onto heavily floured surface; knead until smooth and elastic, about 10 minutes. Place in greased bowl; turn greased side up. Cover; let rise in warm place until double, about 1½ hours. (Dough is ready if indentation remains when touched.)

Punch down dough; divide into halves. Roll each half into rectangle, 15 × 10 inches, on lightly floured surface. Roll up tightly, beginning at a 15-inch side. Pinch edge of dough into roll to seal. Roll gently back and forth to taper ends. Sprinkle lightly greased cookie sheet with cornmeal. Place loaves on cookie sheet. Make ¼-inch deep slashes across loaves at 2-inch intervals, or make ¼-inch deep slash down loaves. Brush tops of loaves with cold water. Let rise until slightly more than double, about 1 hour.

Heat oven to 375°. Brush loaves with cold water. Bake on middle oven rack 20 minutes. Beat egg white and 2 tablespoons cold water; brush over loaves. Bake until loaves sound hollow when tapped, about 25 minutes longer. Cool on wire rack.

Sourdough Starter

1 teaspoon active dry yeast
¼ cup warm water (105 to 115°)
¾ cup milk
1 cup all-purpose flour

Dissolve yeast in warm water in 3-quart glass bowl. Stir in milk. Gradually stir in flour. Beat until smooth. Cover with towel or cheesecloth; let stand in warm, draft-free place until starter begins to ferment, about 24 hours (bubbles will appear on surface of starter). If starter has not begun fermentation after 24 hours, discard and begin again. If fermentation has begun, stir well; cover tightly with plastic wrap and return to warm, draft-free place. Let stand until foamy, 2 to 3 days.

When starter has become foamy, stir well. Pour into 1-quart crock or glass jar with tight-fitting cover. Store in refrigerator. Starter is ready to use when a clear liquid has risen to the top. Stir before using. Use 1 cup starter in recipe; reserve remaining starter. Add ¾ cup milk and ¾ cup flour to reserved starter. Store covered at room temperature until bubbles appear, about 12 hours; refrigerate.

Use starter regularly (every 7 to 10 days). If the volume of the breads begins to decrease, dissolve 1 teaspoon active dry yeast in ¼ cup warm water. Stir in ½ cup milk, ¾ cup flour and the remaining starter.

2 loaves (20 slices each); 70 calories per slice.

☆ ☆ ☆ ☆ ☆

Sourdough Bread

2½   cups all-purpose flour
2   cups warm water (105 to 115°)
1   cup Sourdough Starter (page 202)
3¾   to 4¼ cups flour
3   tablespoons sugar
3   tablespoons vegetable oil
1   teaspoon salt
¼   teaspoon baking soda
     Cold water

Mix 2½ cups flour, 2 cups warm water and the Sourdough Starter in 3-quart glass bowl with wooden spoon until smooth. Cover; let stand in warm, draft-free place 8 hours.

Add 3¾ cups of the flour, the sugar, oil, salt and baking soda to sourdough mixture. Stir with wooden spoon until dough is smooth and flour is completely absorbed. (Dough should be just firm enough to gather into ball.) If necessary, gradually add remaining ½ cup flour, stirring until all flour is absorbed.

Turn dough onto heavily floured surface; knead until smooth and elastic, about 10 minutes. Place in greased bowl; turn greased side up. Cover; let rise in warm place until double, about 1½ hours. (Dough is ready if an indentation remains when touched.)

Punch down dough; divide into halves. Shape each half into round, slightly flat loaf. (Do not tear dough by pulling.) Place loaves in opposite corners of greased cookie sheet. Make three ¼-inch deep slashes across loaves. Let rise until double, about 45 minutes.

Heat oven to 375°. Brush loaves with cold water. Place on middle oven rack. Bake until loaves sound hollow when tapped, about 50 minutes, brushing occasionally with water. Cool on wire rack.

2 loaves (16 slices each); 105 calories per slice.

☆ ☆ ☆ ☆ ☆

Hearty Dark Rye Bread

3   packages active dry yeast
1½   cups warm water (105 to 115°)
2½   cups all-purpose flour
½   cup whole bran cereal
½   cup dark molasses
¼   cup cocoa
1   tablespoon salt
1   tablespoon caraway seed
2   tablespoons vegetable oil
2   to 2½ cups dark rye flour
     Cornmeal
¼   cup cold water
½   teaspoon cornstarch

Dissolve yeast in warm water in large bowl. Add all-purpose flour, bran cereal, molasses, cocoa, salt, caraway seed and vegetable oil. Beat on low speed until moistened; beat on medium speed, scraping bowl occasionally, 3 minutes. Stir in enough rye flour to make dough easy to handle.

Turn dough onto lightly floured surface. Cover; let rest 15 minutes. Knead until smooth and elastic, 10 minutes. Place in greased bowl; turn greased side up. Cover; let rise in warm place until double, about 1 hour. (Dough is ready if indentation remains when touched.)

Sprinkle greased cookie sheet with cornmeal. Punch down dough; divide into halves. Shape each half into a round, slightly flat loaf. Place loaves in opposite corners of cookie sheet. Let rise until double, 40 to 50 minutes.

Heat oven to 375°. Bake 30 minutes. Mix cold water and cornstarch in saucepan; heat to boiling, stirring constantly. Brush cornstarch mixture over loaves. Bake until loaves sound hollow when tapped, about 15 minutes longer. Cool on wire racks.

2 loaves (12 slices each); 125 calories per slice.

☆ ☆ ☆ ☆ ☆

Whole Wheat Bread

1   package active dry yeast
1¼ cups warm water (105 to 115°)
2   cups all-purpose flour
¼   cup honey
2   tablespoons shortening
1½ teaspoons salt
1¾ to 2¼ cups whole wheat flour

Dissolve yeast in warm water in large bowl. Add all-purpose flour, honey, shortening and salt. Beat on low speed until moistened; beat on medium speed, scraping bowl occasionally, 3 minutes. Stir in enough whole wheat flour to make dough easy to handle.

Turn dough onto lightly floured surface; knead until smooth and elastic, about 5 minutes. Place in greased bowl; turn greased side up. Cover; let rise in warm place until double, about 1 hour. (Dough is ready if indentation remains when touched.)

Punch down dough; roll into rectangle, 18 × 9 inches. Fold 9-inch sides crosswise into thirds, overlapping ends. Roll up tightly, beginning at narrow end. Pinch edge of dough into roll to seal well; press in ends of roll. Press each end with side of hand to seal; fold ends under. Place loaf, seam side down, in greased loaf pan, 9 × 5 × 3 inches. Brush with margarine or butter; sprinkle with whole wheat flour or crushed rolled oats if desired. Let rise until double, about 1 hour.

Heat oven to 375°. Place pan on low oven rack so that top of pan is in center of oven. Bake until loaf is deep golden brown and sounds hollow when tapped, 40 to 45 minutes. Immediately remove from pan. Brush top of loaf with margarine or butter if desired; cool on wire rack.

1 loaf (20 slices); 115 calories per slice.

CHEESE WHEAT TWIST: Prepare Cheese Filling (below). Punch down dough; divide into halves. Roll each half into rectangle, 18 × 5 inches. Spread each rectangle with half of the Cheese Filling. Roll each rectangle up tightly, beginning at 18-inch side. Pinch edge of dough into roll to seal. Place rolls side by side on ungreased cookie sheet; twist together gently and loosely. Pinch ends to fasten. Let rise until double, about 40 minutes.

Heat oven to 350°. Bake until twist sounds hollow when tapped, 35 to 40 minutes; brush with margarine or butter if desired. Remove from cookie sheet; cool twist on wire rack.

Cheese Filling

1   small onion, chopped (about ¼ cup)
2   tablespoons margarine or butter
⅓   cup grated Parmesan cheese
¼   cup snipped parsley

Cook and stir onion in margarine over medium heat until onion is tender. Stir in cheese and parsley; cool.

☆ ☆ ☆ ☆ ☆

WHAT IS WHOLE WHEAT FLOUR?

Whole wheat or graham flour is made from the complete wheat kernel or berry which contains the bran, germ and endosperm. It is never enriched because it is naturally nutritious.

There are different granulations of whole wheat flour — from medium to coarse. Stone-ground whole wheat flour is a very coarse granulation. The recipes in this cookbook have been tested with a medium-fine granulation and a stone-ground whole wheat flour, and both give satisfactory results.

Because whole wheat flour contains the germ, which is high in oil, it becomes rancid if not stored correctly. To keep whole wheat flour longer than eight months, refrigerate or freeze in a moistureproof, vaporproof plastic bag.

Molasses Wheat Bread

2 packages active dry yeast
1/2 cup warm water (105 to 115°)
2 cups all-purpose flour
2 cups milk (scalded then cooled)
1/3 cup molasses
1/4 cup vegetable oil
2 tablespoons sugar
2 teaspoons salt
3/4 cup yellow cornmeal
1/4 cup wheat germ
4 to 4 1/2 cups whole wheat flour

Dissolve yeast in warm water in large bowl. Add all-purpose flour, milk, molasses, oil, sugar and salt. Beat on low speed until moistened; beat on medium speed, scraping bowl occasionally, 3 minutes. Stir in cornmeal, wheat germ and enough whole wheat flour to make dough easy to handle.

Turn dough onto lightly floured surface; knead until smooth and elastic, about 5 minutes. Place in greased bowl; turn greased side up. Cover; let rise in warm place until double, about 1 hour. (Dough is ready if indentation remains when touched.)

Punch down dough; divide into halves. Roll each half into rectangle, 18 × 9 inches. Fold 9-inch sides crosswise into thirds, overlapping ends. Roll up tightly, beginning at narrow end. Pinch edge of dough into roll to seal well; press in ends of roll. Press each end with side of hand to seal; fold ends under. Place loaves, seam sides down, in 2 greased loaf pans, 9 × 5 × 3 inches. Let rise until double, about 1 hour.

Heat oven to 375°. Place pans on low oven rack so that tops of pans are in center of oven. Bake until loaves sound hollow when tapped, 40 to 45 minutes. Immediately remove from pans. Brush tops of loaves with margarine or butter if desired; cool on wire rack.

2 loaves (20 slices each); 110 calories per slice.

☆ ☆ ☆ ☆ ☆

Cracked Wheat Bread

1 package active dry yeast
1/2 cup warm water (105 to 115°)
2 cups all-purpose flour
1 cup cracked wheat
1 cup lukewarm milk (scalded then cooled)
1/4 cup molasses
1 tablespoon shortening
2 teaspoons salt
1 cup whole wheat flour
3/4 to 1 cup all-purpose flour
    Margarine or butter, softened
    Cracked wheat

Dissolve yeast in warm water in large bowl. Add 2 cups all-purpose flour, the cracked wheat, milk, molasses, shortening and salt. Beat on low speed until moistened; beat on medium speed, scraping bowl occasionally, 2 minutes. Stir in whole wheat flour and enough all-purpose flour to make dough easy to handle.

Turn dough onto lightly floured surface; knead until smooth and elastic, about 10 minutes. Place in greased bowl; turn greased side up. Cover; let rise in warm place until double, about 1 hour. (Dough is ready if indentation remains when touched.)

Punch down dough; roll into rectangle, 18 × 9 inches. Fold 9-inch sides crosswise into thirds, overlapping ends. Roll up tightly, beginning at narrow end. Pinch edge of dough into roll to seal well; press in ends of roll. Press each end with side of hand to seal; fold ends under. Place loaf, seam side down, in greased loaf pan, 9 × 5 × 3 inches. Brush with margarine; sprinkle with cracked wheat. Let rise until double, about 1 hour.

Heat oven to 400°. Place pan on low oven rack so that top of pan is in center of oven. Bake until loaf sounds hollow when tapped, 30 to 35 minutes. Immediately remove from pan; cool on wire rack.

1 loaf (20 slices); 140 calories per slice.

☆ ☆ ☆ ☆ ☆

Rye Bread

2   packages active dry yeast
1½   cups warm water (105 to 115°)
2½   cups all-purpose flour
⅓   cup packed brown sugar
⅓   cup molasses
1   tablespoon salt
1   tablespoon finely shredded orange peel
2   tablespoons vegetable oil
1   teaspoon anise seed
2   to 2½ cups medium rye flour

Dissolve yeast in warm water in bowl. Add all-purpose flour, brown sugar, molasses, salt, orange peel, oil and anise seed. Beat on low speed until moistened; beat on medium speed, scraping bowl occasionally, 3 minutes. Stir in enough rye flour to make dough easy to handle.

Turn dough onto lightly floured surface. Cover; let rest 10 to 15 minutes. Knead until smooth and elastic, about 5 minutes. Place in greased bowl; turn greased side up. Cover; let rise in warm place until double, about 1 hour. (Dough is ready when an indentation remains when touched.)

Punch down dough; divide into halves. Roll each half into rectangle, 15 × 10 inches. Roll up tightly, beginning at a 15-inch side. Pinch edge of dough to seal. Roll gently back and forth to taper ends. Place loaves on greased cookie sheet. Make ¼-inch deep slashes across loaves at 2-inch intervals. Let rise until double, about 1½ hours.

Heat oven to 375°. Bake until loaves are golden brown, 25 to 30 minutes. Brush tops of loaves with margarine or butter if desired; cool on wire rack.

2 loaves (20 slices each); 70 calories per slice.

Rye Bread

English Muffins

1   package active dry yeast
1   cup warm water (105 to 115°)
3   cups all-purpose flour
¼   cup shortening
2   tablespoons honey
1   teaspoon salt
    Cornmeal

Dissolve yeast in warm water in large bowl. Add flour, shortening, honey and salt. Stir until water is absorbed and dough cleans side of bowl. Turn dough onto floured surface. Knead lightly just until dough is easy to handle, 5 to 10 times. Roll dough ¼ inch thick. (Check surface occasionally while rolling and add more flour as needed to prevent sticking.) Cut into 3½-inch circles.

Sprinkle ungreased cookie sheet with cornmeal. Place circles about 1 inch apart on cookie sheet; sprinkle with cornmeal. Cover; let rise in warm place until light and airy, about 1 hour. (Dough is ready if indentation remains when touched; dough does not double.)

Heat ungreased electric griddle or skillet to 375°. Cook circles until deep golden brown, about 7 minutes on each side; cool. To serve, split with fork, toast and spread with margarine and marmalade if desired.

About 12 muffins; 150 calories per muffin.

CORNMEAL ENGLISH MUFFINS: Substitute 1 cup cornmeal for 1 cup all-purpose flour.

SOURDOUGH ENGLISH MUFFINS: Decrease water to ¾ cup. Add ½ cup Sourdough Starter (page 202) with the shortening.

WHOLE WHEAT ENGLISH MUFFINS: Substitute 1½ cups whole wheat flour for 1½ cups all-purpose flour.

☆ ☆ ☆ ☆ ☆

Whole Wheat Pocket Breads

Good source of thiamin

1   package active dry yeast
1⅓   cups warm water (105 to 115°)
2   cups all-purpose flour
1   tablespoon vegetable oil
1   teaspoon sugar
1   teaspoon salt
1   to 1½ cups whole wheat flour

Dissolve yeast in warm water in large bowl. Add all-purpose flour, oil, sugar and salt. Beat on low speed until moistened; beat on medium speed, scraping bowl occasionally, 3 minutes. Stir in enough whole wheat flour to make dough easy to handle.

Turn dough onto lightly floured surface; knead until smooth and elastic, about 10 minutes. Place in greased bowl; turn greased side up. Cover; let rise in warm place until double, about 1 hour. (Dough is ready if indentation remains when touched.)

Punch down dough; divide into 6 equal parts. Shape each part into ball; place on very lightly floured surface. Cover; let rise 30 minutes. Roll each ball into 6- to 7-inch circle ⅛ inch thick on floured surface. Place 2 circles in opposite corners on each of 3 ungreased cookie sheets. Let rise 30 minutes.

Heat oven to 450°. Bake until breads are puffed and golden brown, about 10 minutes. Cut or tear crosswise into halves; fill with desired meat filling or salad.

6 pocket breads; 250 calories per pocket bread.

TRADITIONAL POCKET BREADS: Substitute all-purpose flour for the whole wheat flour.

☆ ☆ ☆ ☆ ☆

Whole Wheat Croissants

2 packages active dry yeast
1¼ cups warm water (105 to 115°)
2 cups all-purpose flour
¼ cup butter, softened
3 tablespoons sugar
1½ teaspoons salt
2 eggs
1½ to 2 cups whole wheat flour
1 cup butter, softened
1 egg, beaten

Dissolve yeast in warm water in large bowl. Add all-purpose flour, ¼ cup butter, the sugar, salt and 2 eggs. Beat on low speed until moistened. Beat on medium speed, scraping bowl occasionally, 3 minutes. Stir in enough of the whole wheat flour to make dough easy to handle.

Turn dough onto lightly floured surface; knead until smooth and elastic, about 5 minutes. Place in greased bowl; turn greased side up. Cover; let rise in warm place until double, about 1 hour. (Dough is ready if indentation remains when touched.) Punch down dough; refrigerate 1 hour.

Punch down dough; roll into rectangle, 25 × 10 inches. Spread with ⅓ cup of the butter. Fold rectangle crosswise into thirds, overlapping 10-inch edges to make 3 layers; roll into rectangle, 25 × 10 inches. Spread with ⅓ cup of the butter. Fold into thirds; roll into rectangle, 25 × 10 inches. Spread with remaining ⅓ cup butter. Fold into thirds (do not roll into rectangle). Cut dough into halves; refrigerate 1 hour.

Roll one half into rectangle, 18 × 12 inches. (Keep other half refrigerated.) Cut lengthwise into halves; then cut crosswise into 3 squares. Cut each square diagonally into 2 triangles. Flatten triangles slightly with rolling pin. Roll up each triangle, beginning at long side. Place rolls, with points underneath, on greased cookie sheet; curve to form crescents. Cover; let rise at room temperature about 1 hour.

Heat oven to 425°. Brush croissants with beaten egg. Bake until croissants are brown and crisp, 14 to 16 minutes.

24 croissants; 170 calories each.

CHOCOLATE-FILLED CROISSANTS: Place 1 teaspoon chocolate chips at the long side of each triangle before rolling.

HAZELNUT-FILLED CROISSANTS: Mix ½ cup finely chopped hazelnuts, 2 tablespoons sugar, ¼ teaspoon vanilla and 1 egg. Spread each triangle with 1 heaping teaspoon.

TRADITIONAL CROISSANTS: Substitute all-purpose flour for the whole wheat flour.

══════ ☆ ☆ ☆ ☆ ☆ ══════

Shaping Whole Wheat Croissants

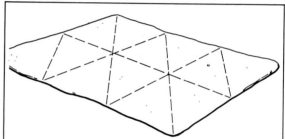

Cut rectangle into 6 squares. Cut each square into 2 triangles.

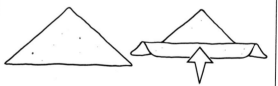

Roll each slightly flattened triangle up, beginning at longer side.

Place rolls on greased cookie sheet; curve to form crescents.

Cinnamon Rolls

Good source of thiamin

1	package active dry yeast
½	cup warm water (105 to 115°)
1¼	cups all-purpose flour
¼	cup sugar
¼	cup shortening
¼	cup lukewarm milk (scalded then cooled)
½	teaspoon salt
1	egg
¾	to 1 cup whole wheat flour
2	tablespoons margarine or butter, softened
¼	cup sugar
2	teaspoons ground cinnamon
	Orange Glaze (below)

Dissolve yeast in warm water in bowl. Add all-purpose flour, sugar, shortening, milk, salt and egg. Beat on low speed until moistened; beat on medium speed, scraping bowl occasionally, 3 minutes. Stir in enough whole wheat flour to make dough easy to handle.

Turn dough onto lightly floured surface; knead until smooth and elastic, about 5 minutes. Place in greased bowl; turn greased side up. Cover; let rise in warm place until double, about 1½ hours. (Dough is ready if indentation remains when touched.)

Punch down dough; roll into rectangle, 15 × 9 inches. Spread with margarine. Mix ¼ cup sugar and the cinnamon; sprinkle over rectangle. Roll up, beginning at a 15-inch side. Pinch edge of dough into roll to seal well; stretch roll to make even. Cut into nine 1½-inch slices. Place slightly apart in greased square pan, 8 × 8 × 2 inches. Cover; let rise until double, about 45 minutes. Heat oven to 375°. Bake until rolls are light brown, 25 to 30 minutes. Prepare Orange Glaze; spread rolls with glaze while warm.

Orange Glaze

Mix 1 cup powdered sugar, ¼ teaspoon finely shredded orange peel and 2 tablespoons orange juice until smooth.

9 rolls; 290 calories each.

☆ ☆ ☆ ☆ ☆

Cinnamon Rolls

Cheese-Carob Rolls

1 package active dry yeast
¼ cup warm water (105 to 115°)
1 cup all-purpose flour
¼ cup lukewarm milk (scalded then cooled)
¼ cup shortening
2 tablespoons carob powder
2 tablespoons honey
½ teaspoon salt
1 egg
1¼ to 1½ cups all-purpose flour
    Cheese Filling (below)
½ cup apricot jam
¼ cup finely chopped nuts

Dissolve yeast in warm water in large bowl. Add 1 cup flour, the milk, shortening, carob powder, honey, salt and egg. Beat on low speed until moistened; beat on medium speed, scraping bowl occasionally, 3 minutes. Stir in enough remaining flour to make dough easy to handle.

Turn dough onto lightly floured surface; knead until smooth and elastic, about 5 minutes. Place in greased bowl; turn greased side up. Cover; let rise in warm place until double, about 1½ hours. (Dough is ready if indentation remains when touched.)

Prepare Cheese Filling. Punch down dough; roll into 15-inch square. Cut into twenty-five 3-inch squares. Place one square on greased cookie sheet. Spoon 1 heaping teaspoon Cheese Filling onto center of square. Bring diagonally opposite corners to center of square, overlapping slightly; pinch. Repeat with remaining squares. Let rise until almost double, about 40 minutes.

Heat oven to 375°. Bake until rolls are done, 12 to 15 minutes. Heat jam until melted; brush over hot rolls and sprinkle with nuts.

Cheese Filling

1 package (8 ounces) Neufchâtel cheese, softened
¼ cup sugar
3 tablespoons all-purpose flour
1 egg yolk
½ teaspoon grated lemon peel
1 tablespoon lemon juice

Beat cheese and sugar until light and fluffy. Stir in remaining ingredients.

25 rolls; 135 calories each.

CHEESE-CHOCOLATE ROLLS: Substitute ⅓ cup cocoa for the carob powder.

☆ ☆ ☆ ☆ ☆

Cheese-Carob Rolls, and Honey Twist Coffee Cake

Honey Twist Coffee Cake

1　package active dry yeast
¼　cup warm water (105 to 115°)
1½　cups all-purpose flour
1　cup plain yogurt
2　tablespoons granulated sugar
2　tablespoons margarine or butter, softened
1　teaspoon salt
1　egg
1　to 1½ cups all-purpose flour
　　Honey-Nut Filling (below)
¼　cup margarine or butter, melted
⅓　cup packed brown sugar
¼　cup honey

Dissolve yeast in warm water in large bowl. Add 1½ cups flour, the yogurt, granulated sugar, 2 tablespoons margarine, the salt and egg. Beat on low speed until moistened; beat on medium speed, scraping bowl occasionally, 3 minutes. Stir in enough remaining flour to make dough easy to handle.

Turn dough onto lightly floured surface; knead until smooth and elastic, about 5 minutes. Place in greased bowl; turn greased side up. Cover; let rise in warm place until double, about 1 hour. (Dough is ready if indentation remains when touched.)

Prepare Honey-Nut Filling. Mix ¼ cup margarine, the brown sugar and honey in rectangular pan, 13 × 9 × 2 inches; spread evenly in pan. Punch down dough; roll into rectangle, 24 × 9 inches. Spread Honey-Nut Filling crosswise over half of rectangle; fold crosswise in half. Seal edges; cut rectangle crosswise into six 2-inch strips. Twist each strip loosely; place strips crosswise in pan. Let rise until double, about 1 hour.

Heat oven to 375°. Bake until coffee cake is golden brown, 20 to 25 minutes. Immediately invert pan on heatproof serving plate. Let pan remain a minute so honey mixture can drizzle over coffee cake.

Honey-Nut Filling

Mix ⅓ cup margarine or butter, softened, ¼ cup honey and ¼ cup finely chopped nuts.

1 coffee cake (18 servings); 200 calories per serving.

☆ ☆ ☆ ☆ ☆

Shaping Fruit and Nut Turban

Fit circle of dough in round pan. Roll up fruit-covered rectangle from 18-inch side.

Place roll, seam side down, in dough-lined pan; pinch ends together to form a ring.

Bring sides of dough up over roll into center, pleating dough into loose folds.

Fruit and Nut Turban

1 package active dry yeast
1/2 cup warm water (105 to 115°)
2 cups all-purpose flour
1/2 cup lukewarm milk (scalded then cooled)
1/3 cup granulated sugar
1/3 cup margarine or butter, softened
1 teaspoon salt
1 egg
1 1/2 to 2 cups all-purpose flour
Fruit and Nut Filling (below)
2 tablespoons margarine or butter, softened
Powdered sugar

Dissolve yeast in warm water in large bowl. Add 2 cups flour, the milk, granulated sugar, 1/3 cup margarine, the salt and egg. Beat on low speed until moistened; beat on medium speed, scraping bowl occasionally, 3 minutes. Stir in enough remaining flour to make dough easy to handle.

Turn dough onto lightly floured surface; knead until smooth and elastic, about 5 minutes. Place in greased bowl; turn greased side up. Cover; let rise in warm place until double, about 1 1/2 hours. (Dough is ready if indentation remains when touched.)

Prepare Fruit and Nut Filling. Punch down dough; remove 1/3 and reserve remaining dough. Roll dough into 22-inch circle; place circle in greased round pan, 9 × 1 1/2 inches. Roll reserved dough into rectangle, 18 × 12 inches; spread with 2 tablespoons margarine. Spread with Fruit and Nut Filling. Roll up tightly, beginning at an 18-inch side. Pinch

edge of dough into roll to seal. Place roll, seam side down, in a ring in dough-lined pan; pinch ends together.

Heat oven to 375°. Place a tent of aluminum foil over coffee cake, being careful foil does not touch dough. Bake until coffee cake is golden brown, about 30 minutes. Immediately remove from pan; sprinkle with powdered sugar. Cool on wire rack.

Fruit and Nut Filling

1 cup golden raisins
1 cup cut-up dried apricots
2/3 cup water
1/3 cup brown sugar
1 teaspoon finely shredded orange peel
1 teaspoon finely shredded lemon peel
1/4 teaspoon ground nutmeg
1/8 teaspoon ground allspice
1/2 cup chopped toasted almonds

Cook all ingredients except almonds over medium heat, stirring constantly, until thickened, about 6 minutes. Stir in nuts; cool.

1 coffee cake (16 servings); 270 calories per serving.

CHERRY ALMOND TURBAN: Omit Fruit and Nut Filling and 2 tablespoons margarine or butter. Beat 1 cup almond paste, 1/4 cup margarine or butter, softened, and 1 egg white until of spreading consistency, about 1 1/2 minutes. Spread over rectangle; spread 2/3 cup cherry preserves over almond mixture. Continue as directed.

Wheat with Vegetables

Good source of vitamin A

1   cup uncooked wheat berries
4   cups water
8   ounces mushrooms, sliced (about 3 cups)
1   medium onion, chopped (about 1/2 cup)
2   tablespoons vegetable oil
1   medium carrot, shredded (about 1 cup)
1   cup frozen green peas
1/3 cup water
2   teaspoons instant beef bouillon
1/2 teaspoon dried basil leaves
1/4 teaspoon pepper

Wash wheat berries by placing in wire strainer; run cold water through berries, lifting with fingers to clean thoroughly. Heat berries and 4 cups water to boiling in 3-quart saucepan; boil 2 minutes. Remove from heat; cover and let stand 1 hour.

Heat to boiling; reduce heat. Cover and simmer until tender, 1¾ to 2 hours; drain. (Wheat berries can be covered and refrigerated no longer than 3 days.)

Cook and stir mushrooms and onion in oil in 10-inch skillet over medium heat until onion is tender, about 5 minutes. Stir in wheat berries and remaining ingredients. Heat to boiling; reduce heat. Cover and simmer until liquid is absorbed, about 10 minutes.

8 servings (about 1/2 cup); 130 calories each.

☆ ☆ ☆ ☆ ☆

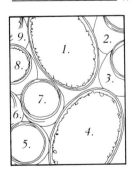

1. *Mexican-Style Kasha*
2. *Buckwheat (Kasha)*
3. *Millet*
4. *Wheat with Vegetables*
5. *Wheat Berries*
6. *Barley*
7. *Cracked Wheat (Bulgur)*
8. *Brown Rice*
9. *Wild Rice*

Mexican-Style Kasha

1   cup medium buckwheat kernels (kasha)
1   egg
2   medium onions, sliced
1   clove garlic, finely chopped
2½ cups water
2   tablespoons margarine or butter
1   teaspoon salt
1   teaspoon red wine vinegar
1/4 teaspoon ground cumin
1   medium tomato, chopped (about 1 cup)
1   medium avocado, chopped (about 1 cup)

Mix buckwheat kernels and egg. Cook buckwheat mixture in ungreased 10-inch skillet over medium-high heat, stirring constantly, until kernels separate and dry. Stir in onions, garlic, water, margarine, salt, vinegar and cumin. Heat to boiling, stirring constantly; reduce heat. Cover and simmer until kernels are tender and liquid is absorbed, about 5 minutes. Stir in tomato and avocado.

8 servings (about 3/4 cup); 125 calories each.

☆ ☆ ☆ ☆ ☆

BUCKWHEAT (KASHA)

Buckwheat, which is related to the rhubarb plant, produces a seed which is technically a fruit, but is used as a grain. When the seed is split, the kernel inside the hull is removed; this is known as a buckwheat groat. When the groat is roasted, it has a distinctive nutty flavor and is called kasha.

Kasha, which is available whole or in fine, medium or coarse grinds, is growing in popularity because buckwheat is recognized as a source of protein in the plant world. It is also as rich in B vitamins as wheat. Kasha makes a hearty side dish with nutlike flavor to serve with meats, poultry and fish or can be part of a main dish.

Barley and Vegetables

3   cups water
1   cup uncooked barley
1   tablespoon instant beef bouillon
2   small zucchini, cut into ¼-inch slices
        (about 1¾ cups)
2   medium stalks celery, sliced (about 1 cup)
1   small onion, chopped (about ¼ cup)
1   cup sliced mushrooms
¾   teaspoon dried basil leaves
2   tablespoons margarine or butter
1   jar (2 ounces) diced pimiento, drained
½   teaspoon salt
1   tablespoon lemon juice

Heat water, barley and bouillon to boiling in 3-quart saucepan; reduce heat. Cover and simmer until barley is tender and all liquid is absorbed, about 1 hour. Cook and stir zucchini, celery, onion, mushrooms and basil in margarine in 10-inch skillet until celery is crisp-tender, about 10 minutes. Stir in barley, pimiento and salt. Cook over medium heat, stirring occasionally, until barley is hot, about 5 minutes. Stir in lemon juice.

8 servings (about ¾ cup); 130 calories each.

☆ ☆ ☆ ☆ ☆

Rice-Cracked Wheat Casserole

½   cup uncooked regular rice
½   cup uncooked cracked wheat (bulgur)
2   medium stalks celery, sliced (about 1 cup)
1   medium onion, chopped (about ½ cup)
¼   to ½ teaspoon curry powder
2   tablespoons margarine or butter
1   can (11 ounces) mandarin orange segments,
        drained (reserve liquid)
1   tablespoon instant beef bouillon
¼   cup snipped parsley

Cook and stir rice, cracked wheat, celery, onion and curry powder in margarine in 10-inch skillet until onion and celery are crisp-tender, about 5 minutes. Turn into ungreased 1½-quart casserole. Add enough boiling water to orange liquid to measure 2¼ cups; pour over rice mixture. Stir in bouillon. Cover and cook in 350° oven until grains are tender and liquid is absorbed, 25 to 30 minutes. Carefully stir in orange segments and parsley.

7 servings (about ¾ cup); 105 calories each.

☆ ☆ ☆ ☆ ☆

CRACKED WHEAT AND BULGUR — THERE IS A DIFFERENCE

It is important to distinguish between cracked wheat and bulgur — the two kinds of cracked wheat available for use in recipes. Both are made from whole wheat kernels or berries; but there the similarity ends.

Cracked wheat, made from any variety of wheat except durum, has been cleaned and cracked or cut into fine, angular fragments and is used as flour. Bulgur is whole wheat, which has been parboiled, dried and partially debranned, then cracked into coarse, angular fragments. It is prepared and served like rice, and its kernels retain their shape and chewy texture. Cooked bulgur can be combined with fruits, vegetables or other grains for a hearty side dish or with fish, poultry or meat in main dishes. This versatile grain also can be combined with other ingredients and chilled for a salad.

Both cracked wheat and bulgur provide protein, niacin and thiamin. Both also contain some of the wheat germ, rich in oils which can become rancid. To preserve freshness, store tightly covered at room temperature, or place in moistureproof, vaporproof plastic bags in the refrigerator or freezer.

Millet Pilaf

4 slices bacon
1 medium onion, thinly sliced
1 medium green pepper, chopped (about 1 cup)
1 cup uncooked millet
3 cups water
1 tablespoon instant chicken bouillon
1/8 teaspoon ground ginger
1 medium apple, coarsely chopped (about 1 cup)

Fry bacon in 10-inch skillet until crisp. Remove from skillet and drain; crumble and reserve. Cook and stir onion, green pepper and millet in bacon fat until onion is crisp-tender, about 5 minutes. Stir in water, bouillon and ginger. Heat to boiling; reduce heat. Cover and simmer until millet is tender, about 30 minutes. Stir in apple; heat until hot. Sprinkle with reserved bacon.

6 servings (about 3/4 cup); 190 calories each.

☆ ☆ ☆ ☆ ☆

Rice and Pine Nuts

1 cup uncooked brown rice
1 medium onion, chopped (about 1/2 cup)
2 cloves garlic, finely chopped
2 tablespoons vegetable oil
2 1/2 cups water
1/2 cup raisins
1 tablespoon instant chicken bouillon
1/2 teaspoon dry mustard
1/8 teaspoon pepper
1 jar (1 ounce) pine nuts
1/4 cup snipped parsley

Cook and stir rice, onion and garlic in oil in 2-quart saucepan over medium heat until onion is tender, about 5 minutes. Stir in water, raisins, bouillon, mustard and pepper. Heat to boiling; reduce heat. Cover and simmer until rice is tender and water is absorbed, about 45 minutes. Stir in pine nuts and parsley.

8 servings (about 1/2 cup); 180 calories each.

☆ ☆ ☆ ☆ ☆

Savory Mixed Rice

3/4 cup uncooked brown rice
1/4 cup uncooked wild rice
1 medium stalk celery, chopped (about 1/2 cup)
1 medium onion, chopped (about 1/2 cup)
3 tablespoons margarine or butter
3 cups chicken broth
1/2 teaspoon salt
1/4 teaspoon ground sage
1 can (4 ounces) mushroom stems and pieces, drained
1/2 cup plain yogurt
2 tablespoons snipped parsley

Cook and stir brown rice, wild rice, celery and onion in margarine in 2-quart saucepan over medium heat until onion is tender, about 6 minutes. Stir in broth, salt, sage and mushrooms. Heat to boiling; reduce heat. Cover and simmer until rice is tender, about 1 hour. Stir in yogurt and parsley.

5 servings (about 3/4 cup); 250 calories each.

☆ ☆ ☆ ☆ ☆

Fruited Cold Cereal

1 cup quick-cooking oats
3/4 cup water
2 medium apples, coarsely chopped (about 3 cups)
1/2 cup raisins
1/4 cup packed brown sugar
2 tablespoons lemon juice
1/3 cup sliced almonds
   Milk

Mix oats and water in 1 1/2-quart bowl. Let stand until oats are soft, about 10 minutes. Stir in apples, raisins, brown sugar and lemon juice. Sprinkle with almonds. Serve with milk.

8 servings (about 1/2 cup); 190 calories each.

☆ ☆ ☆ ☆ ☆

Wheat-Date Cereal

1   cup uncooked wheat berries
4   cups water
½   cup milk
⅓   cup cut-up dates
¼   cup chopped almonds
1   tablespoon packed brown sugar
¼   teaspoon ground nutmeg
    Milk

Wash wheat berries by placing in wire strainer; run cold water through berries, lifting with fingers to clean thoroughly. Heat berries and water to boiling in 3-quart saucepan; boil 2 minutes. Remove from heat; cover and let stand 1 hour.

Heat to boiling; reduce heat. Cover and simmer until tender, 1¾ to 2 hours; drain. (Wheat berries can be covered and refrigerated no longer than 3 days.)

Heat wheat berries, ½ cup milk, the dates, almonds, brown sugar and nutmeg just to boiling; reduce heat. Simmer uncovered, stirring occasionally, until milk is absorbed, about 5 minutes. Serve hot with milk and, if desired, additional brown sugar.

6 servings (about ½ cup); 190 calories each.

☆ ☆ ☆ ☆ ☆

Granola

Good source of vitamin A and thiamin

3   cups oats
2   cups golden raisins
1   cup sunflower nuts
1   cup coarsely chopped raw cashews or
        blanched almonds
1   cup coconut
1   cup cut-up dried apricots, apples, pears
        or mixed fruit
½   cup packed brown sugar
½   cup vegetable oil
½   cup honey
1   tablespoon vanilla
¾   teaspoon ground allspice
½   teaspoon salt

Mix oats, raisins, sunflower nuts, cashews, coconut and dried apricots in 4-quart bowl. Mix remaining ingredients; pour over oat mixture. Toss until oat mixture is evenly coated. Spread in 2 ungreased jelly roll pans, 15½ × 10½ × 1 inch. Cook in 325° oven, stirring frequently, until golden brown, about 30 minutes; cool. Store tightly covered in refrigerator no longer than 2 months.

About 10 cups granola; 645 calories per cup.

☆ ☆ ☆ ☆ ☆

KNOW YOUR GRAINS

Various grains, which date from early history, are becoming more popular in today's cooking. Rice, brown rice, wild rice and pearl barley are popular grains which have long been eaten as hearty side dishes or as part of a main dish. Cracked wheat or bulgur (page 216) and buckwheat kernels or kasha (page 215) are now being used more widely.

Two varieties, millet and wheat berries, are relatively new to American cooking. If they cannot be found in the supermarket, they are available at health food stores. Millet is a small, round, yellowish seed, which originated in Africa and Asia. It can be boiled or steamed and served alone as a side dish or combined with other grains or ingredients.

Wheat berries are the whole wheat kernels. Presoaking and long, slow cooking, similar to dried bean cookery, is necessary to make the slightly sweet, nutlike kernels tender. This versatile berry can be used in cereals, side dishes and main dishes. Because wheat berries contain the wheat germ, they should be stored in a tightly covered container in the refrigerator to help prevent rancidity.

Macaroni with Marinated Tomatoes

Macaroni with Marinated Tomatoes

Good source of vitamin C

2   medium tomatoes, chopped (about 2 cups)
2   green onions (with tops), chopped
2   cloves garlic, finely chopped
¼   cup snipped parsley
½   teaspoon salt
½   teaspoon dried basil leaves
⅛   teaspoon coarsely cracked pepper
2   tablespoons olive oil or vegetable oil
1   package (7 ounces) macaroni shells

Mix tomatoes, onions, garlic, parsley, salt, basil, pepper and oil. Cover and refrigerate at least 2 hours but no longer than 24 hours.

Prepare macaroni as directed on package; drain. Immediately toss with tomato mixture.

6 servings (about ¾ cup); 95 calories each.

☆ ☆ ☆ ☆ ☆

Tomato-Artichoke Spaghetti

8   ounces uncooked thin spaghetti
1   can (14 ounces) artichoke hearts
2   medium tomatoes, chopped (about 2 cups)
3   green onions, chopped
½   teaspoon dried oregano leaves
¼   teaspoon salt

Cook spaghetti in 3 quarts boiling salted water (1 tablespoon salt) until tender, 4 to 6 minutes; drain. Drain artichoke hearts, reserving ¼ cup liquid. Cut artichokes into halves. Cook and stir artichokes, tomatoes, onions, oregano, salt and reserved artichoke liquid just until hot, about 7 minutes; toss with hot spaghetti.

6 servings (about ¾ cup); 95 calories each.

☆ ☆ ☆ ☆ ☆

Pasta in Green Sauce

Good source of vitamin A

2   cups uncooked elbow macaroni
2   cups spinach leaves
½   cup parsley sprigs
1   or 2 large cloves garlic, coarsely chopped
2   tablespoons lemon juice
½   teaspoon pepper
3   tablespoons firm margarine or butter

Cook macaroni in 3 quarts boiling salted water (1 tablespoon salt) until tender, 12 to 15 minutes; drain. Place spinach, parsley, garlic, lemon juice and pepper in blender container. Cover and blend on medium speed, stopping blender frequently to scrape sides, until spinach leaves are finely chopped, about 3 minutes. Add margarine; cover and blend on medium speed, stopping blender frequently to scrape sides, until mixture is smooth, about 2 minutes. Toss with hot macaroni; sprinkle with grated Parmesan cheese if desired.

8 servings (about ½ cup); 150 calories each.

□ *Food Processor Directions:* Place spinach, parsley, garlic, lemon juice and pepper in workbowl fitted with steel blade. Cover and process until leaves are finely chopped, about 15 seconds. Add margarine; cover and process until smooth, about 15 seconds.

☆ ☆ ☆ ☆ ☆

DO-AHEAD NOODLES

Making homemade noodles can be fun and rewarding, as well as time consuming. However, you can make both the Green Fettuccine (right) and Egg Noodles (page 221) ahead of time and dry them, to cook when you want a special treat for family and friends.

To make noodles in advance, prepare them according to the recipe, then cut and unfold the strips. Place the strips in a single layer on towels and let stand at room temperature until they are stiff and thoroughly dry, at least 2 hours. The dry noodles can be wrapped securely in aluminum foil or placed in an airtight container. Store them up to 1 month at room temperature.

Green Fettuccine

Good source of vitamin A

8   ounces spinach*
2   eggs
1   tablespoon olive or vegetable oil
1   teaspoon salt
2   cups all-purpose flour
4½   quarts water
1   tablespoon salt
1   tablespoon olive or vegetable oil

Wash spinach; drain. Cover and cook with just the water that clings to leaves, 3 to 10 minutes. Rinse spinach with cold water; drain. Place spinach, eggs, 1 tablespoon oil and 1 teaspoon salt in blender container. Cover and blend on medium speed until smooth, about 20 seconds.

Make a well in center of flour in large bowl. Add spinach mixture; mix thoroughly. (Sprinkle with few drops water if dough is dry; mix in small amount flour if dough is sticky.) Gather dough into ball. Knead on lightly floured cloth-covered board until smooth and elastic, about 5 minutes. Let stand 10 minutes.

Divide dough into 4 equal parts. Roll dough, one part at a time, into paper-thin rectangle on well-floured cloth-covered board (keep remaining dough covered). Loosely fold rectangle lengthwise into thirds; cut crosswise into ¼-inch strips. Unfold strips and place on towel until dry, at least 30 minutes.

Heat water to boiling; stir in 1 tablespoon salt, 1 tablespoon oil and the noodles. Cook until almost tender, 5 to 7 minutes; drain.

8 servings (about ¾ cup); 100 calories each.

*1 package (10 ounces) frozen spinach can be substituted for the fresh spinach. Cook as directed on package; drain.

□ *Food Processor Directions:* Place cooked spinach, eggs, 1 tablespoon oil and 1 teaspoon salt in workbowl fitted with steel blade. Cover and process until smooth, about 15 seconds. Continue as directed.

☆ ☆ ☆ ☆ ☆

Egg Noodles

2 cups whole wheat or all-purpose flour
3 egg yolks
1 egg
2 teaspoons salt
1/4 to 1/2 cup water

Make a well in center of flour in large bowl. Add egg yolks, egg and salt; mix thoroughly. Mix in water, 1 tablespoon at a time, until dough is stiff but easy to roll. Divide dough into 4 equal parts. Roll dough, one part at a time, into paper-thin rectangle on well-floured cloth-covered board (keep remaining dough covered). Loosely fold rectangle lengthwise into thirds; cut crosswise into 1/8-inch strips for narrow noodles, 1/4-inch strips for wide noodles. Unfold strips and place on towel until stiff and dry, about 2 hours.

Break strips into smaller pieces. Cook in 3 quarts boiling salted water (1 tablespoon salt) until tender, 5 to 7 minutes; drain. (To cook half of the noodles, use 2 quarts water and 2 teaspoons salt.)

7 servings (about 3/4 cup); 115 calories each.

☐ *Food Processor Directions:* Place flour, egg yolks, egg, salt and 1/4 cup of the water in workbowl fitted with steel blade. Cover and process until mixture is moist and crumbly, about 10 seconds. Add remaining water, if necessary, by tablespoonfuls; cover and process until dough forms a ball, 10 to 15 seconds longer. (Do not add any more water than necessary.) Continue as directed.

CORNMEAL NOODLES: Substitute 1/2 cup cornmeal for 1/2 cup of the flour.

SESAME SEED NOODLES: Substitute 1/3 cup sesame seed for 1/3 cup of the flour. Do not fold dough; cut with serrated knife.

☆ ☆ ☆ ☆ ☆

Herbed Noodles, and Orange Almond Trout (page 20)

Herbed Noodles

6 ounces uncooked egg noodles
2 ounces uncooked egg noodles
1/4 cup margarine or butter
1 tablespoon snipped chives
1/2 teaspoon salt
1/4 teaspoon dried basil leaves
1/4 teaspoon dried thyme leaves
1/4 teaspoon white pepper

Cook 6 ounces noodles in 3 quarts boiling salted water (1 tablespoon salt) until tender, 7 to 10 minutes; drain. Wrap 2 ounces noodles in towel or place in plastic bag; crush with rolling pin until pieces resemble crushed cornflakes. Cook and stir crushed noodles and margarine in 10-inch skillet over medium heat, stirring constantly, until golden brown, about 3 minutes. Stir in cooked noodles; toss gently. Stir in remaining ingredients. Heat until noodles are hot, about 3 minutes.

6 servings (about 1/2 cup); 115 calories each.

☆ ☆ ☆ ☆ ☆

Nutrition Information Per Serving or Unit

Recipe and Page Number	Protein	Carbo-hydrates	Fat	Sodium	Potas-sium	Protein	Calcium	Iron
		Grams		Milligrams		Percent U.S. Recommended Daily Allowance		
BREADS								
Apple-Granola Coffee Cake, 198	5	41	7	335	145	8	8	6
Apricot-Date Bread, 196	3	23	5	55	150	4	2	8
Buttermilk Pancakes, 194	3	14	5	295	110	6	6	4
Carrot-Whole Wheat Coffee Cake, 197	6	41	13	285	190	10	6	8
Cheese-Carob Rolls, 210	3	19	5	85	60	4	2	4
Cinnamon Rolls, 209	5	48	9	170	125	8	4	8
Cottage Herb Bread, 200	3	11	3	100	30	4	0	2
Cracked Wheat Bread, 205	4	26	2	235	125	6	4	8
English Muffins, 207	3	25	4	185	42	6	0	6
Four-Grain Batter Bread, 200	3	15	1	75	65	4	2	4
Fruit and Nut Turban, 213	5	44	8	215	255	8	4	10
Gruyère Puff Ring, 197	9	13	13	195	105	14	16	6
Hearty Dark Rye Bread, 203	3	24	2	295	185	4	4	8
Honey-Nut Muffins, 196	4	22	10	205	125	6	6	6
Honey Twist Coffee Cake, 211	3	27	9	220	85	6	2	6
Honey Wheat Batter Bread, 199	3	15	2	220	65	4	0	4
Molasses Wheat Bread, 205	3	19	2	150	115	4	4	6
Oatmeal-Raisin Bread, 199	3	25	2	230	145	4	2	6
Oven Crunchy French Toast, 194	12	50	15	550	200	20	6	16
Pear Oven Pancake, 195	9	53	22	370	285	14	10	12
Rye Bread, 206	1	14	1	165	75	2	0	4
Sesame Loaves, 201	5	25	5	60	290	8	4	6
Sourdough Bread, 203	3	19	2	70	30	4	0	4
Sourdough French Bread, 202	2	13	1	95	30	2	0	2

Nutrition Information Per Serving or Unit

Recipe and Page Number	Protein	Carbo-hydrates	Fat	Sodium	Potas-sium	Protein	Calcium	Iron
		Grams		Milligrams		Percent U.S. Recommended Daily Allowance		
Waffles, 195	7	27	15	518	175	22	25	10
Whole Wheat Bread, 204	3	21	2	165	75	4	0	4
Whole Wheat Croissants, 208	3	15	11	245	65	6	2	4
Whole Wheat Pocket Breads, 207	8	48	3	365	155	12	2	12
Whole Wheat Popovers, 195	6	17	4	135	120	8	6	6
GRAINS Barley and Vegetables, 216	4	22	3	385	240	6	2	6
Fruited Cold Cereal, 217	5	30	6	35	300	8	10	6
Granola, 218	11	87	28	130	710	18	8	26
Mexican-Style Kasha, 215	3	13	7	320	255	6	2	6
Millet Pilaf, 217	6	33	4	380	275	10	2	16
Rice-Cracked Wheat Casserole, 216	2	15	4	290	150	4	2	6
Rice and Pine Nuts, 217	4	29	6	250	165	6	2	4
Savory Mixed Rice, 217	8	34	9	795	310	12	6	8
Wheat with Vegetables, 215	5	20	4	165	280	8	2	8
Wheat-Date Cereal, 218	6	32	5	30	290	10	10	8
PASTA Egg Noodles, 221	5	17	3	450	100	8	2	6
Green Fettuccine, 220	4	16	2	210	120	6	2	8
Herbed Noodles, 221	2	9	8	275	25	2	0	4
Macaroni with Marinated Tomatoes, 219	2	11	5	185	165	2	2	4
Pasta in Green Sauce, 220	4	22	5	65	160	6	2	8
Tomato-Artichoke Spaghetti, 219	3	19	1	80	130	4	2	14

Desserts, Appetizers & Snacks

★★★

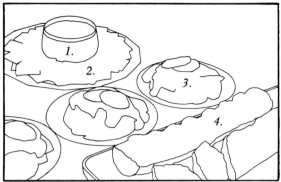

1. Peanut Butter, 2. Whole Wheat Crackers, 3. Papaya Dessert, 4. Apple-Cheese Slices

Papaya Dessert

Good source of vitamins A and C

3   papayas
1/2 cup chilled whipping cream
2   tablespoons powdered sguar
2   tablespoons orange-flavored liqueur
1/2 lime
1   kiwi, sliced

Cut 2 of the papayas lengthwise into slices. Cut remaining papaya into pieces. Place papaya pieces in blender container. Cover and blend on high speed, stopping blender occasionally to scrape sides, until smooth, about 1 minute. Beat whipping cream and powdered sugar in chilled bowl until thick but not stiff. Fold in puréed papaya and liqueur. Arrange papaya slices on 4 plates; squeeze juice from lime over papaya. Spoon whipped cream mixture over papaya; top with kiwi.

4 servings; 225 calories each.

CANTALOUPE DESSERT: Substitute 1 small cantaloupe for the 3 papayas. Cut 3/4 of the cantaloupe into slices. Cut remaining 1/4 into pieces. Place pieces in blender container and continue as directed.

☆ ☆ ☆ ☆ ☆

Cherry-Wine Dessert

Custard Sauce (below)
1/4 cup sugar
1   envelope unflavored gelatin
2   cups medium dry white wine
1 1/2 cups pitted bing cherry halves

Prepare Custard Sauce. Mix sugar and gelatin in 1-quart saucepan. Stir in wine. Heat over medium heat, stirring constantly, just until gelatin is dissolved. Refrigerate uncovered until gelatin begins to thicken, about 2 hours. Fold cherries into thickened gelatin mixture. Spoon into 6 dishes. Refrigerate until firm, at least 4 hours. Top each dessert with Custard Sauce. Garnish with pitted whole bing cherry if desired.

Custard Sauce

3   egg yolks
1/4 cup sugar
1 1/2 cups half-and-half
1   teaspoon vanilla

Beat egg yolks until thick and lemon colored, about 5 minutes. Gradually beat in sugar. Heat half-and-half in 1 1/2-quart saucepan over medium heat just until hot. Stir at least 3/4 cup of the hot half-and-half gradually into egg yolks. Blend into hot half-and-half in saucepan. Cook, stirring constantly, until mixture thickens, about 5 minutes (do not boil). Remove from heat; stir in vanilla. Refrigerate at least 2 hours.

6 servings; 275 calories each.

CHERRY-GRAPE JUICE DESSERT: Substitute 2 cups white grape juice for the white wine; omit sugar.

STRAWBERRY-WINE DESSERT: Substitute 1 1/2 cups strawberry halves for the cherries.

☆ ☆ ☆ ☆ ☆

Fruit with Rum Custard Sauce

Good source of vitamin C

Rum Custard Sauce (below)
1   *pint strawberries, cut into halves (about 2 cups)*
½   *medium pineapple, cut into bite-size pieces (about 2 cups)*
1   *kiwi fruit, sliced (about ½ cup)*
½   *cup seedless green or red grapes*
1   *medium banana, sliced (about 1 cup)*
Ground nutmeg

Prepare Rum Custard Sauce. Reserve 6 strawberry halves. Toss remaining strawberries, the pineapple, kiwi and grapes; cover and refrigerate. Just before serving, add banana; toss. Divide fruit among 6 dishes. Spoon custard sauce over fruit. Sprinkle with nutmeg; top with reserved strawberries.

Rum Custard Sauce

4   *egg yolks, slightly beaten*
¼   *cup sugar*
¼   *teaspoon salt*
1   *cup milk*
2   *tablespoons rum or brandy*

Mix egg yolks, sugar and salt in heavy 2-quart saucepan. Gradually stir in milk. Cook over low heat, stirring constantly, until mixture coats a metal spoon, about 30 minutes. (Do not boil; custard sauce will thicken slightly as it cools.) Remove from heat; stir in rum. Place saucepan in cold water until sauce is cool. Cover and refrigerate at least 2 hours but no longer than 48 hours.

6 servings; 185 calories each.

☆ ☆ ☆ ☆ ☆

Chocolate-Dipped Strawberries

Good source of vitamin C

8   *large strawberries with leaves*
1   *package (6 ounces) semisweet chocolate chips, melted*
½   *cup chilled whipping cream*
1   *tablespoon cherry brandy*

Cover each strawberry ¾ of the way with melted chocolate (top of strawberry and leaves should be visible); place on waxed paper. Refrigerate uncovered until chocolate is firm, about 30 minutes.

Beat whipping cream and brandy in chilled 1½-quart bowl until stiff. Divide whipped cream among 4 dishes; top each with 2 chocolate-dipped strawberries.

4 servings; 365 calories each.

WHITE CHOCOLATE-DIPPED STRAWBERRIES: Substitute 2 squares (2 ounces each) white chocolate candy coating, melted, for the chocolate chips.

☆ ☆ ☆ ☆ ☆

Strawberry-Yogurt Frost

Good source of vitamin C

1   *cup plain yogurt*
¾   *cup nonfat dry milk*
¼   *cup sugar*
1   *package (16 ounces) frozen unsweetened strawberries*

Place yogurt, dry milk and sugar in blender container. Cover and blend on high speed 20 seconds. Add about ½ cup of the strawberries. Cover and blend on high speed 10 seconds; stir. Repeat with remaining strawberries, about ½ cup at a time. Pour into glasses; serve with cocktail straws.

6 servings (about ½ cup); 115 calories each.

☆ ☆ ☆ ☆ ☆

Avocado-Fruit Whip

Good source of vitamin C

2   medium fully ripe avocados
1/3 cup powdered sugar
1/4 cup chilled whipping cream
3   tablespoons lemon juice
1   banana, sliced
1   cup sliced strawberries

Cut avocados into pieces. Place avocado, powdered sugar, whipping cream and lemon juice in blender container. Cover and blend on high speed, stopping blender occasionally to scrape sides, until smooth and creamy, about 1 minute. Pour into 2-quart bowl; fold in banana and strawberries.

5 servings (about 1/2 cup); 220 calories each.

☆ ☆ ☆ ☆ ☆

Brandied Peach Sundaes

1 1/2 teaspoons cornstarch
1 1/2 teaspoons cold water
     Dash of salt
1/2 cup grenadine syrup
1/4 cup brandy
2   medium peaches, cut into halves
1   pint vanilla ice cream

Mix cornstarch, water and salt in 1-quart saucepan. Stir in grenadine syrup. Heat to boiling; reduce heat. Cook and stir over low heat until thickened, about 3 minutes. Stir in brandy. Cover and refrigerate until chilled, about 2 hours. Place 1 peach half, cut side up, in each of 4 dishes. Spoon sauce over peaches. Top with ice cream.

4 servings; 300 calories each.

☆ ☆ ☆ ☆ ☆

Peach Surprise

     Custard Sauce (page 226)
1/3 cup cherry brandy
6   macaroon cookies
3   peaches, sliced
2   tablespoons sugar

Prepare Custard Sauce. Pour brandy over cookies; cover and let stand at room temperature at least 2 hours. Toss peaches with sugar. Place 1 cookie in each of 6 dishes. Spoon peaches over cookies; top with Custard Sauce.

6 servings; 275 calories each.

☆ ☆ ☆ ☆ ☆

Peaches with Yogurt

Good source of vitamin A

4   peaches, sliced
2   tablespoons wheat germ
1/4 teaspoon ground ginger
1   cup plain yogurt
1   tablespoon packed brown sugar
1/4 cup packed brown sugar

Toss peaches, wheat germ and ginger; divide among 4 dishes. Mix yogurt and 1 tablespoon brown sugar; spoon 1/4 cup yogurt mixture over fruit in each dish. Top with remaining brown sugar; sprinkle with granola if desired.

4 servings; 155 calories each.

BANANAS WITH YOGURT: Substitute 2 medium bananas, sliced, for the peaches. Sprinkle with ground nutmeg if desired.

STRAWBERRIES WITH YOGURT: Substitute 1 pint strawberries, cut into halves, for the sliced peaches.

☆ ☆ ☆ ☆ ☆

Pears with Amber Sauce

6   large pears
1/3 cup finely chopped pecans
2   tablespoons margarine or butter, softened
1   teaspoon finely shredded lemon peel
    Amber Sauce (below)

Core pears; pare upper half of each to prevent splitting. Place pears upright in ungreased rectangular baking dish, $12 \times 7\frac{1}{2} \times 2$ inches. (If necessary, cut thin slices from bottoms of pears so they will stand upright.) Mix pecans, margarine and lemon peel. Place about 2 teaspoons pecan mixture in center of each pear. Pour water (1/4 inch deep) into baking dish. Cover tightly with aluminum foil. Cook in 350° oven until pears are tender when pierced with fork, 40 to 50 minutes. Prepare Amber Sauce; serve over warm pears.

Amber Sauce

1/2 cup packed brown sugar
1/4 cup light corn syrup
1/4 cup milk
2   tablespoons margarine or butter

Mix all ingredients in 1-quart saucepan. Cook over low heat, stirring occasionally, until sugar is dissolved and sauce is hot, about 5 minutes.

6 servings; 345 calories each.

☐ *Microwave Directions:* Prepare pears as directed. Arrange in circle in microwavable pie plate, $10 \times 1\frac{1}{2}$ inches. Cover tightly and microwave on high (100%) 3 minutes; rotate pie plate 1/2 turn. Microwave until pears are tender when pierced with fork, 3 to 5 minutes longer. Cover and let stand 10 minutes. Prepare Amber Sauce except — decrease milk to 3 tablespoons. Mix all ingredients in 4-cup microwavable measure. Microwave uncovered on high (100%), stirring every minute, until sugar is dissolved, 2 to 3 minutes.

☆ ☆ ☆ ☆ ☆

Pears with Amber Sauce

Chocolate Soufflé Crepes

Chocolate Soufflé Crepes

Crepes (below)
½   cup granulated sugar
½   cup cocoa
3   tablespoons cornstarch
¼   teaspoon salt
1   cup water
2   egg yolks, slightly beaten
1   teaspoon vanilla
2   egg whites
⅛   teaspoon cream of tartar
¼   cup granulated sugar
½   cup chilled whipping cream
1   tablespoon powdered sugar
¼   teaspoon almond extract
⅓   cup toasted sliced almonds

Prepare Crepes. Mix ½ cup granulated sugar, the cocoa, cornstarch and salt in 2-quart saucepan. Stir in water gradually. Cook over medium heat, stirring constantly, until mixture thickens and boils. Boil and stir 1 minute. Stir at least half of the hot mxiture gradually into egg yolks. Blend into hot mixture in saucepan. Boil and stir 1 minute. Remove from heat; stir in vanilla. Cool, stirring occasionally to prevent film from forming.

Beat egg whites and cream of tartar in large bowl until foamy. Beat in ¼ cup granulated

sugar, 1 tablespoon at a time; continue beating until stiff and glossy. Do not underbeat. Fold cocoa mixture into meringue.

Heat oven to 350°. Spoon about 2 tablespoons cocoa mixture down center of each crepe; roll up. Place crepes, seam sides down, in ungreased rectangular baking dish, 13 × 9 × 2 inches. Bake uncovered until centers spring back when touched lightly, 15 to 20 minutes.

Beat whipping cream, powdered sugar and almond extract in chilled bowl until stiff. Place 2 crepes on each plate. Top with whipped cream; sprinkle with almonds.

Crepes

¾   cup all-purpose flour
1½   teaspoons sugar
¼   teaspoon baking powder
¼   teaspoon salt
1   cup milk
1   egg
1   tablespoon margarine or butter, melted
¼   teaspoon vanilla

Mix flour, sugar, baking powder and salt. Stir in remaining ingredients. Beat with hand beater until smooth. Lightly butter 6-inch skillet; heat over medium heat until butter is bubbly. For each crepe, pour about 2 tablespoons of the batter into skillet; immediately rotate skillet until thin film of batter covers bottom. Cook until light brown. Run wide spatula around edge to loosen; turn and cook other side until light brown. Stack crepes, placing waxed paper between each. Keep crepes covered to prevent them from drying out.

8 servings (2 crepes); 310 calories each.

NOTE: Crepes can be assembled and refrigerated up to 4 hours before baking.

☆ ☆ ☆ ☆ ☆

Orange Dessert Omelets

Good source of vitamin C

2   egg whites
⅛   teaspoon cream of tartar
2   tablespoons granulated sugar
2   egg yolks
2   tablespoons water
2   tablespoons all-purpose flour
3   oranges, pared and sectioned
    Powdered sugar

Beat egg whites and cream of tartar in large bowl until foamy. Gradually beat in 2 tablespoons granulated sugar; continue beating until stiff and glossy. Do not overbeat. Beat egg yolks and water until thick and lemon colored, about 5 minutes. Stir in flour. Fold egg yolk mixture into egg whites.

Heat oven to 400°. Grease and flour 2 round pans, 9 × 1½ inches. Divide egg mixture between pans. Bake until puffy and light brown, 8 to 10 minutes. Remove omelets from pans; spoon half of the oranges onto half of each omelet. Fold other half of each omelet over oranges; sprinkle with powdered sugar. Garnish with orange sections if desired.

6 servings (⅓ omelet); 100 calories each.

☆ ☆ ☆ ☆ ☆

Carob Pudding Cake

1   cup all-purpose flour
¾   cup granulated sugar
2   tablespoons carob powder
2   teaspoons baking powder
¼   teaspoon salt
½   cup milk
2   tablespoons vegetable oil
1   teaspoon vanilla
1   cup chopped nuts
1   cup packed brown sugar
¼   cup carob powder
1¾   cups hottest tap water

Heat oven to 350°. Mix flour, granulated sugar, 2 tablespoons carob powder, the baking powder and salt in ungreased square pan, 9 × 9 × 2 inches. Mix in milk, oil and vanilla with fork until smooth. Stir in nuts. Spread in pan. Sprinkle with brown sugar and ¼ cup carob powder. Pour hot water over batter. Bake 40 minutes. Let stand 10 minutes. Spoon into individual dishes; spoon sauce over each serving. Top with ice cream if desired.

9 servings; 355 calories each.

FUDGE PUDDING CAKE: Substitute cocoa for the carob powder. Continue as directed.

☆ ☆ ☆ ☆ ☆

Strawberry-Almond Torte

Good source of vitamins A and C

2 *pints strawberries*
2 *tablespoons powdered sugar*
4 *tablespoons almond-flavored liqueur*
3 *eggs*
¾ *cup granulated sugar*
⅓ *cup water*
½ *teaspoon vanilla*
½ *teaspoon almond extract*
½ *cup all-purpose flour*
½ *cup ground almonds*
1 *teaspoon baking powder*
¼ *teaspoon salt*
   Powdered sugar
   Almond Cream Filling (below)
1 *cup chilled whipping cream*
3 *tablespoons powdered sugar*
½ *teaspoon almond extract*

Reserve 6 small strawberries; slice remaining strawberries. Toss sliced strawberries with 2 tablespoons powdered sugar and 1 tablespoon of the almond-flavored liqueur. Let stand at room temperature at least 1 hour.

Heat oven to 375°. Line jelly roll pan, 15½ × 10½ × 1 inch, with aluminum foil or waxed paper; grease generously. Beat eggs in small bowl on high speed until very thick and lemon colored, about 5 minutes. Pour eggs into large bowl. Beat in granulated sugar gradually. Beat in water, vanilla and ½ teaspoon almond extract on low speed. Add flour, almonds, baking powder and salt gradually, beating just until blended. Pour into pan. Bake until wooden pick inserted in center comes out clean, 12 to 15 minutes. Cover wire rack with towel; sprinkle towel generously with powdered sugar. Immediately loosen cake from edges of pan; invert on towel. Carefully remove foil; cool cake.

Prepare Almond Cream Filling. Drain strawberries, reserving juice. Place cake on cutting surface; remove towel. Trim off stiff edges of cake if necessary. Cut cake crosswise into 3 equal pieces, about 10½ × 5 inches each. Place one piece on plate; sprinkle with 1 tablespoon of the reserved strawberry juice and 1 tablespoon of the almond-flavored liqueur. Spread half of the Almond Cream Filling on cake to within ⅜ inch of edges. Spread half of the strawberries over filling. Place second cake piece on strawberries; sprinkle with 1 tablespoon strawberry juice and 1 tablespoon almond-flavored liqueur. Spread with remaining Almond Cream Filling and strawberries; top with third cake piece. Sprinkle cake with 1 tablespoon strawberry juice and remaining liqueur. Cover with plastic wrap and refrigerate at least 4 hours.

Beat whipping cream, 3 tablespoons powdered sugar and ½ teaspoon almond extract in chilled bowl until stiff. Spread sides and top of torte with about 1½ cups of the whipped cream. Place remaining whipped cream in decorators' tube or bag; make rosettes and pipe border around edge of torte with star tip. Cut each of the 6 reserved strawberries into slices, not cutting all the way through. Separate slices slightly to form fans. Garnish torte with strawberry fans.

10 servings; 530 calories each.

Almond Cream Filling

1 *cup milk*
¼ *cup all-purpose flour*
1 *cup powdered sugar*
1 *cup margarine or butter, softened*
½ *teaspoon almond extract*
⅛ *teaspoon salt*

Stir milk into flour in 1-quart saucepan until smooth. Cook, stirring constantly, over medium heat until thickened; cool. Beat powdered sugar, margarine, almond extract and salt in 1-quart bowl on medium speed until fluffy. Gradually add flour mixture, beating on high speed until light and fluffy, about 2 minutes.

☆ ☆ ☆ ☆ ☆

Strawberry-Almond Torte

Assembling Strawberry-Almond Torte

Cut cooled and trimmed cake crosswise into 3 equal pieces, about 10½×5 inches each.

Spread remaining half of the Almond Cream Filling on cake to within ⅜ inch of edges.

Apple-Raisin Pastry

Apple-Raisin Pastry

½   *cup granulated sugar*
⅓   *cup all-purpose flour*
½   *teaspoon ground cinnamon*
5   *cups thinly sliced pared tart apples*
½   *cup golden raisins*
   Pastry Dough (below)
1   *tablespoon margarine or butter*
½   *cup powdered sugar*
1   *teaspoon light corn syrup*
¼   *teaspoon vanilla*
2   *to 3 teaspoons hot water*

Heat oven to 350°. Mix granulated sugar, flour and cinnamon; toss with apples and raisins. Prepare Pastry Dough. Roll dough into 15-inch circle on lightly floured surface. Fold dough into quarters; carefully place on greased cookie sheet and unfold. Spoon fruit mixture onto center of dough to within 3 inches of edge; dot with margarine. Bring edge of dough up and over fruit mixture, stretching slightly to make 4-inch opening in center. Bake until crust is golden brown and fruit is tender, about 45 minutes. Cool 15 min-utes. Mix powdered sugar, corn syrup and vanilla. Stir in water, 1 teaspoon at a time, until mixture is smooth and desired consistency. Drizzle over warm crust.

Pastry Dough

1   *package active dry yeast*
½   *cup warm water (105 to 115°)*
1   *cup all-purpose flour*
⅓   *cup sugar*
¼   *teaspoon salt*
½   *cup margarine or butter, softened*
1   *to 1¼ cups whole wheat or all-purpose flour*

Dissolve yeast in warm water in large bowl. Add all-purpose flour, sugar, salt and marga-rine. Beat until smooth. Stir in enough re-maining whole wheat flour to make dough easy to handle. Turn dough onto lightly floured surface; knead until smooth, about 1 minute.

12 servings; 290 calories each.

☆ ☆ ☆ ☆ ☆

Apple Cake

1/3   *cup boiling water*
2   *cups chopped pared apples (about 2 medium)*
1   *cup all-purpose flour*
1   *cup whole wheat flour*
1 1/4   *cups sugar*
1/2   *cup vegetable oil*
1 1/4   *teaspoons baking soda*
1   *teaspoon ground cinnamon*
1   *teaspoon vanilla*
1/2   *teaspoon salt*
1/2   *teaspoon ground cloves*
3   *eggs*
   Nut Topping (below)

Heat oven to 350°. Grease and flour rectangular pan, 13 × 9 × 2 inches. Pour water over apples in 3-quart bowl. Add remaining ingredients except Nut Topping. Blend on low speed, scraping bowl constantly, 1 minute. Beat on medium speed, scraping bowl occasionally, 2 minutes. Pour batter into pan; sprinkle with Nut Topping. Bake until wooden pick inserted in center comes out clean, 40 to 45 minutes.

Nut Topping

Mix 1/2 cup chopped nuts and 2 tablespoons packed brown sugar.

15 servings; 250 calories each.

CARROT CAKE: Substitute 2 cups shredded carrots for the apples.

RHUBARB CAKE: Substitute 2 cups cut-up rhubarb for the apples.

☆ ☆ ☆ ☆ ☆

Frozen Chocolate Cream

   Chocolate Sauce (below)
14   *ladyfingers*
2   *tablespoons orange-flavored liqueur*
1   *tablespoon water*
3   *cups chilled whipping cream*
1/4   *cup orange-flavored liqueur*

Prepare Chocolate Sauce. Remove 1 cup of the sauce; cool. Cover and refrigerate remaining sauce. Split ladyfingers lengthwise into halves. Mix 2 tablespoons liqueur and the water; dip each ladyfinger half into liqueur mixture. Place ladyfingers on bottom and upright around side of 7-inch springform pan. Beat whipping cream in chilled 2 1/2-quart bowl until stiff. Mix the 1 cup Chocolate Sauce and 1/4 cup liqueur; fold into whipped cream. Spoon into pan; smooth top. Freeze until firm, about 8 hours.

Place in refrigerator at least 1 hour but no longer than 2 hours before serving. Heat refrigerated Chocolate Sauce, stirring occasionally, just until warm. Cut Frozen Chocolate Cream into wedges; serve with remaining Chocolate Sauce.

Chocolate Sauce

1   *can (13 ounces) evaporated milk*
1   *package (12 ounces) semisweet chocolate chips*
1   *cup sugar*
1   *tablespoon margarine or butter*
2   *teaspoons orange-flavored liqueur*

Heat milk, chocolate chips and sugar over medium heat, stirring constantly, until chocolate is melted and mixture boils; remove from heat. Stir in margarine and liqueur.

18 servings; 360 calories per serving.

☆ ☆ ☆ ☆ ☆

Pineapple Ice

4   cups 1-inch pieces pineapple
      (about 1 medium pineapple)
½   cup light corn syrup
2   tablespoons lemon juice

Place all ingredients in blender container. Cover and blend on high speed until smooth, about 5 seconds. Pour into metal refrigerator tray or loaf pan, 9 × 5 × 3 inches. Freeze until firm around edges but soft in center, about 2 hours. Spoon into blender container. Cover and blend on high speed until smooth. Pour into refrigerator tray. Freeze until firm, about 3 hours.

8 servings (about ½ cup); 105 calories each.

☐ *Food Processor Directions:* Place all ingredients in workbowl fitted with steel blade. Cover and process until smooth, about 10 seconds. Continue as directed.

CANTALOUPE ICE: Substitute 4 cups 1-inch pieces cantaloupe for the pineapple.

WATERMELON ICE: Substitute 4 cups 1-inch pieces watermelon for the pineapple.

——————— ☆ ☆ ☆ ☆ ☆ ———————

Honey-Vanilla Bean Ice Cream

½   cup milk
½   cup honey
¼   teaspoon salt
3   egg yolks, beaten
1   vanilla bean (3 inches)
2   cups chilled whipping cream

☐ *Crank-type Freezer Directions:* Mix milk, honey, salt, egg yolks and vanilla bean in saucepan. Cook over medium heat, stirring constantly, just until bubbles appear around edge. Remove vanilla bean; split bean lengthwise into halves. Scrape seeds into cooked mixture with tip of small knife; discard bean. Cool to room temperature. Stir in whipping cream.

Pour into freezer can; put dasher in place. Cover and adjust crank. Place can in freezer tub. Fill freezer tub ⅓ full of ice; add remaining ice alternately with layers of rock salt (6 parts ice to 1 part rock salt). Turn crank until it turns with difficulty. Drain water from freezer tub. Remove lid; take out dasher. Pack mixture down; replace lid. Repack in ice and rock salt. Let stand to ripen several hours.

☐ *Refrigerator Directions:* Mix milk, honey, salt, egg yolks and vanilla bean in saucepan. Cook over medium heat, stirring constantly, just until bubbles appear around edge. Remove vanilla bean; split bean lengthwise into halves. Scrape seeds into cooked mixture with tip of small knife; discard bean. Cool to room temperature.

Pour into metal refrigerator tray or loaf pan, 9 × 5 × 3 inches. Freeze until mixture is mushy and partially frozen, 1 to 2 hours. Beat whipping cream in chilled bowl until soft peaks form. Spoon partially frozen mixture into another chilled bowl; beat until smooth. Fold in whipped cream. Pour into 2 metal refrigerator trays or loaf pans, 9 × 5 × 3 inches. Cover to prevent crystals from forming. Freeze, stirring frequently during first hours, until firm, 4 to 5 hours.

8 servings (about ½ cup); 315 calories each.

NOTE: Recipe can be doubled.

PISTACHIO ICE CREAM: For crank-type freezer, stir in ½ cup chopped pistachio nuts, ½ teaspoon almond extract and few drops green food color after stirring in whipping cream.

For refrigerator, stir ½ teaspoon almond extract and few drops green food color into cooled honey mixture. Fold in ½ cup chopped pistachio nuts with whipped cream.

——————— ☆ ☆ ☆ ☆ ☆ ———————

Frozen Mocha-Almond Dessert

Frozen Mocha-Almond Dessert

Almond Crunch (below)
7   egg yolks
½   cup corn syrup
½   cup semisweet chocolate chips, melted
        and cooled
1   teaspoon coffee-flavored liqueur
1   teaspoon freeze-dried coffee
1   teaspoon almond-flavored liqueur
2   cups chilled whipping cream

Prepare Almond Crunch. Beat egg yolks on high speed until thick and lemon colored, about 8 minutes. Stir in corn syrup. Pour mixture into 2-quart saucepan. Cook over medium heat, stirring constantly, until hot but not boiling, about 6 minutes. Cool to room temperature.

Place ⅓ of the egg yolk mixture in each of three 2-quart bowls. Stir melted chocolate chips into mixture in one bowl, coffee-flavored liqueur and coffee into mixture in another bowl and Almond Crunch and almond-flavored liqueur into remaining egg mixture.

Beat whipping cream in chilled bowl until stiff. Fold ⅓ of the whipped cream into egg yolk mixture in each bowl.

Spread chocolate mixture in ungreased 7-inch springform pan; cover and freeze 30 minutes. Cover remaining bowls and refrigerate. After 30 minutes, spread Almond Crunch mixture over chocolate layer; cover and freeze 30 minutes. Spread coffee mixture over Almond Crunch layer; cover and freeze until firm, about 8 hours.

Loosen edge of Frozen Mocha-Almond Dessert with knife before removing side of pan. Return dessert to freezer until serving time. Garnish with chocolate curls if desired.

Almond Crunch

Cook 3 tablespoons sugar in 6- or 7-inch skillet over low heat, stirring constantly, until sugar melts and turns light brown. Stir in 3 tablespoons toasted whole almonds. Pour into buttered shallow pan; cool. Break into pieces and crush.

12 servings; 285 calories each.

☆ ☆ ☆ ☆ ☆

Chicken Pâté Puff

Preparing Chicken Pâté Puff

Spread remaining Chicken Pâté over spinach layer. Bring sides of pastry up and over pâté; seal ends.

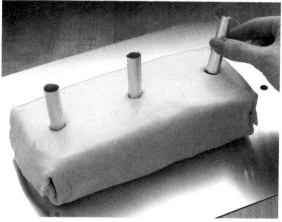

Insert aluminum foil tube in each opening in pastry to allow steam to escape.

Chicken Pâté Puff

Good source of vitamin A and riboflavin

Chicken Pâté (below)
1/2 *package (17¼-ounce size) frozen puff pastry, thawed (1 sheet)*
1 *package (10 ounces) frozen chopped spinach, thawed and drained*
1 *egg*
1 *tablespoon cold water*
1 *envelope unflavored gelatin*
2 *cups cold chicken broth (page 56)*

Prepare Chicken Pâté. Roll pastry into rectangle, 12 × 10 inches, on lightly floured surface. Spread half of the pâté crosswise into rectangle, 8 × 3 inches, on center of pastry. Squeeze spinach dry between paper towels; spread over pâté. Spread remaining pâté over spinach. Bring 10-inch sides of pastry up and over pâté; seal seam and ends tightly. Place seam side down on ungreased cookie sheet.

Cut three ½-inch round openings in top of pastry to allow steam to escape (cut one opening near each end and one in the middle). Mix egg and water; brush pastry with half of the egg mixture. Refrigerate Chicken Pâté Puff and remaining egg mixture 20 minutes.

Heat oven to 425°. Fold 12 × 4-inch strip aluminum foil lengthwise in half. Cut strip crosswise into three 4 × 2-inch pieces. Roll each piece into 4 × ½-inch tube. Brush pastry with reserved egg mixture. Insert aluminum foil tube in each opening in pastry. Bake 15 minutes. Reduce oven temperature to 325°. Bake until pastry is deep golden brown and a skewer inserted in center of pâté through middle steam opening comes out hot, about 1 hour. Remove aluminum foil tubes. Refrigerate puff until cold, at least 8 hours.

Sprinkle gelatin on ½ cup of the chicken broth; stir until softened. Add remaining chicken broth. Heat over low heat, stirring constantly, until gelatin is dissolved. Chill until slightly thickened. Pour or spoon gelatin mixture into steam openings, tilting puff so gelatin mixture fills air spaces on sides and top. (Entire gelatin mixture may not be used.) Refrigerate until gelatin is firm, at least 4 hours. To serve, cut into ⅝-inch slices.

Chicken Pâté

8 *ounces chicken livers*
1 *small onion, chopped (about ¼ cup)*
½ *cup water*
¼ *teaspoon salt*
1 *whole chicken breast (about 1 pound)*
4 *ounces mushrooms, cut into quarters (about 1½ cups)*
¼ *cup margarine or butter, softened*
2 *tablespoons snipped parsley*
⅛ *teaspoon ground sage*
⅛ *teaspoon pepper*

Heat chicken livers, onion, water and salt to boiling; reduce heat. Simmer uncovered until livers are tender, about 15 minutes; drain and cool. Remove bones and skin from chicken breast; chop chicken. Place livers, onion, chicken breast and remaining ingredients in food processor workbowl fitted with steel blade. Cover and process until smooth, about 30 seconds.

12 slices; 205 calories each.

☐ *Blender Directions:* Place ¼ of the cooked livers, onion, chicken breast, mushrooms, margarine and parsley in blender container. Cover and blend on high speed, stopping blender frequently to scrape sides, about 1 minute. Repeat three times, adding sage and pepper last time. Stir all mixtures together.

CHICKEN PÂTÉ APPETIZER: Prepare Chicken Pâté. Place mixture in greased 1-quart casserole. Cook uncovered in 325° oven until firm to touch and skewer inserted in center comes out hot, about 1 hour. Let stand 15 minutes; invert on serving plate. Cover and refrigerate until cold, at least 8 hours. Garnish with snipped parsley; serve with chopped onion and assorted crackers.

☆ ☆ ☆ ☆ ☆

Apple-Cheese Slices

1   cup packed parsley sprigs
1/4 cup walnuts
1   tablespoon dried basil leaves
3   tablespoons olive or vegetable oil
1   tablespoon lemon juice
1/2 teaspoon salt
1   medium apple, cut into 16 slices
1   tablespoon lemon juice
1/2 baguette, cut lengthwise into halves
1   cup shredded Swiss cheese (about 4 ounces)
1/2 teaspoon freshly ground or coarse
     ground pepper

Place parsley, walnuts, basil, olive oil, 1 table-spoon lemon juice and the salt in blender container. Cover and blend on high speed, stopping blender occasionally to scrape sides, until mixture is the consistency of paste, about 5 minutes. Toss apple slices with 1 tablespoon lemon juice.

Place bread halves, cut sides up, on ungreased cookie sheet. Set oven control to broil and/or 550°. Broil halves with tops 5 to 6 inches from heat until golden brown (if bread arches in center, turn crust sides up and broil until flat). Spread parsley mixture over each bread half; arrange apple slices diagonally on top, leaving small space between each slice. Sprinkle cheese over apples; sprinkle with pepper. Broil with tops 5 to 6 inches from heat until cheese is melted, 3 to 4 minutes. To serve, cut between apple slices.

16 slices; 95 calories each.

☐ *Food Processor Directions:* Place parsley, walnuts, basil, olive oil, 1 tablespoon lemon juice and the salt in workbowl fitted with steel blade. Cover and process until mixture is the consistency of paste, about 30 seconds. Continue as directed.

☆ ☆ ☆ ☆ ☆

Sauerkraut Appetizers

1   pound ground pork
1   medium onion, finely chopped (about 1/2 cup)
1/2 pound ground fully cooked smoked ham
1   cup all-purpose flour
1/2 teaspoon dry mustard
2   to 4 drops red pepper sauce
1/2 cup milk
1   can (16 ounces) sauerkraut, rinsed, well
     drained and chopped
1/4 cup snipped parsley
1/3 cup margarine or butter
2   eggs
1/4 cup cold water
3/4 cup dry bread crumbs
     Mustard Sauce (below)

Cook and stir ground pork and onion in 10-inch skillet over medium heat until pork is done; drain. Stir in ham, flour, mustard and pepper sauce until blended. Stir in milk. Cook over medium heat, stirring constantly, until mixture is hot, about 5 minutes; remove from heat. Stir in sauerkraut and parsley; cool.

Heat margarine in jelly roll pan, 15½ × 10½ × 1 inch, in 400° oven until melted. Mix eggs and water. Shape pork mixture into 1-inch balls; dip in egg mixture. Coat evenly with bread crumbs. Place in margarine in pan. Cook uncovered 15 minutes; turn. Cook until hot and golden brown, about 15 minutes longer. Prepare Mustard Sauce. Serve appetizers with Mustard Sauce.

Mustard Sauce

1/4 cup dairy sour cream
1/4 cup mayonnaise or salad dressing
1   tablespoon dry mustard
1/4 teaspoon sugar

Mix all ingredients until smooth.

About 5 dozen appetizers; 70 calories each.

☆ ☆ ☆ ☆ ☆

Mini Oriental Rolls

8   ounces bean sprouts (about 4 cups)
1   pound ground pork
½   cup chopped mushrooms
¼   cup chopped water chestnuts
¼   cup sliced green onions (with tops)
1   teaspoon cornstarch
1   teaspoon five spice powder
1   teaspoon soy sauce
½   teaspoon salt
8   frozen phyllo sheets, thawed
2   tablespoons margarine or butter, melted
¼   cup dry mustard
3   tablespoons cold water

Rinse bean sprouts under running cold water; drain. Cook and stir ground pork in 10-inch skillet until brown; drain. Stir in bean sprouts, mushrooms, water chestnuts and onions; cook and stir 2 minutes. Stir in cornstarch, five spice powder, soy sauce and salt.

Cut stack of phyllo sheets lengthwise into halves. Cut each half crosswise into thirds to make 24 squares, each 5½ × 5¼ inches. Cover squares with waxed paper, then with damp towel to prevent them from drying out.

Heat oven to 350°. For each roll, use 2 phyllo squares. Place about 2 tablespoons pork mixture slightly below center of square. Fold corner of square closest to filling over filling, tucking point under filling. Fold in and overlap the two opposite corners. Roll up; place seam side down on greased cookie sheet. Repeat with remaining phyllo squares. Brush rolls with margarine. Bake until golden brown, about 25 minutes. Mix dry mustard and water until smooth; let stand 5 minutes. Serve with rolls.

24 rolls; 115 calories each.

DO-AHEAD TIP: Place rolls on greased cookie sheet. Cover tightly with plastic wrap. Refrigerate no longer than 3 hours. Brush rolls with margarine. Bake at 350° until golden brown, about 25 minutes.

☆ ☆ ☆ ☆ ☆

Mini Oriental Rolls

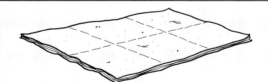

Cut phyllo lengthwise into halves; crosswise into thirds.

Spoon the pork mixture slightly below center of square.

Fold corner over filling; fold in opposite corners and roll up.

Shrimp Triangles

1   can (4¼ ounces) tiny shrimp, drained
2   tablespoons chili sauce
½   teaspoon prepared horseradish
    Pastry (below)
    Margarine or butter, melted
    Sesame, poppy or caraway seed

Heat oven to 450°. Rinse shrimp under running cold water; drain. Chop shrimp finely; mix with chili sauce and horseradish. Prepare Pastry. Roll into rectangle, 18 × 15 inches, on lightly floured cloth-covered board. Cut into thirty 3-inch squares. Place scant teaspoonful shrimp mixture on each square. Fold one corner to opposite corner to form triangle; press edges together with fork to seal. Place triangles on ungreased cookie sheet. Brush with margarine; sprinkle with sesame seed. Bake until brown, about 10 minutes. Serve warm.

Pastry

⅔   cup plus 2 tablespoons shortening
2   cups all-purpose flour
1   teaspoon salt
4   to 5 tablespoons cold water

Cut shortening into flour and salt until particles are size of small peas. Sprinkle in water, 1 tablespoon at a time, tossing with fork until all flour is moistened and pastry almost cleans side of bowl (1 to 2 teaspoons water can be added if necessary). Gather pastry into ball.

30 triangles; 95 calories each.

CHEESE TRIANGLES: Substitute 1 cup shredded sharp Cheddar, Swiss or Monterey Jack cheese (about 4 ounces) for the shrimp, chili sauce and horseradish. Continue as directed.

DEVILED HAM TRIANGLES: Substitute 1 can (4¼ ounces) deviled ham and 1 tablespoon prepared mustard for the shrimp, chili sauce and horseradish. Continue as directed.

☆ ☆ ☆ ☆ ☆

Fruit with Smoked Salmon

½   lime or lemon
12 pieces honeydew melon, 2 × 1 inch
24 thin strips smoked salmon, 3 × 1 inch
2   large kiwi, each cut lengthwise into 6 wedges

Squeeze juice from lime over melon pieces; toss until evenly coated. Wrap 1 strip salmon around center of each piece of melon and each wedge of kiwi.

24 appetizers; 15 calories each.

FRUIT WITH HAM: Substitute 24 thin strips fully cooked smoked ham, 3 × 1 inch, for the smoked salmon.

☆ ☆ ☆ ☆ ☆

Brie with Almonds

1   whole round brie cheese (4½ ounces)
2   tablespoons margarine or butter
¼   cup toasted sliced almonds
1   tablespoon brandy, if desired
24 assorted crackers

Set oven control to broil and/or 550°. Broil cheese with top 3 to 4 inches from heat until soft and warm, about 2½ minutes. Heat margarine until melted; stir in almonds and brandy. Pour over cheese. Garnish with snipped parsley if desired. Serve with crackers.

☐ *Microwave Directions:* Microwave cheese uncovered on medium (50%) just until soft and warm, 2 to 3 minutes. Microwave margarine uncovered on high (100%) until melted, about 1 minute; stir in almonds and brandy. Pour over cheese. Garnish with snipped parsley if desired. Serve with crackers.

8 servings; 140 calories each.

☆ ☆ ☆ ☆ ☆

Chili Bows, Fruit with Smoked Salmon, and Broiled Camembert

Chili Bows

2   cups uncooked pasta bows (farfalle)
     Vegetable oil
2   tablespoons grated Parmesan cheese
1/2 teaspoon chili powder
1/4 teaspoon seasoned salt
     Dash of garlic powder

Cook bows as directed on package just until tender; drain. Rinse under running cold water; drain thoroughly. Heat oil (1 inch) to 375°. Fry bows, about 1 cup at a time, until crisp and golden brown, about 2 minutes. Drain on paper towels. Mix remaining ingredients; toss with bows until evenly coated.

4 cups bows (about 12 per serving); 120 calories each.

☆ ☆ ☆ ☆ ☆

Broiled Camembert

1   whole round camembert cheese (4 1/2 ounces)
1   egg
1   tablespoon cold water
3   tablespoons wheat germ
2   apples, each cut into 12 wedges

Cut cheese into 12 wedges. Mix egg and water with fork until smooth. Dip each cheese wedge into egg mixture; sprinkle with wheat germ. Dip again into egg and sprinkle with wheat germ. Place wedges on heatproof serving plate. Set oven control to broil and/or 550°. Broil wedges with tops 4 to 6 inches from heat until warm, 3 to 5 minutes (shape of wedges should be retained). Serve immediately with apple wedges.

12 appetizers; 50 calories each.

☆ ☆ ☆ ☆ ☆

Tortilla Cheese Wedges

1   egg
½   teaspoon red pepper sauce
¼   teaspoon salt
1   package (13⅓ ounces) large flour tortillas (about 7 inches in diameter)
5   teaspoons mild taco sauce
1¼   cups shredded Monterey Jack or mozzarella cheese
⅔   cup sliced green onions (with tops)
¼   cup vegetable oil

Beat egg, pepper sauce and salt until smooth. Brush each of 5 tortillas with about 2 teaspoons egg mixture and 1 teaspoon taco sauce. Sprinkle each of the 5 tortillas with ¼ cup of the cheese to within ½ inch of edge; sprinkle with 2 tablespoons green onions. Top each with 1 tortilla, pressing edges firmly together to seal.

Heat oil in 10-inch skillet over medium heat until hot. Fry 1 tortilla sandwich at a time, turning once, until golden brown, 2 to 3 minutes; drain. Place on ungreased cookie sheet; keep warm in 200° oven. Repeat with remaining tortilla sandwiches, adding more oil if necessary. Cut each tortilla sandwich into 6 wedges.

30 wedges; 70 calories each.

☆ ☆ ☆ ☆ ☆

Garlic Spiced Olives

1   teaspoon dried oregano leaves
¼   teaspoon red pepper flakes
3   small cloves garlic, slivered
1   jar (7 ounces) large green olives

Place oregano, pepper flakes and garlic in jar of olives. Cover tightly and shake until seasonings are well distributed. Refrigerate at least 4 days but no longer than 2 weeks.

About 20 olives; 10 calories each.

☆ ☆ ☆ ☆ ☆

Fruit Flautas

Good source of niacin

1   package (13⅓ ounces) 6- or 7-inch flour tortillas
1¼   cups chunky-style peanut butter
⅔   cup fruit preserves (grape, peach, apricot, pineapple, cherry or strawberry)
Vegetable oil
Powdered sugar

Spread each tortilla with 2 tablespoons peanut butter. Spread 1 tablespoon preserves across one end of each tortilla; roll up. Heat oil (1 inch) in 10-inch skillet to 350°. Fry 3 or 4 roll-ups at a time, seam sides down, until golden brown, turning once, about 1½ minutes. Drain; sprinkle with powdered sugar. Serve warm or cool.

10 flautas; 415 calories each.

☆ ☆ ☆ ☆ ☆

Chili-Cheese Bars

1   egg
1   cup whole wheat or all-purpose flour
¾   cup margarine or butter, softened
½   cup cornmeal
½   teaspoon salt
¼   teaspoon chili powder
2   cups shredded sharp Cheddar cheese (about 8 ounces)
1   can (4 ounces) chopped green chilies, drained
2   tablespoons chopped onion

Heat oven to 350°. Mix egg, flour, margarine, cornmeal, salt and chili powder. Press in ungreased rectangular pan, 13×9×2 inches. Bake until firm, about 25 minutes. Mix remaining ingredients; spread over baked layer. Bake until cheese is melted, about 20 minutes. Cool; cut into bars, about 3×1 inch.

36 bars; 80 calories each.

☆ ☆ ☆ ☆ ☆

Granola Bars

1/2 cup margarine or butter, softened
1/3 cup honey
1   egg
1   cup oats
1/2 cup whole bran cereal
1/2 cup whole wheat flour
1/2 cup flaked coconut
1/2 cup coarsely chopped almonds
1/2 teaspoon salt
1/2 teaspoon ground cinnamon

Heat oven to 350°. Mix margarine, honey and egg. Stir in remaining ingredients. Spread oat mixture in greased rectangular pan, 13 × 9 × 2 inches. Bake until golden brown, about 20 minutes. Cool 10 minutes; cut into bars, about 3 × 1 inch.

36 bars; 70 calories each.

☆ ☆ ☆ ☆ ☆

Trail Mix

2   cups oats
1   cup banana chips
1   cup roasted salted pumpkin seeds
1   cup salted peanuts
1   cup raisins
1/4 cup margarine or butter, melted

Mix oats, banana chips, pumpkin seeds, peanuts and raisins in ungreased rectangular pan, 13 × 9 × 2 inches. Pour margarine over mixture; toss until evenly coated. Cook uncovered in 350° oven, stirring occasionally, 15 minutes, cool. Store in tightly covered container no longer than 4 weeks.

12 servings (1/2 cup); 295 calories each.

☆ ☆ ☆ ☆ ☆

Snack Cookies

1/2 cup shortening
1/2 cup granulated sugar
1/2 cup packed brown sugar
1   egg
3   tablespoons milk
1/2 teaspoon vanilla
1   cup whole wheat or all-purpose flour
1   cup quick-cooking oats
1   cup whole wheat flake cereal
1/2 cup chopped nuts
1/2 cup raisins
1/2 teaspoon baking soda
1/4 teaspoon baking powder
1/4 teaspoon salt

Heat oven to 375°. Mix shortening, granulated sugar, brown sugar, egg, milk and vanilla. Stir in remaining ingredients. Drop dough by rounded teaspoonfuls about 2 inches apart onto ungreased cookie sheet. Bake until light golden brown, 8 to 10 minutes. Remove from cookie sheet; cool.

About 4 1/2 dozen cookies; 60 calories per cookie.

☆ ☆ ☆ ☆ ☆

Snack Sticks

Good source of vitamin C

2   tablespoons honey
1   tablespoon water
1   can (8 ounces) pineapple chunks in
       juice, drained
1/4 cup finely chopped pecans
20   3/4-inch Swiss cheese cubes
20   3/4-inch green pepper squares
20   3/4-inch fully cooked smoked ham cubes

Mix honey and water; stir in pineapple until evenly coated. Toss pineapple with pecans until evenly coated. Alternate pineapple, cheese, green pepper and ham on skewers.

20 sticks; 75 calories each.

☆ ☆ ☆ ☆ ☆

Whole Wheat Soft Pretzels

1	package active dry yeast
1½	cups warm water (105 to 115°)
2½	cups all-purpose flour
2	teaspoons sugar
½	teaspoon salt
1	to 1½ cups whole wheat flour
1	egg
1	tablespoon cold water
2	tablespoons coarse salt

Dissolve yeast in warm water in large bowl. Add all-purpose flour, sugar and ½ teaspoon salt. Beat on low speed until moistened. Beat on medium speed, scraping bowl occasionally, 3 minutes. Stir in enough whole wheat flour to make dough easy to handle.

Turn dough onto lightly floured surface; knead until smooth and elastic, about 5 minutes. Place in greased bowl; turn greased side up. Cover; let rise in warm place until double, about 1 hour. (Dough is ready if indentation remains when touched.)

Heat oven to 425°. Punch down dough; divide into halves. Cut each half into 6 equal pieces. Roll each piece into rope 15 inches long. Place rope on greased cookie sheet. Bring left end of rope over to the middle of the rope to form a loop. Bring right end of rope up and over the first loop to form a pretzel shape. Enlarge the holes in the loops so they do not bake together. Place pretzels about 3 inches apart. Mix egg and cold water; brush pretzels with egg mixture and sprinkle with coarse salt. Bake until pretzels are brown, 15 to 20 minutes; cool on wire rack. Serve with prepared mustard if desired.

12 pretzels; 135 calories each.

TRADITIONAL SOFT PRETZELS: Substitute 1 to 1½ cups all-purpose flour for the whole wheat flour.

☆ ☆ ☆ ☆ ☆

Whole Wheat Soft Pretzels

Shaping Soft Pretzels

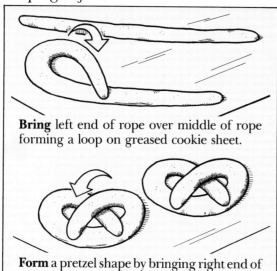

Bring left end of rope over middle of rope forming a loop on greased cookie sheet.

Form a pretzel shape by bringing right end of rope up and over first loop.

Spicy Beef Jerky

1¼ - pound beef boneless top round
¼   cup soy sauce
¼   cup water
1   tablespoon sugar
1   teaspoon garlic powder
1   teaspoon onion powder
¼   teaspoon red pepper sauce

Trim all excess fat and connective tissue from beef. Freeze beef until partially frozen, about 1 hour. Cut beef diagonally across grain into ⅛-inch slices. Mix remaining ingredients; stir in beef. Cover and refrigerate at least 1 hour; drain. Place beef in single layer on racks in 2 jelly roll pans, 15½×10½×1 inch (do not overlap slices).

Dry beef in 200° oven, rotating pans every 2 hours, in oven with door slightly ajar until beef bends and cracks but does not break, about 4½ hours. Cool; store in airtight container at room temperature no longer than 4 weeks.

About 48 slices (6 ounces); 35 calories per slice.

☐ *Microwave Directions:* Prepare beef as directed. Arrange half of beef slices close together on microwavable bacon rack. Cover with waxed paper and microwave on low (30%) 21 minutes. Arrange drier strips in center of rack; rotate rack ½ turn. Microwave 21 minutes longer. Rotate rack ½ turn and microwave until dry but slightly pliable, about 10 minutes. Cool on towel; cover with additional towel. Repeat with remaining beef slices. Let stand 24 hours before storing.

SPICY FISH JERKY: Substitute 1-pound skinless cod fillet for beef. Cut partially frozen fish into ¼-inch slices. Reduce marinade time to 15 minutes. Increase drying time to about 5 hours.

☆ ☆ ☆ ☆ ☆

Whole Wheat Crackers

⅓   cup shortening
⅓   cup milk
2   tablespoons honey
1   cup whole wheat flour
⅔   cup all-purpose flour
2   tablespoons yellow cornmeal
2   tablespoons wheat germ
½   teaspoon baking powder
¼   teaspoon salt

Heat oven to 350°. Mix shortening, milk and honey in 2-quart bowl; stir in remaining ingredients until well blended. Divide dough into halves. Roll one half into rectangle, 15×10 inches, on lightly greased cookie sheet. (Place cookie sheet on damp towel to prevent it from sliding while rolling.) Cut dough into about 1½-inch squares. Bake until light brown and firm, 10 to 12 minutes. Repeat with other half.

10 dozen crackers; 15 calories each.

WHOLE WHEAT ANIMAL CRACKERS: Roll dough 1/16 inch thick on lightly floured surface. Cut with animal-shaped cookie cutters. Place on ungreased cookie sheets. Bake until edges are very light brown, 8 to 10 minutes.

☆ ☆ ☆ ☆ ☆

Peanut Butter

Place 2 cups salted or unsalted roasted peanuts in blender container. Cover and blend on low speed until finely chopped, about 1 minute. Blend on high speed, stopping blender occasionally to scrape sides, until smooth, about 7 minutes. Cover and refrigerate.

1 cup (16 tablespoons); 115 calories per tablespoon.

☐ *Food Processor Directions:* Place nuts in workbowl fitted with steel blade. Cover and process until smooth, stopping if necessary to scrape side, about 3 minutes.

CASHEW BUTTER: Substitute 2 cups unsalted cashews and 1 tablespoon vegetable oil for the peanuts.

☆ ☆ ☆ ☆ ☆

Nutrition Information Per Serving or Unit

Recipe and Page Number	Protein	Carbo-hydrates	Fat	Sodium	Potas-sium	Protein	Calcium	Iron
		Grams		Milligrams		Percent U.S. Recommended Daily Allowance		
DESSERTS								
Apple Cake, 235	4	32	12	185	100	6	2	6
Apple-Raisin Pastry, 234	4	49	9	155	180	6	2	8
Avocado-Fruit Whip, 228	2	22	14	10	545	4	2	4
Brandied Peach Sundaes, 228	3	47	7	140	240	4	10	4
Carob Pudding Cake, 231	3	57	13	165	235	4	8	10
Cherry-Wine Dessert, 226	5	29	10	35	235	8	8	6
Chocolate-Dipped Strawberries, 227	3	30	26	15	250	4	4	8
Chocolate Soufflé Crepes, 230	7	37	15	215	255	10	8	10
Frozen Chocolate Cream, 235	4	32	24	50	160	8	8	4
Frozen Mocha-Almond Dessert, 237	3	19	22	30	85	4	6	8
Fruit with Rum Custard Sauce, 227	4	29	6	120	345	6	8	8
Honey-Vanilla Bean Ice Cream, 236	3	20	25	105	85	4	6	2
Orange Dessert Omelets, 231	3	18	2	25	215	4	2	4
Papaya Dessert, 226	2	30	11	20	555	2	6	4
Peach Surprise, 228	4	31	12	75	205	6	8	6
Peaches with Yogurt, 228	3	31	2	30	375	6	10	8
Pears with Amber Sauce, 229	2	55	13	115	335	4	6	10
Pineapple Ice, 236	0	26	0	15	120	0	2	6
Strawberry-Almond Torte, 232	6	50	34	370	240	10	10	8
Strawberry-Yogurt Frost, 227	5	20	2	65	330	8	16	4
APPETIZERS								
Apple-Cheese Slices, 240	3	7	6	145	70	6	10	4
Brie with Almonds, 242	5	5	11	195	70	8	4	2
Broiled Camembert, 243	3	3	3	95	60	4	4	2
Chicken Pâté Puff, 239	11	9	14	355	225	22	4	16

Nutrition Information Per Serving or Unit

Recipe and Page Number	Protein	Carbo-hydrates	Fat	Sodium	Potas-sium	Protein	Calcium	Iron
		Grams		Milligrams		Percent U.S. Recommended Daily Allowance		
Chili Bows, 243	4	22	2	95	60	6	2	4
Garlic Spiced Olives, 244	0	0	1	220	10	0	0	0
Fruit with Smoked Salmon, 242	1	1	1	10	50	2	0	0
Mini Oriental Rolls, 241	6	7	7	85	150	10	0	6
Sauerkraut Appetizers, 240	3	3	5	90	55	6	0	2
Shrimp Triangles, 242	2	6	7	110	15	2	0	2
Tortilla Cheese Wedges, 244	2	6	4	60	15	2	6	2
SNACKS Chili-Cheese Bars, 244	2	4	6	145	25	4	6	0
Fruit Flautas, 244	10	36	26	225	225	16	10	10
Granola Bars, 245	1	7	4	70	45	2	0	2
Peanut Butter, 247	5	3	9	75	120	8	0	2
Snack Cookies, 245	1	8	3	30	40	0	0	2
Snack Sticks, 245	4	4	5	20	65	6	8	2
Spicy Beef Jerky, 247	3	1	2	95	50	8	0	2
Trail Mix, 245	9	26	17	100	220	14	2	14
Whole Wheat Crackers, 247	0	2	1	10	5	0	0	0
Whole Wheat Soft Pretzels, 246	5	27	1	1200	90	8	2	8

Index
★★★